BEFORE FREEDOM AND AFTER

BEFORE FREEDOM AND AFTER

PERSONAL RECOLLECTIONS OF ONE OF THE KEY WITNESSES OF INDIAN EVENTS OVER THE LAST HALF A CENTURY

By

Ansar Harvani

GYAN

Before Freedom and After

ISBN : 978-81-212-0284-8

First Published 1989, reprint 2013 in India by
Gyan Publishing House
23, Main Ansari Road, Daryaganj,
New Delhi - 110002
Phones : 23282060, 23261060
Fax : (011) 23285914
E-mail: books@gyanbooks.com
website: gyanbooks.com

Printed at : Sagar Color Scan, New Delhi.

PREFACE

I have spent almost sixty years of my life in the service of the nation. In the course of my political activities I had the opportunities of working with and observing at close quarters a number of contemporary eminent public figures. Some well-meaning friends have been suggesting to me to write my memoirs. I always pointed out that who would read the memoirs of an obscure person like me. However, I cannot refrain from temptation of writing some interesting episodes and my impressions of personalities and panoramas in the era from Gandhi to Rajiv.

Having been in the thick of Indian struggle for freedom, I have my own assessment about different personalities and various events. I have read a number of autobiographies of contemporary politicians and bureaucrats and I find that they left many gaps.

As I have said, I have seen some of the architects of modern India from close quarters, and I have my own assessment of them. It is true that while describing contemporary historical events, it is very difficut to be objective, but I have tried to demolish many myths which are associated with some of our top leaders.

Having been born in a Muslim home, by accident of birth I have been especially touched by the events that led to the partition of Indian sub-continent and carving of two sovereign neighbouring States of India and Pakistan. I have tried with documentary evidences to expose those who blessed and later accepted the partition of India, and pointed out its consequences.

I have been a freedom fighter and I have spent the best period of my youth languishing in British jails. But I refuse to claim that the freedom of India could come only through our efforts. It were the extraordinary domestic and international compulsions of the British government that transference of power to India, came.

I have witnessed the rise and fall of India's major political party the Congress Party. I have witnessed the double talks and hypocrisy of many who occupied high pedestal in our imagination.

I have been a member of Lok Sabha and have seen three Prime Ministers, Nehru, Lal Bahadur and Indira Gandhi, in action. I have my own assessment about their contribution to parliamentary democracy.

My impression about many of the India's leaders may shock their devotees and admirers, but I have based them on my personal assessment, though they may appear to many as subjective. However, as a citizen of free India, I have every right to have my views provided they are based on hard facts.

Now, I have become old; I still like good faces. I am still thrilled by achievement of my fellow country-men. I feel distressed and disappointed when I find that the suffering of many of my countrymen has gone in vain.

The collapse of what was known as Congress culture hurts me, and I am depressed when I find the young Indians are more interested in career and money than intrinsic values of life.

I have tried my best that my views are supported by facts. It is inevitable then in a work like this one cannot be completely objective, for I myself have played a role, however, minor it might have been in the drama of India's liberation and its partition.

I offer no apology, but I expect the readers to treat my narrative on its own merit.

23/24 Janpath Lane
New Delhi 110001.

ANSAR HARVANI

CONTENTS

Chapter 1

EARLY REMINISCENCES

IF contraceptives were known most probably I would have never been born. I was the ninth child of my parents. I was born in a small town Rudauli in Barabanki District of United Provinces of Agra and Oudh, now known as Uttar Pradesh, at a time when first Great War was in full swing.

My father was the first graduate of his town. He was a petty landlord, and a lawyer; later, he joined the Provincial Civil Service.

According to family traditions, my first introduction in literacy was with Arabic script. A Hafiz and Maulvi was engaged to teach me how to read the Holy Quran and he taught me and my elder brother Asrar who later on came to be known as Majaz, a celebrated revolutionary and progressive poet. My heart was not in reading the holy script and in spite of my teacher's thrashing, I could not complete the reading of the full text of the holy book.

I was the youngest and favourite child of my father. Though he was not in active politics, he was regular subscriber of newspapers, and in the evening, he would discuss politics with his friends. I used to hear these discussions with curiosity and interest. It was then that I heard the name of Gandhi, Ali Brothers, Abul Kalam Azad and many other leaders. I did not only listen to the word of 'Congress', but also Bolshevik being talked over.

At the age of six, I was admitted to Municipal School. The non-cooperation and Khilafat movement was in full swing. People in the streets, used to sing *"Boli Aman Mohammad Ali Ki Jan Bata Khilafat Per de do"* and anti-British songs, instead of present day filmi songs.

The whole atmosphere was vibrating with the sound of *"Mahatma Gandhi Ki Jai"*, *"Ali Brothers Zindabad"*. By now, I could read Urdu, though I could not understand much; I regularly read *'Zamindar'* edited by Maulana Zafar Ali Khan. My father also subscribed for me an Urdu children's magazine *Ghunja* which devoted its last two pages to the summary of weekly news in Urdu language.

Mustafa Kamal Pasha, later to be known as Kamal Ata Turk, the liberator of Turkey, was my hero. The Muslims, all over India, inspired by Khilafat movement, were attracted to Pan-Islamic movement. In middle class homes, the portraits of Ottoman Caliphs, and their generals were prominently displayed. While Gandhi cap has become popular among Congress workers, the Muslims wore Enver Cap worn by the last Commander- in-Chief of Ottoman Empire, Enver Pasha.

Later, my father, who was a lawyer in Barabanki, moved to Lucknow, as a civil servant. My house was near Aminudula Park, where in the evening most of the neighbourhood boys used to assemble to play. In those days, Aminudula Park was the venue of the public meetings in Lucknow. Nearby was situated Ganga Prasad Memorial Hall, which housed a library and reading room. I was not much interested in games. I used to sneak to reading room to read newspapers and I attended the public meeting, where I listened to the speeches of visiting leaders.

I still recollect that Maulana Mohammad Ali was to address a public meeting and a fair-looking young man wearing a khadi tweed sherwani, dhoti and Gandhi cap was making arrangement. He asked the assembled young men and children to spread *durries* on the floor, and I was one of them. He was none else but Pandit Jawaharlal Nehru who was later to become the first Prime Minister of India. It was here that I had my first glimpse of Mahatma Gandhi, C.R. Das, Hasrat Mohani, Lala Lajpat Rai, Mrs. Sarojini Naidu, Madan Mohan Malaviya and other leading lights of the time.

I was admitted in Aminabad Municipal School. On Friday the school used to have an hour long interval, while other boys, spent their leisure in playing, I used to sneak to nearby mosque where, after prayers, the mullas used to deliver political speeches. I delivered my first speech here exhorting the Muslims to liberate their own country, and Muslim holy land occupied by the British after the defeat of Germans and Turks in the First World War.

During summer vacation, we used to go to our home in Rudauli My two recollections of childhood still haunt me. In our town during summers there used to be a *mela,* in which the children of local zamindars used to go on palanquin. I was hardly four or five when I was to go to fair with my elder brother

Asrar. The palanquin bearers, who used to be brought from our zamindari villages, as forced labour, were late, and we became restless.

On their arrival, they explained that they could not realise the time, and one of my uncles asked one of his hangers-on from our zamindari, to thrash them with shoes. This memory in later life haunted me and made me deeply antagonistic to zamindari and feudal system. The other memory that deeply affected in my future life was our visit to Nainital, the summer capital of our province. Here, round the lake, there are two roads, one was meant for the white men and the other for Indians. One day I walked on the road meant for white men and tried to talk to a white boy who snubbed me by calling me a black nigger.

Apart from my parents, I was much influenced by Choudhari Mohammad Ali, known as Chmroo Mian, a relation of ours; he was a nationalist and often used to advise me and his son Saliman, who was of my age, not to accept anything without questioning. Saliman later on became Pakistani Ambassador to Moscow and High Commissioner in London.

He wrote a book on sex explaining the harm, that masturbation and homosexuality caused to human beings. Sixty five years ago, such pieces of advice by any elder were unthinkable.

His book written in Urdu, entitled Salhakar, on sex even today can be a good text-book for schools.

He was elected as a Member of U.P. Legislative Council, where he vehemently opposed the Immoral Traffic Bill, pointing out that prostitutes were necessary for those members of working class in towns who cannot afford to bring their families from villages. He felt that the oldest profession in the world cannot be checked by legislation alone. He was a great conversationalist, and was very popular in his social circles.

It is his influence that never allowed me to be a bigot and led me to rationalism. He was a great scholar of Urdu and Persian and though did not actively join freedom movement, but all sympathies were with it. In his house, I saw pandit Motilal as a house guest, and it was from him that I heard about the activities of Tilak and Gokhale, and earlier Congress leaders.

Chapter 2

MY BAPTISM IN FREEDOM STRUGGLE

AS a school boy, my main hobby was to attend public meetings in Amindula Park, and listen to the speeches of local and visiting national leaders. Lucknow Congress was led by Choudhari Khaliquz-Zaman who, later on, became one of the architects of Pakistan, and Mohan Lal Saksena; Pandit Jawaharlal Nehru who was a regular visitor of Lucknow, was often seen organising meetings and addressing them.

I was fascinated, like many young men of my generation, by his personality, though not impressed by his orations. He took particular interest, in the younger set who attended these meetings and I was probably the youngest among them.

It was in 1928, that is when Simon Commission appointed by the British Government was to visit India. The Congress and the Muslim League factions led by M.A. Jinnah had decided to boycott it. The Congress had decided to organise massive demonstrations in all those cities which were to be visited by the Commission headed by Sir John Simon, who, later on, became a Foreign Secretary in British Cabinet and among its members was Major Clement Attlee who, as British Prime Minister, presided over the liquidation of the British Empire in India.

At one of the massive meetings, Pandit Motilal Nehru, Jawaharlal Nehru, Choudhari Khaliquz-Zaman and others appealed to the citizens of Lucknow, to assemble at Aminudala Park, the day Simon Commission was to visit Lucknow and to march to Lucknow Railway Station shouting the slogan "Simon, Go Back", carrying Congress and black flags. On the appointed day, more than twenty thousand young men and women assembled and under the guidance of young Nehru, a procession marched to Railway Station headed by Pandit Jawaharlal Nehru, and Pandit Pant who was the leader of

Swaraj Party in U.P. Legislative Council, in orderly fashion shouting the slogan, "Simon Go Back", and "Mahatma Gandhi Ki Jai". The moment it reached near the Railway Station, it was stopped by mounted policemen mostly consisting of Anglo-Indian sargeants. Khan Bahadur Syed Anuddin, who was the City Magistrate, was on the horseback, and was seen asking Pandit Pant and Nehru to ask the processionists to disperse. On their refusal, he ordered *lathi* charge, and I saw Pandit Pant and Jawaharlal Nehru falling down on the ground. Most of the processionists ran away, and some of us who stood firm were rounded up. While the elders were taken away to jail, we, the youngsters, were taken to Faizabad Road and were left stranded about twelve miles from the city.

I walked back to my house reaching there late in the night and was scolded by my anxious parents. I did not tell them that I was one of the processionists, and lied that I went to some friend's house, and got late. This was my first baptism in active politics.

Next day, Simon Commission was to be entertained at a reception by British India Taluqdar Association at Butler Park, in the heart of Kaiserbag, which was once the palace of Don Juan King of Oudh, Wajid Ali Shah, and was later distributed among Oudh taluqdars for their meritorious services in the mutiny of 1957. We assembled at the residence of Maharaja of Mahomodabad who was a personal friend of Pandit Motilal Nehru and was sympathetic to national cause. The police will not allow anyone to go near the venue of reception. But Choudhari Khaliquz Zaman and Dr. Jaykar Nath Misra, Head of the Law Department of Lucknow University and Deputy Leader of Swaraj Party, were too resourceful to be discouraged. They had brought kites, inscribed with the slogan of "Simon Go Back", and flew them with an angle that they were visible by the British loyalists and the members of the Simon Commission much to the embarrassment of Sir William Morris, the Governor of U.P., and the taluqdars who had assembled to show their solidarity with him. We climbed a nearby wall and shouted the much popular slogan and were dispersed by the police.

It was the same year that the British Secretary of State for India, Lord Birkenhead had announced in British Parliament that India could obtain Dominion Status, if all the political parties, and communities agreed upon a Constitution. The challenge was accepted by the Congress, and I remember that Maulana Mohammad Ali at a meeting at Lucknow announced that we Indians will unite and prove that Lord Birkenhead, the

British Secretary of State for India is Lord 'Brokenhead'. We were much amused by this description.

Later, at the Madras session of the Indian National Congress presided over by Dr. M.A. Ansari, a committee was formed under the Chairmanship of Motilal Nehru to prepare a report on the constitutional reforms in India. It was at Madras session of the Congress that Subhas Bose, who was only thirty years old was elected as one of the General Secretaries of the Congress along with Jawaharlal Nehru, and Shoib Qureshi who later on came as the High Commissioner of Pakistan in India.

Twenty-nine organisations were represented in this committee. Later, a sub-committee was set up to frame the proposed Indian Constitution. The sub-committee with Motilal Nehru, as Chairman, had Sir Tej Bahadur Sapru, Sir Ali Imam, M.S. Aney, Sardar Mangal Singh and Shoib Qureshi and Subhas Bose as Member Secretaries.

After twenty five sittings the committee came out with a report which was to be discussed and adopted at an all-party conference to be held at Lucknow.

The arrangements of this Conference were entrusted to Jawaharlal Nehru, and Lucknow City Congress Committee. I got myself enrolled as volunteer, and since I was the youngest among them, I was attached to Dr. Ansari, the Congress President as his page-boy. In my whole life, no other assignment could have given me more satisfaction and pride than to be a page-boy of one of the noblest patriots of this country.

I helped Jawaharlal Nehru in arranging seats, putting buntings and decorations. Obviously he was happy with my devotion.

It was here that I saw Madan Mohan Malviya, Lala Lajpat Rai, Mrs. Annie Besant, Sir Sankaran Nair, Dr. Saifuddin Kitchlu, Maulana Azad and many other national dignitaries.

As a page-boy of the President, I had to attend on member General-Secretary, Subhas Bose. I fell in love with him at first sight, though I had to wait for almost ten years to come in closer contact with him and to enjoy the position of one of his few confidants.

At this Conference, Jinnah had agreed to have joint electorate with some reservations. But, Hindu Mahasabha leaders led by Madan Mohan Malaviya and Lajpat Rai would not agree for separation of Sind from Bombay Presidency and reforms in N.W.F.P. to my young mind, Jinnah appeared to be more compromising than Pandit Madan Mohan Malaviya and his Hindu supporters.

Incidentally, it was at this Conference, that I noticed a young girl in frock with her bespectacled mother sitting in gallery. She was none other than Indira Gandhi, in future to be the most powerful and assertive ruler of India.

This conference was a landmark in the history of Indian struggle for freedom. Ali Brothers who were till then close associates of Gandhi, were disgusted with the arrogance of Pandit Motilal Nehru and at a later stage they had to part company with the Congress.

Maulana Mohammad Ali, issued a statement after the conclusion of this Conference, that he had no place in the Congress because it was controlled by father and son and holy ghost meaning thereby Motilal, Jawaharlal and Gandhi.

Though Nehru Committee Report got a sizeable support from the Muslim leaders like Sir Ali Amam, Abul Kalam Azad, Dr. Saifuddin Kitchlu and Choudhari Khaliquz-Zaman, Dr. M.A. Ansari but the British stooges like Sir Mian Mohammad Shafi, Sir Fazal Hussain, Sir Mohammad Yakub dubbed it as anti-Muslim, and the challenge of Lord Birkenhead, Secretary of State for India went by default.

The salient points of the report of the Motilal Nehru Committee constituted in answer to Birkenhead's challenge to produce a blueprint for India's Constitution were:

> "All power of Government and all authority, legislative, executive and judicial, are derived from the people and the same shall be exercised in the commonwealth of India through organisations established by, or under, and in accord with, this Constitution."
>
> "There shall be no state religion, men and women shall have equal rights as citizens".
>
> "Separate electorates shall be abolished. Every person of the age of 21 shall have the vote".
>
> "A Supreme Court shall be set up".
>
> "The re-distribution of provinces shall take place on a linguistic basis on the demand of the majority of the area concerned subject to financial and administrative considerations".

The report having recommended adult franchise, attempted to appease communal sentiment by proposing a 'balance' between the Hindu majority and Muslim majority provinces. It recommended the advancement of the North-West Frontier to full provincial status and the separation of Sind from Bombay Presidency.

The All-Party Convention at Calcutta adopted the report,

disregarding the pleas of the Muslim extremists for the retention of separate electorates, the reservation of a third of the seats in the Central Assembly for Muslims and for a federal, rather than unitary, Constitution with the province holding residuary powers.

I started speaking at a Congress meeting in Lucknow and became a great favourite with local Congress leaders. I developed personal friendship with many Congressmen though most of them were much older in age than me and that friendship continued throughout their lives.

Chapter 3

DAYS AT ALIGARH

I was sent to Aligarh with a view to dissuading me from involving myself in political activities. In entering the portals of Aligarh Muslim University, in those days, one entered the heart of Muslim India, for it was a meeting ground of the Muslim students not only from all over India, but it attracted students from Middle East, Burma, Malaya, Indonesia, then known as Dutch East Indies, and Maldives.

The British encouraged Aligarh boys to be loyal subjects of His Majesty the King and Emperor, and the British stooges often visited Aligarh to impress upon the young minds the benefit of British Raj, and the danger of domination by Hindus.

Aligarh, if on one side was well known for producing loyalists like Sir Nazimuddin, Sir Mohammad Yakub, Sir Sikander Hayat Khan and host of other British stooges, it also produced men like Hasrat Mohani and Raja Mahendra Pratap, who established the first Provisional Indian Government during the First World War in Berlin.

If on one side it gave Pakistan Field Marshal Ayub, on the other, it sent Khan Abdul Ghaffar Khan, the legendary Pathan leader, who spent most of his life either in exile or in jail, after the partition of India.

Before I departed for Aligarh, I had heard from some Aligarh students, the name of Khwaja Ahmad Abbas who had already made a mark as a good debator among Aligarh undergraduates. I was determined to seek his friendship. He has described my encounter with him in his autobiography, *I Am Not An Island*, and he writes:

> "Then one day I saw an unknown student he looked like a junior, for I had not seen him before wearing a fez which was made of maroon coloured khadi made stiff by using buchram in its lining. He looked extraordinarily smart in his *khaddar* pyjama, tight-fitting black khadi

Turkish coat, the stiffened khadi fez set at rakish angle on his head, and very impressive gold rimmed glasses on his eyes.

"Generally, it was considered undignified for a senior to speak to a junior, but I could not resist the temptation to ask him how, and where he had his khadi fez made. He told me the address of his tailor who lived and worked in the city. That day half a dozen of us were there, ordering our caps, and the tailor must have made quite a packet of our patriotism.

"That was how I came to know Ansarul Haq Harvani, then an intermediate student, and through him, his elder brother, Asrarul Haq Majaz, the poet, who died young but who has left behind an astonishingly rich treasure of progressive and revolutionary poems of great beauty and power. They were also semi-boarders like us, their father was an excise inspector, and along with their parents and sisters, they lived in a little house almost opposite the Women's College, where their sisters were studying. And nearly forty five years later, I have to admit that the geography of his house had much to do with the speed with which my friendship with Ansar developed.

"Ansar had one speciality peculiar to him, he always managed to look smart. A midnight visit to the railway station was a must for us in those days, and knowing Bhaijan to be an early sleeper, we would creep out of our rooms at about eleven and bicycle our way to the station (Later, when Bhaijan bought a sporting car for two, we would steal it, pushing it out of the bungalow, and starting it with a duplicate key which my cousin Mehboob had made out of a sardine tin opener. Then we would go to the station, at least four or five of us clinging to various parts of the car.)

"Since my newly formed friendship with Ansar, I suggested we cycle round to Marris Road to pick him up on the way. This also had to be done by stealth, he slept in the room next to his father, and the connecting door was kept open. We stimulated a dog's howling, and in answer would climb out the window of his room. The very first day it took him a long time to come out and my companions were getting fidgety, for we missed the midnight mail train from Delhi. I asked Ansar what he was doing, taking such a long time. He calmly replied "I could not find my jar of cold cream. I had to grope for it, for I couldn't switch on the light".

"Damn fool", I exclaimed, "what was the necessity of applying cold cream to your face at this hour?"

And he calmly replied, "You never know when you might meet the girl". However foolish his concern for his impeccable appearance might be, Ansar with characteristic frankness and forthrightness, had put his finger on the real purpose of our visit to the station which none of us was prepared to admit even to ourselves.

"It was true that the railway station book stall, at this late hour, could be open, and now and then we might be tempted to buy a magazine or even a book from there. It was also true that at the tea stall one could get hot tea and home-made biscuits which we relished at this hour, especially, in the cold season. But it was also true that none of these things would, or could, take us cycling two miles in the cold to the station. It was the off chance of seeing a pretty face in a women's compartment, or among the entraining or detraining passengers, that took us there. Occasionally, the elegant wife of the Bengali Joint Magistrate would arrive by the train, in the company of her husband, and we would make a mental note to invite them, but really it was her that we meant for the next debate in the Union, or some Women's College girls would come by that train, wearing burquas, but their faces tantalizingly uncovered, and it would be a thrill for us if one of them happened to look in our direction and smile, for each of us imagined that smile to be directed at himself.

"And this would give us an idea why not have a purdah enclosure for girls' college students at Union debates and annual mushaira? The girls should also be given a chance to develop culturally and socially. Even in the midst of these nocturnal outings, we never forgot that we were intellectuals and social reformers. And even while parading up and down the platform,our eyes focussed on some fair face in the train compartment, making our rounds shorter and shorter we would be loudly discussing the pros and cons of Gandhiji's departure for London to attend the Round Table Conference or the consequences of Pandit Jawaharlal Nehru's latest arrest. Love and liberty were the two obsession of our lives and we found nothing incongruous in the just a position."

This was a period when Aligarh like rest of India was seething with discontent. Sir Ross Masud, the grandson of Sir Syed Ahmed Khan, was the Vice-Chancellor of the University. He was considered to be too liberal to handle the situation and was made to resign.

At a memorable meeting of the University court, in spite of the opposition of the nationalist Muslims led by Dr. M.A. Ansari, Dr. Sir Ziauddin Ahmed, who was earlier ousted as a result of the findings of a committee presided over by Sir Ibrahim Rahmatullah, the then President of Central Legislative Assembly from Pro-Vice-Chancellorship, was brought back. Even the Chancellor of the University, Nawab Sir Hamidullah Khan of Bhopal, who was a suspect in Lord Willingdon's eyes for having acted as a host of Gandhi had to quit, and was replaced by His Exalted Highness Mir Usman Ali Khan, the Nizam of Hyderabad, who had earned the title of faithful ally of the British from Queen Victoria, the Empress of India.

On assumption of office, Dr. Sir Ziadduin started victimising the nationalist students by stopping their stipends and withdrawing concession of their fees. The students went on an indefinite strike, and locked the doors of the hostels. The University was closed for indefinite period, and the guardians were telegraphically called to take charge of their wards.

When the next session started, a number of students were refused admission, prominent among whom were well known poet Ali Sardar Jafri and Kazi Jalal Abbasi who is now a Member of Lok Sabha.

I would like to mention the names of some of my friends and contemporaries at Aligarh, of course, my closest friend was Khwaja Ahmad Abbas, who made a mark as a writer, journalist and film maker. But, my other friends were M.N.M. Badiduddin who later on became Education and Information Minister in Sri Lanka, Ali Sardar Jafri and, of course, my brother, Majaz, celebrated Urdu poets, Sibte Hasan and Akhtar Raipuri, prominent Urdu writers, and Ibrahim Hilmi, Prime Minister of Maldives Island.

The atmosphere in Aligarh University was different from most of the other Universities. In the evening, we used to visit our teacher for a cup of tea and had informal discussion.

In my days, the most popular teachers were Prof. Habib, a great scholar of medieval history, whose son Irfan Habib is a Marxist historian. The other was Prof. K.G. Saydain, Principal of Teachers' Training College. He was a cousin of Abbas who lived with him. I often visited him and he guided me in public-speaking and writing.

Prof. Habib was one of the most popular teachers. He was a great philanthrophist and used to give financial help to poor students without disclosing to anybody. So many students were his beneficiaries.

The Historical Society under Prof. Habib organised a trip to Afghanistan to study its historic sites. In those days, a visit to a foreign land was a great event. I was thrilled. We applied for passport and described our nationality as "British subject by birth". While all the applicants were granted passport, Abbas was refused because he belonged to Panipat which was, in those days, in Punjab, which was seething with revolutionary activities, and British authorities felt that he may make contact with many revolutionaries living in exile in Afghanistan.

We were about a dozen students and Badiduddin was with us. We went to Peshawar by train, and from there crossed the Khyber Pass on a bus to reach Kabul.

Afghanistan had recently undergone a revolution. The previous King Amanullah, who had toured Europe, was greatly impressed by the modernisation scheme of Kamal Ata Turk. He had also visited Soviet Union as Stalin's guest. On his return, he abolished purdah and made available modern education facilities. He opened two schools in Kabul, one with the help of Germans and the other with that of French.

The British India had taken keen interest in Afghanistan affairs. It considered it as a backward buffer state between India and Soviet Union. It was alarmed at the modernisation scheme of Amanullah. They instigated and financed Afghan mullas to revolt against him.

The picture of queen Suraya, the wife of the Afghan King, were distributed among the tribes showing her dressed in European costumes. The King was painted as an atheist and enemy of Islam.

Even small Afghan army was influenced by this campaign launched by the Imperialist agents. King Amanullah had to abdicate and fly to Rome *via* Bombay. He was succeeded by a bandit, formerly a water carrier.

The British had cultivated General Nadir Khan, who had spent most of his life in Dehradun as an Afghan exile. He was rushed back along with his three brothers who, after a token fight, overthrew the bandit and was enthroned as His Majesty King Nadir Shah.

He appointed his second brother General Hashim Khan as Prime Minister, Wali Khan as Foreign Minister and Mahmood

Khan as Minister of War.

The destiny ordained that the son of Mahmood Khan overthrew his cousin King Zahir Shah, last king and proclaimed Afghanistan to be a Republic.

During our stay, we were cordially received by His Majesty, Crown Prince and his minister. Though they were brought to power by British, they apparently did not trust them.

Obviously, he wanted Indian Muslims to be on their side, and he proved that a neighbouring country is being ruled by a Muslim King. The Khilafat movement in India had made a deep impact on Muslim World, and they felt that the British will give at least some weight to the opinion of their Muslim subjects in India.

During my stay at Aligarh, I came in contact with a number of national figures. Aligarh was considered to be the heart of Muslim India, and every notable Muslim was eager to visit this seat of learning.

Rabindranath Tagore came here and I met him. Halida Adib Khanum, a legendary figure of Turkish Revolution, who had wielded gun against imperialism in the trenches of Anatolia, visited us. She was given a rousing reception by the students, and my elder brother Majaz wrote one of his classic poems in her honour.

When I was in Aligarh, it had only an intermediate college for the women students. They were kept in strict purdah, and it was a job to persuade the Muslim families of the country to send their daughters to the college.

We were a small band of students who were interested in social reforms. We became very close to Sheikh Abdullah, a Kashmiri Pandit converted to Islam, who had established an educational institution for girls in spite of great opposition of conservatives of the community. He was denounced even by a section of the University teachers who were influenced by Muslim fundamentalists. Myself and Abbas often visited him and offered our support to him.

During summer vacation, we undertook a tour of U.P., meeting former students of Aligarh and seeking their support for the education of Muslim girls. At many places, we were dubbed as atheist and anti-Islamic, but by and large the response was encouraging and a number of middle class families in the cities agreed to send their girls for education.

During my Aligarh days, I came in close contact with most of the Muslim leaders of that period. Aligarh University often invited leading public men to address the students or to participate in debates organised by its union.

Aga Khan was the most prominent British stooge among the Muslims. He led Indian delegation to the Peace Conference at Paris after he First World War and represented the country at League of Nations. He was not only a prominent figure of the empire, but was known all over the world for possessing best horses for turf. He won the races in many European and American countries.

Once he came to Aligarh, and was given red carpet reception for he was mainly responsible for raising M.A.O. College, founded by Sir Syed Ahmed Khan to the status of the University. He was invited by the students union and offered its honorary membership.

Having addressed the students on the role that they can play to lead the Muslims in British Empire, it was customary that after a lecture the students were permitted to put questions.

I got up and asked Aga Khan whether he knew more about poor Indian Muslims or qualities of Arab, Australian and Indian horses. This evoked laughter among the audience, and obviously, Aga Khan was embarrassed.

Once M.A. Jinnah while addressing the students, put his monocle and declared that politics is a game of chess. I shouted, "Whose pawn are you?" Jinnah was not man to be ruffled, and declared that this young man sitting looked like Ceylon in the map of India, and my remarks were drowned in laughter.

We invited Jawaharlal Nehru to address the students, Sir Syed Ross Masud, the Vice-Chancellor, was embarassed. But he was a very resourceful man. While Sir John Hewett, Lt. Governor of U.P., had sponsored Nehru for Harrow, Sir Ross, Chief Justice of Allahabad High Court, has got him admitted to Eton. Sir Ross received him at Railway Station, took him to his residence, and accompanied him to union, and himself presided over the function and declared that in him the University was not receiving a political leader but the son of a personal friend of his father. Obviously Nehru was flattered and our plan to seek political advantage was foiled by clever diplomacy of Sir Ross Masud.

We invited a number of national leaders such as Bhulabhai Desai, the leader of the Congress Party in Central Assembly, and Khan Abdul Ghaffar Khan. I was much impressed by the simplicity of M. Hasrat Mohani, who had moved the Independence Resolution, at Ahmedabad A.I.C.C. session as early as 1920.

He was a mystic and Marxist. He was a rebel against establishment. I had seen Ali Brothers but had never come in close contact with them. Mohammad Ali who had attended the First Round Table Conference in London had died, but his elder brother, Shahukat Ali often visited Aligarh. I became very close to him.

While at Aligarh, I was a correspondent of *Hindustan Times*. I used to send university news with nationalist slant.

A debate was held in the University Union, the participants, were Nawab Sir Ahmad Syed Khan Chetri, then Home Member of U.P., Sir Sikandar Hayat Khan, Home Minister of Punjab, and Nawabzada Liquat Ali Khan, Deputy President of U.P. Legislative Assembly. While I was given a chance, I made a frontal attack on these British stooges. After the meeting was over, I rushed to Railway Station and filed its report through Railway Mail Service.

The following day it appeared with screaming headline that Muslim landlords had the taste of frontal attack from University students.

They were the days when British Government used to depute their most reliable educationists to Aligarh, and various colleges meant for the wards of Indian Princes. Their main task was to see that the students are not influenced by national and patriotic tendencies. Mr. R.B. Ramsbottom who later on became education Minister in Winston Churchill's War Cabinet was the Pro-Vice-Chancellor. He was furious with this report.

He called me to his office and told me that all those whom I denounced were the benefactors of the University. He called me a traitor to University.

He had two typed sheets in his drawer. He drew them and gave me, one was a letter of unconditional apology to those dignitaries to be signed by me, the other was an order of rustications to be signed by him.

I was in a dilemma if I sign one, my political career comes to end, and if he signs the other, my educational prospects were doomed. I was nervous to make a decision. Then a brainwave came to me, and I said, "It will be much better if both of us go to Nawab of Chatari and I sign this letter in his presence and also personal apologise to him. For a moment, he was reluctant but ultimately agreed. Nawab Sahib was a perfect gentleman. He was sitting in his garden under an umbrella. On seeing us, he got up, took me in his arms, congratulated me on my oration but cautioned me to be more restrained.

I told him that the Pro-Vice-Chancellor wants me to sign a

letter of apology. He remarked that it was not at all necessary since a firebrand like me had come to him was more than enough, and thus he closed the chapter.

Though Nawabzada Liaquat Ali Khan was one of his proteges, but he never joined the movement for the partition of this country. In fact, as Prime Minister of Nizam of Hyderabad, he tried his best to persuade him to come to term with New Delhi. On his failure, he resigned in disgust and left Hyderabad which had to face Sardar Patel's police action resulting in great humiliation and harassment of Muslim nobility in particular and Muslim masses in general.

While I was a student at Aligarh, I visited Nainital the summer capital of U.P. The bus conductor refused to take me as none with Gandhi cap could go to the seat of U.P. Government. I had to walk all the way from railhead to Nainital. I never imagined that in later years the same cap could come to symbolise blackmarketing and corruption.

Chapter 4

STUDENT UNREST

WHILE at Aligarh, I was closely associated with the Aligarh Muslim University Union which, in the past, claimed Ali Brothers, Hasarat Mohani and Dr. Zakir Hussain as its active members and office holders. I had visited almost every University in India to participate in inter-University debating contest along with Khwaja Ahmad Abbas.

It was in thirties that Sir Malcolm Hailey who, later on, became Lord Hailey, was transferred from Punjab as the Governor of United Provinces of Agra and Oudh, now known as Uttar Pradesh.

He was very much concerned with the revolutionary and terrorist activities of youth and students like Bhagat Singh and his associates. He wanted to canalise the activities of youth and students to"constructive activities". He appointed a Committee under the Chairmanship of Sir Tej Bahadur Sapru to study the problems of unemployed youth. He prompted Dr. Paranjapye, the Vice-Chancellor of Lucknow University, to form a Federation of all the Universities Unions in the provinces.

It was decided to hold a Conference of the representatives of Allahabad, Banaras, Aligarh, Lucknow and Agra Universities Unions. It was presided over by Sir Mohammed Yakub, Deputy President of Central Legislative Assembly.

I attended this Conference as representative of Aligarh Muslim University. After the usual presidential address, the Chair moved a condolence resolution on the death of King George V, Emperor of India. It was in 1936, in the same year, the Communist Member of British House of Commons, Shapurji Saklatwala had died. I myself and Anwar Jamal Kidwai who later retired as Secretary of Ministry of Information and Broadcasting got up to move an amendment that Saklatwala's name may be added to the Resolution.

This created an uproar in the gathering and Sir Mohammad Yakub adjourned the Conference and left the venue by the back door. We captured the rostrum, and elected M.M.N. Badiuddin, who later on became the Minister of Education and Information and Broadcasting in Bhandaranaika Government in Ceylon (now, Sri Lanka) as President.

It was decided to call a Convention of Students from all over India to form an All India Students' Federation. I had already built up my contacts in various Universities and I wrote letters to most of them who eagerly appreciated the idea and expressed their willingness to attend the Conference. We decided that the Conference should be presided over by Mrs. Sarojini Naidu and inaugurated by Pandit Jawaharlal Nehru.

I proceeded to Bombay to sound Mrs. Naidu, who had a permanent suite in Taj Mahal Hotel. She advised me to approach M.A. Jinnah, who had recently come back from his voluntary exile in Great Britain, and was working for Congress and Muslim League unity. I sought an appointment with Mr. Jinnah who asked me to see him at 5.30 p.m. in his chamber in Bombay High Court. It was my first encounter with the Ambassador of 'Hindu Muslim Unity', who, in later days, as Quaid-e-Azam, was to mobilise Muslim frenzy demanding the partition of sub-continent. He came back from the court a few minutes later and apologised to me. I was much impressed by the courtesy and manner and he agreed to come to Lucknow to preside over the Conference. He appeared to be overjoyed to know that the Conference will be inaugurated by the son of his old and close friend, Motilal Nehru.

The Conference was held in Ganga Prasad Memorial Hall and was represented by the students from all over India. The Communist Party of India which was still banned took special interest to send their student cadres to this Conference. As the subsequent events will show, they were most active in mobilising the students.

Incidentally, this was the last occasion when Jinnah and Nehru shared a platform. Very shortly, the parting of ways was to come and both of them had to be bitterest critics of each other.

In those days, after Calcutta, Lahore was the hub of the student and youth unrest. The Navjavan Bharat Sabha, to which Bhagat Singh belonged, was banned. The students of Punjab were in search of an avenue to express themselves. Probodh Chand, who later, became a Minister and Speaker in Punjab came to Lucknow to attend the Convention. He invited the special session of the All India Students Federation, to be held at Lahore to adopt a regular Constitution.

The Lahore Session was presided over by Sarat Chandra Bose, elder brother of Subhas Bose, and inaugurated by Pandit Gobind Ballabh Pant, the Deputy Leader of the Congress Party in Central Legislative Assembly. It was at this Session that I came into contact with the Communist, Royist and Congress Socialist students.

It was decided to bring out an organ of the students movement to be named 'Students Tribune", edited by Probodh Chandra. After Lahore Session, myself and Probodh Chandra went to Burma. We helped to organise the Burma Unit of the Federation headed by Aungsan, who was later on to become the First Prime Minister of Burma, and to be described as father of Burmese Nation.

I also contacted the students in Great Britain. On our instruction, they formed a Federation of Indian Students. Prominent among its promoters were Mohan Kumaramangalam, Renu Chakravartty and Rajni Patel.

Though Nehru inaugurated the First Session of the Students' Conference at Lucknow, the right wing of Congress Leadership was hostile to the students movement.

All India Students Federation, drew the cadres of Communist Party of India, Congress Socialist Party, M.N. Roy, followers and small groups like Revolutionary Socialist Party, Revolutionary Communist Party, headed by Somen Tagore but a very insignificant number of students came who believed in Gandhian ideology.

The Lahore Session finally constituted All India Students Federation into a well knit organisation. Its regular session was held in Madras in December 1937. It was inaugurated by Mrs. Kamala Devi Chattopadhyaya and M.R. Masani, one of the Secretaries of the Congress Socialist Party presided. The Communist faction of the Federation wanted to control the organisation. The strength of the Communist and other elements was almost balanced. Since I was supported by Masani and Kamaladevi, they looked upon me with suspicion, and attempted to oust me from the helm of affairs.

Masani, as President, disallowed the Resolution of congratulating Joseph Stalin for having introduced a new Soviet Constitution. The Communists walked out of the Conference and showed black flag to Masani. They went still further, and expelled me from the Federation and formed a parallel organisation, though Revolutionary Communists, R.S.P., Royists and unattached delegates, fully supported me.

In course of my work in student movement, an interesting

incident took place. The Communist elements of Students' Federation were determined to reduce it to be a front organisation. Obviously their cadre was more active but, certainly, less popular than those from other parties and groups. They were working to capture local units. I wanted the student movement to continue as National Front instead of being run by a single party.

In Banaras, the Communists were gaining ground. They were being helped by some University teachers who had recently returned from Britain deeply impressed by the Communist leaders like Rajani Palme Dutt. I approached Acharya Narender Dev, Former Vice-Chancellor of Kashi Vidyapith to give me introduction to some non-communist students in Banaras whom I could mobilise.

He promptly obliged and gave me the names of about a dozen students of Banaras Hindu University and Kashi Vidyapith. I left for Banaras. I found most of them in their hostels but was told that Raj Narain stays in the city. We went there on an *eka* to the city and stopped in front of a street and it was pointed out that it was so narrow that no vehicle could move. We alighted and entered the street and found some young men using vulgar language and pushing one another. We were embarrassed but asked one of them, the house of Raj Narain. The young man introduced himself to me as Raj Narain.

Later on, he became a storm trooper of Socialist Party. He was appointed as Health Minister when Janata Party formed the Government in 1977. But till his untimely death he did not change the image that he had created in my mind in our first meeting. It was Raj Narain who defeated Indira Gandhi in Rai Bareli and was mainly responsible for the fall of Morarji Desai and Charan Singh, as Prime Ministers.

In due course, the All India Students' Federation developed into a very powerful organisation. In fact, it overshadowed the Indian National Congress in the urban areas. The Congress leaders became jealous of students and often we were accused of irresponsibility.

Even Gandhi did not approve of its frequent calls for political strike and pointed out that the schools and colleges were temples of learning where there was no justification for strike conveniently forgetting that in 1921, during the Khilafat and Non-cooperation movement, he himself has given the call for boycott of schools and colleges.

The more I saw Gandhi and read him the more I became

disappointed and disillusioned with him. My assessment of him is that he was a Hindu revivalist. His talk of Ram Raj, though well meaning, could not create any impression among Muslims who constituted one-fifty population of sub-continent. By joining hands with the mullas in the demand for restoration of Ottoman Empire in Turkey under the garb of Khilafat Movement, he encouraged Muslim revivalism and fundamentalism.

The concept of Mahatma and Maulana was against my rational thinking. If the national movement was led by one who was shaped in Science and Technology, probably, the shape of modern India would have been different.

As a student leader, I was deeply impressed by Jawaharlal. But, I was disappointed when he always compromised with Gandhi at every stage. I was more impressed by militancy of Subhas Bose. I will describe later my relationship with him.

Even after I had ceased to be a student, I continued my connection with the students' movements. At Calcutta Session of the All India Students' Federation, in spite of the opposition of the Communists, M.L. Shah who was sponsored by Congress Revolutionary Socialist Party, Royists and unattached groups were elected to succeed me.

Though he was General Secretary, the moving spirit behind him were myself and Probodh Chandra. We toured through length and breadth of India mobilising the students for anti-imperialist struggle.

I had shifted from Aligarh to Lucknow. The Lucknow University Union was very well organised. Most of my time, I used to spend in the University Union building. We captured the Union, by getting D.P. Dhar elected as President, who, later on, became a leading figure in Kashmir liberation and joined as Planning Minister in Indira Gandhi Government and represented India as its ambassador in Moscow, Sardar Jafri celebrated Urdu Poet as Secretary and Shankar Dayal Sharma, the present Vice-President of India as Librarian.

We organised at Lucknow, an all India Women Students' Conference. It was inaugurated by Mrs., Sarojini Naidu, and Renu Roy who was Secretary of our unit in Britain presided. Later, as Mrs. Renu Chakravartty became a prominent Member of Parliament. The Conference was attended by women students from all over India, and when Quit India Movement was launched in August 1942, many of them played a leading role as underground workers.

The All India Students' Federation, generated tremendous discontent among students all over India. It became a recruiting ground for leftist parties in India. The movement was completely neglected by Congress leadership, and often it was discouraged.

Among the non-students who played a prominent role in building up the students movements were Yousuf Mehar Ali, Dr. Ram Manohar Lohia, Acharya Narender Dev, M.R. Masani of the Congress Socialist Party, P.C. Joshi, Dr. K.M. Ashraf of the Communist Party. But, real inspiration came from Subhas Bose.

The election of Subhas Bose as Congress President gave a great fillip to the Students' Movement. Unlike other Congress leaders who looked upon students and youth with suspicion, he had a great faith in the youth power. During his first term as Congress President, he toured through length and breadth of the country, and in spite of the advice of local Congress Committees not to accept the invitation of Students' Federation he made it a point not only to address the meetings arranged by them, but built up personal contact with local as well as provincial students leaders.

He used to receive a big mail from students all over the country, and reply to them personally. He used to send those letters to me for being followed up.

Jawaharlal Nehru, who till then, was the hero of youths and students, felt neglected. In fact, during one of his visits to Lucknow, Mrs. Vijaya Lakshmi Pandit personally approached me to arrange a meeting of the students to be addressed by him. C.B. Gupta who was then the boss of the Lucknow City Congress Committee used to organise a Swadeshi Exhibition which was meant to give employment to his Congress workers. He invited Subhas Bose, as Congress President, to inaugurate the Exhibition. In his programme, he did not provide any time for him to address the students. He was curtly told by Subhas Bose that he would burn midnight candles to meet the student leaders and to address their meeting.

When Subhas decided to contest the election of Congress President for second term, I myself from U.P. and Probodh Chandra from Punjab were summoned by him to Calcutta for advice. We told him that though most of the students were not Congress delegates, with voting rights, they would still exert their influence on the voters to re-elect him as Congress President, in spite of the opposition of the right wing of the Congress and M.K. Gandhi.

For Subhas Bose's triumph over Gandhi, the workers of All India Students' Federation can take some credit. The Congress

Socialist Party headed by Jaiprakash Narain who had always been very close to Gandhi was forced to support Bose for fear of revolt of Student Cadres of his party.

The election of Subhas Bose, made Congress right wing more suspicious of the students. When Subhas Bose resigned from the Congress following the famous Pant Resolution, forcing him to form his Working Committee with the approval of Gandhi, the students of India solidly stood by him. His call for left Consolidation Committee, received response from the youths and students of the country.

When the Congress amended the Independence Pledge, which was supposed to have been drafted by Pandit Jawaharlal Nehru, but was just paraphrase of Declaration of Independence composed by Jafferson in America, inserting a clause that, we pledge to play *charkha* and wear *khadi.* Subhas Bose vehemently opposed the hypocrisy and futility of playing *charkhas.*

He appealed to his countrymen to organise separate meetings and to take the original pledge which they had taken on the bank of Ravi in Lahore in 1929. He decided to come to Lucknow and asked me to organise a meeting and procession.

The Congress meeting was organised in Amindula Park, the traditional venue of Congress Meeting. We organised a meeting just adjacent to this park. The Congress meeting was addressed by Pandit Pant, besides his Cabinet colleagues like Mrs. Vijaya Lakshmi Pandit, Sampurnanand, Dr. Katju and Rafi Ahmad Kidwai and socialist leader Acharya Narender Dev. It had a very thin gathering.

Subhas Bose addressed a massive rally of youth and students presided over by me in adjacent park and was taken in a huge procession shouting anti-compromise slogans.

On the outbreak of war, most of the student leaders were imprisoned under the Defence of India Rules. Many of them were sent to Deoli detention camps in the heart of the desert of Rajasthan. Till Soviet Union was not attacked by Nazi Germany, the Communist Party students supported us in anti-war activities. Many of them were arrested on some pretext or the other. But, when under the instruction of Communist Party, they declared it was people's war', many of them were released from jails.

After Britain entered in World War II, there was a persistent talk of compromise between Congress and British. Subhas Bose launched an anti-compromise campaign. The mass of the student offered their wholehearted support to him.

Lord Linlithgow invited seventeen Indian leaders to enlist

their support to war efforts. Subhas Bose was in Bombay and he was invited to meet the Viceroy in New Delhi. This was probably to be the first and last meeting between him and the representative of the British Crown.

I received a telegram from him to meet at Jhansi Railway station where he had to break his journey to catch the other train for Delhi. I met him in the waiting room of Jhansi station where he unfolded his plan to organise an anti-compromise conference while the Congress Session was to meet at Ramgarh in Bihar under the Presidentship of Maulana Azad. I expressed my doubt about its success at such a short notice. However, he asked me to proceed to Ramgarh immediately where I was to meet Swami Shajana Saraswati, the legendary kisan leader, Dhanraj Sharma, a prominent forward block leader and to assist them to organise the Conference. On alighting at Ranchi Road Station I found a sprawling township being erected in preparation of Congress Session. Dr. Rajendra Prasad who was the Chairman of the reception committee had all the resources of Birlas and Dalmias at his disposal. In fact, Dalmia was camping in Ramgarh, personally supervising the arrangements.

When I proceeded further, I found a small tent with a banner of anti-compromise conference. It housed Swami and some of his dedicated workers.

Within a few days, thousands of kisans and Adivasi volunteers poured in carrying thatch from neighbouring forests to erect the township. These volunteers lived on parched grain of gram and rice and worked throughout the whole day and night with unknown devotion in modern Indian history.

Within a few days, a car fitted with loudspeaker arrived from Calcutta and I took charge of it. I selected some local young men and started touring the neighbouring mining areas exhorting the workers and peasants to assemble at Ramgarh to attend anti-compromise conference to challenge the British to Quit India.

Krishna Ballabh Sahi, who later on, became Chief Minister and strong man of Bihar represented this area in Legislative Assembly. He used to follow me in other car campaigning against my campaign. But it appeared that he did not cut much ice with eager workers and peasants.

The Congress Socialist Party led by Jai Prakash Narayan had issued a statement dissociating his party from this Conference, I used to meet Dr. Ram Manohar Lohia in Congress, who was a close personal friend of mine. He used to make a fun of my optimism for he felt that Gandhi's influence was too great to be challenged.

However, on appointed day I was in sleep. Subhas Bose came and I was woken by a soft touch of hand and when I saw Subhas Bose, I was shocked and surprised but he explained that he would arrive by 9 a.m. by train. He came down from neighbouring railway station just to satisfy himself about the arrangements.

I took him round the camp. He even inspected urinals and latrines and suggested some improvements in them and left. This was the first glimpse of mine about his thoroughness which was amply displayed when he later on organised the legendary Indian National Army which hastened the retreat of British Imperialism from India.

It was fifty-second session of the Indian National Congress. The tastefully decorated chariot drawn by oxen which carried Subhas Bose and the Chairman, Reception Committee in a procession. It was preceded by fifty-two bullock carts carrying women singing anti-compromise songs. The half-naked Santals carrying their bows and arrows lent colour to the procession. When I passed local PWD Inspection House, I noticed who else but Pandit Jawaharlal Nehru standing behind a pillar watching the panorama with obvious envy.

The arrangement of anti-compromise conference at Ramgarh we made mostly through the effort of students and kisans. On my call, students from all over India had assembled at Ramgarh to offer their support to Subhas Bose to declare that no compromise was made with imperialism, short of complete Independence.

He asked Gandhi and Congress to give six months' ultimatum to Britain to hand over power to Indian people, otherwise, to launch a massive movement to drive them away. He believed that Britain's difficulty was India's opportunity.

But Gandhi and his Congress was reluctant to launch a massive movement. They were hoping against hope that in view of its difficulties Britain would be forced to hand over some limited power to his party men.

But, in the meantime, Britain had created a considerable following of Muslims for M.A. Jinnah and his Muslim League. The feudal elements in U.P. and Bihar and many other provinces had rallied round him. He had taken advantage of Hindu revivalist tendencies of Congress governed Provinces under provincial autonomy. The naming of primary schools in Central Provinces headed by Ravi Shankar Shukla's Vidya

Mandir, insistence on singing of *Vande Mataram,* and preference to Hindi over Urdu by Pant in U.P the cradle of Urdu culture were easy handle in the hand of Jinnah to tell the Muslim masses that 'Islam was in danger.'

Gandhi's plea not to launch a mass movement was that it may result in communal tension and riots. However, Subhas Bose launched a limited movement in Calcutta to remove the Holwell monument which tarnished the image of a Muslim Sultan Sirajuddaula. Even the most rabid Muslim Leaguer could not take objection to this movement and, along with hundreds of students, Subhas Bose courted arrest.

Earlier at Ramgarh, I had acted as his public relation officer. He was staying in a thatched hut and was busy drafting his presidential address. In between, he used to peep out and finding thousands of people making their way towards the venue of anti-compromise conference, with a smile used to remark that what fool Jaya Prakash is for he felt that my conference will be an utter failure.

He had deep contempt for double dealing of Jayaprakash Narayan who posed to be a leftist, but was always on the side of the right.

One incident I remember — I was in Calcutta and J.P. had come to see Subhas Bose; he assured him that in case he launched a movement, he will offer him full support.

I was asked by Subhas Bose to check up that what will be his real attitude. I went to Burra Bazar, where as usual, J.P. was guest of a rich Marwari Seth. I met him and asked him for his reaction. He told me that since Subhas had lot his head who will support him if Gandhi does not bless a movement? I came back, reported to Subhas Bose and he remarked that he was always convinced that the man was a double dealer.

However, undaunted by discouragement of Gandhi, double talks of J.P., Subhas Bose launched a limited direct action in Calcutta in spite of Gandhi's warning this did not generate any hostility among Muslims. In fact, the Muslims came in large number to encourage those who were determined to restore the honour of last Muslim monarch of Bengal.

Subhas Bose was arrested and detained in Presidency Jail of Calcutta. After some time, he wrote a letter to Viceroy which he described as his last testament, and in Gandhian fashion went to fast unto death.

This decision unnerved the Muslim League Ministry of Bengal headed by Sir Nizamuddin. Their emissary, Abdul Rahman Siddiqui, a former leader of Khilafat Movement, who was Mayor of Calcutta visited him and urged him to give up the fast. On Subhas Bose's refusal, Siddiqui persuaded Sir Nizamuddin to release him and to re-arrest him when he is fully recovered.

On his release, he invited me and Probodh Chandra from Lahore by telegram to come to Calcutta to meet him. When I was ushered in his room, I found a bearded Subhas Bose lying on king size bed surrounded by bouquets sent by his admirers. He had a feeble voice obviously he did not take us into confidence as what was to come. It was early January 1941, he told me that Gandhi was going to launch individual satyagraha to send political elements to jail in most peaceful and non-violent fashion. But something big is going to happen before the end of June, when monsoon will set in, and see that as many students cadres remained outside jails as possible. I was bewildered by his advice. I could not imagine in my wildest dream and that he would march to Europe to head an Indian National Army. On my return I organised a meeting to felicitate him on his birthday on January 23. It was on January 26 that we learnt from newspapers that he had disappeared from his 38A, Elgin Road residence heavily surrounded by intelligence people.

In early June 1941, we learnt that Mufti Aminul Hussainia has revolted in Palestine. Rashed Ali the Prime Minister of Iraq has taken arms against British, Pir of Pagaro was in revolt in Sind and Baluchistan border, Reza Shah Pahalvi, father of last Shah of Iran was banished by British forces to South America.

The German Army had overrun Greece, but was halted in rocky Crete, which delayed their march to Asiatic soil.

In spite of Subhas Bose's instruction, I was arrested in April for delivering a speech as I did not offer individual satyagraha, just reciting a mantra handed over to Congressmen by Gandhi.

I was sad that I could not avoid arrest till June as stipulated by my leader. However, I will describe my jail life later.

When I was released by some administrative mistake, for those arrested for satyagraha were given amnesty, Japanese had already taken over British colonies in Far East. They were knocking at the door of Bengal. The Berlin Radio was busy broadcasting message of Subhas Bose telling his people that freedom comes to those who dare and act. Gandhi and his followers were hoping against hopes that British will make some gesture to enlist Indian support. They sent Sir Stafford Cripps who was reputed to be a friend of India in general and Nehru in particular. But, Gandhi in desperation had to learn that he was offering a post dated cheque of a crashing bank.

There was general frustration in the country and among Congress cadres. The Communists had already hitched their wagon with British imperialism after Soviet's entry in the war.

All hopes of Gandhi and his right wing supporters to get some sort of gesture from British to enlist Indian support for war efforts were shattered. The British war Cabinet headed by Sir Winston Churchill, who, time and again, had declared that he was not going to preside over His Majesty's Government to liquidate the empire.

The leftist elements in the Congress were not happy with the efforts to have a compromise with the British. Most of them were arrested. But some of us managed to go underground, and carry on anti-war campaign.

Chapter 5

COMMUNALISM AND STUDENTS

EVER since I joined politics in 1928, I never entertained any communal idea. Aligarh which was the hot-bed of Muslim communalism could not influence many of us to be carried away by the slogan of 'Islam is in Danger' and 'Muslim should be trained for re-conquest of India for Islam?'

As mentioned before, we had a number of brushes with the authorities especially Dr. Sir Ziauddin the lengendary Vice-Chancellor of Aligarh Muslim University.

I had met M.A Jinnah in his chamber at Bombay High Court in 1936 after his return from England as he, disowned by his community and not trusted by Congressmen, had settled down permanently to carry on his legal practice. On his return, he tried to reorganise the Muslim League, which was shattered to pieces after his decision to boycott the Simon Commission.

It may be interesting to describe briefly the background of M.A Jinnah. He started his political career, under the guidance of Dada Bhai Nauroji and Feroze Shah Mehta.

Jinnah, assisted by K.F. Narriman, a young Congress leader, arranged a demonstration against Lord Willingdon, the Governor of Bombay and in appreciation of his services, the people of Bombay raised enough fund to erect 'People's Jinnah Hall', in the heart of Bombay city which housed the Office of the Indian National Congress, even after the partition of Indian sub-continent. He was described as Ambassador of Hindu Muslim Unity by poetess politician, Sarojini Naidu. He was completely innocent of Islamic teaching and Muslim rituals. He enjoyed his smoke and whisky and soda.

He had complete mistrust of Gandhi. He was first shocked when after Gandhi's arrival from South Africa, the Gujaratis of Bombay organised a reception in his honour presided over by Jinnah. While replying to address of welcome, Gandhi described Jinnah as a fellow Muslim Gujarati, not an Indian. His second disappointment came when at Nagpur session of the Indian National Congress, where the Muslim constituted the overwhelming majority of delegates, for Gandhi has come forward to support the Turkish Caliph, who was considered a spiritual head of Muslim world. Every delegate was addressing Gandhi as Mahatma, but Jinnah refused to do so. He was hooted down by delegates mostly long flowing bearded mullas and had to walk away from the Congress, which he had served for almost three decades never to return back again.

I persuaded him to preside over the All India Students' Convention which was to be inaugurated by Jawaharlal Nehru. This was the last time when the two shared the same platform. He gave me an autographed photograph, with slogan work for Hindu Muslim Unity'. The photograph appeared in 'Students' Tribune' published from Lahore. I lost all photographs and papers during the raids in my residence and offices during freedom movement.

The Congress had decided to fight the election of Provincial Legislature in 1937, under Government of India Act, 1935. The Congress was not confident to obtain absolute majority. In U.P., Khaliquz Zaman, and many other Congressmen were persuaded to contest on League's ticket with full assurance that after election, they will be accepted as collaborators of Congress Party. The Congress won unexpected absolute majority and under the influence of communists and Rafi Ahmed Kidwai who was jealous of Khaliquz Zaman, Nehru refused to allow a coalition Government with the league. This deeply hurt Jinnah, who like other moderates, liberals and constitutionalists of the twenties was suspicious of Gandhi's influence and popularity. But he could not help it, by temperament, as he could not discard his London-tailored suit and sacrifice even the crease of his trousers to mix with the masses like Gandhi and his Muslim supporters. In Khalique, he found a useful ally who was brought up in the Congress technique of mass agitation. It was he who suggested at the Lucknow Session of All India Muslim League in 1938, to adopt a flag to enlist volunteers, to hold mass rallies and processions. Though a year earlier Jinnah had presided over All India Students Convention at Lucknow, which gave birth to All India Students' Federation, he mooted the idea of organising an All India Muslim Students' Federation. The Aligarh Muslim University was the most fertile ground for its birth. Choudhari Khaliquz Zaman addressed a meeting of the University Union, where he declared that a time would come when Nehru would realise that there was no better Congressman than him, but urged the Muslim to rally, under the flag of an All India Students' Federation.

Some students aspirant of the patronage of authorities took up the idea and it was decided to organise a Convention at Lucknow, at the same venue where Jinnah and Nehru had helped the birth of the All India Students' Federation.

This was a challenge to me and to most of my Aligarh colleagues. We decided to go to Lucknow to capture the Convention and to foil the move of the Muslim Leaguers. About one hundred of us travelled to Lucknow, mostly without railway tickets as we had no money for it, and occupied the rooms meant for those who were to attend the Convention. We mobilised the support of nationalist minded students of Lucknow. Early in the morning accompanied by some colleagues, I visited Nadwatual Ulema, a University which trained Muslim divines, and offered our prayer in their mosque. After the prayers were over, I made a moving speech urging the Muslim students to foil the move of separatism which was likely not only to hamper the freedom of India but also liberation of Arab world, particularly, the holy places in Palestine which were under foreign occupation.

Later, I met the son of Maulana Abdul Bari, Jamal Mian in Frangi Mahal. Maulana Bari was the main collaborator of Gandhi during the Khilafat Movement, and I reminded him of the anti-imperialist traditions of his house. He readily agreed to lend his support through; later, he became the most trusted Muslim divine and lieutenant of Jinnah and replaced Maulana Abdul Kalam Azad to lead *Id* prayers in Calcutta.

The Convention was to meet in the morning. I knew the entire topography of the venue. We occupied the hall and galleries much before our opponents reached. The Convention was to be presided over by Dr. Abdullah Yousuf Ali, a former I.C.S., whose English translation of *Quran* is considered to be most authentic. He could not even enter the Hall. We had persuaded Mushir Hassain Qidwai, a Pan-Islamist of world fame who presided and we declared our unqualified opposition to formation of Muslim Students' Federation.

The Muslim League leadership and their cadres were not dismayed by their failure at Lucknow. The indiscretions of Congress Governments in U.P. and Central Provinces gave an impetus to their movement.

The revivalist tendencies of some of the Hindu Congress leaders created widespread misunderstanding in Muslim minds. In Bengal, during the General Election of 1937, Congress had collaborated with Krishak Praja Party, headed by

A.K. Fazlul Haq. But, Sarat Bose, elder brother of Subhas Bose, was not allowed to join a coalition government with them, and in sheer desperation, A.K. Fazlul Haq and his party had to join hands with the Leagues to form a Government. Gandhi's well meaning slogan to usher Ram Raj had no appeal to Muslim minds. They were made to believe that it meant Hindu Raj.

Since Bengal was ruled by a coalition of Krishak Praja Party, and Muslim League, they tried to mobilise their force there. The students from Lahore, Aligarh, Delhi, Lucknow and other places reached Calcutta to repeat the performance at Lucknow.

In Calcutta, we got full cooperation from Sarat Bose who was the leader of the Congress Party. We tried to get one of the Muslim Ministers from one of the seven Congress governed provinces to preside. But, all of them, got cold feet.

A.K. Fazlul Haq, one of the most dynamic politicians of his times actively campaigned to mobilise the Muslim students. He went from room to room in Carmichael Hostel which housed the Muslim Students of Calcutta University to mobilise their support. We followed him to counteract his campaign and met with a considerable success.

Backed by their Lucknow experience, they organised the Conference in Mohammad Ali Park in a thickly populated Muslim locality notorious for anti-social elements. We thought discrimination to be a better valour and decided to organise the parallel Conference in Albert Hall at College Street just in front of University Campus.

The Conference in Mohammad Ali Park, Calcutta, was presided over by M.A. Jinnah while our Conference was presided over by Professor Humayun Kabir, Nazrul Islam, the greatest Bangla Poet after Tagore, especially, composed a poem for the Conference and inaugurated it.

The proceedings of our Conference overshadowed the performance of the Conference presided over by Jinnah in national papers. We denounced the separatist move among students and gave full support to anti-imperialist forces.

However, the Muslim Students' Federation got a shot in arm when the Communist Party of India supported the right of self-determination of Muslim nationalities and described the British stooges as League patriots. Some of our best cadres, mostly in Lahore, to name a few, Maher Ali, Mohammad Ali and Miss Mumtaz Shahnawaz, cosmopolitan and modern in their outlook started shouting 'Quid-e-Azam Zindabad' as 'Allah Akbar', and repeating the slogan that Islam is in danger.

This was one of the greatest disservice of the Communist Party of India to the cause of Indian Nationalism and I wonder if posterity will forgive them for this betrayal.

Chapter 6

I GO UNDERGROUND

IN March 1942, U.P. Government issued order of arrest against Rafi Ahmed Kidwai, S.K.D. Paliwal, President of U.P.C.C., Prof. Shibban Lal Saksena, a peasant leader of Gorakhpur and myself.

On getting the news that the police had reached old Councillors' residence, where Rafi was staying after resignation of Congress Ministries, I rushed there. Most of the Congress workers and leaders in Lucknow also happened to be there. Islam Ahmed who later on became the I.G.P., U.P. and during emergency was appointed as Chief Advisor of the Governor, was then an Assistant Superintendent of Police and had come to escort Rafi to Bareily Central Jail, told me that the station officer of my area must be awaiting for me at my house to take me in custody. Having received this tip though given innocently by a police officer, I went underground. I stayed with a non-political lawyer friend, and thence, sent information to Calcutta and Bombay friends, under cover address to help to escape from Lucknow, where my movements were not possible without being noticed by the police.

An emissary arrived from Bombay and it was arranged that I should meet him later in the evening on river bank. An interesting incident took place which needs to be recorded.

A number of Burmese refugees had arrived in Lucknow and the prosperous among them were living in posh localities. A family was staying in a bungalow in front of Wazir Manzil, the residence of Dr. Hussain Zaheer, an eminent scientist who was an active communist. It appears that the family had reported to the police that the neighbouring servants come and make vulgar remarks against Burmese beauties. The house was being watched by the police men and seeing me in the dresses of valet of 'bura sahibs', they pounced on me and asked me to accompany them to the police station. I knew if I was taken to police station, I would at once be recognised and arrested.

However, I had a brainwave and told them that my master, Dr. Zaheer will vouch for my good character. Accompanied by them, I came to Dr. Zaheer's house. Realizing the situation, he asked police to let me go. Dr. Zaheer was a member of Communist Party, which was supporting the war efforts but his gesture belied the accusation that the communists were helping the police to arrest the Congress workers. The hub of political activities were Calcutta and Bombay. Due to revolutionary movement, the British Intelligence and vigilance in Calcutta was strongest, Bombay being a cosmopolitan city was a haven for underground workers. Moreover, many young businessmen were willing to offer financial and other kind of help to political workers.

So, I decided to go to Bombay where already two of the important Secretaries of Forward Block, H.V. Kamath who had resigned from coveted I.C.S. to join Bose and Sheelbhadra Yajee, and Mukundlal Sarkar, a former General Secretary of All India Trade Union Congress were stationed. They had hired an apartment on Chowpatty seaface and staying there. I joined them. Being the youngest among them I was made to travel almost all over India to contact our cadres who were out of jail, to mobilize them for a final struggle. I visited Lahore, Karachi, Peshawar, Rawalpindi and some of the Southern provinces. Though most of our senior friends were in Jail a number of students were willing to come forward to work for us.

In those days, coloured posters were very rare. A friendly press published for us a poster with Subhas Bose's portrait with caption 'Liberator of India'; overnight, it was pasted on the walls of all prominent cities of India much to the surprise of Congress right wing which had hounded him out of India.

Some of the Congress socialists like Dr. Lohia were also staying underground in Bombay. We had close contact with them though not convinced of their revolutionary credentials for their stand at the Tripura remaining neutral on Pant Resolution which had led to the resignation of Subhas Bose. We decided to give them a try. The country was seething with discontent and Subhas Bose's broadcast from Berlin radio were eagerly awaited in homes which possessed radio sets. His moving appeal to throw away British yoke, and request to Gandhi and Congress to give up illusions about British intentions were creating a mass upsurge. Obviously Congress could not remain unmoved by this situation. The British snub was adding fuel to fire and reluctantly Gandhi and Congress had to take up militant attitude by giving slogan of 'Quit India'. Aware of the impatience of the Indian people Gandhi and Congress Working Committee were constantly meeting, awaiting for some response from their British masters. But in spite of defeats in Europe as well as in South East the British Government headed by Winston Churchill still held belief in 'white man's burden' and imperialism and was in no mood to oblige them.

However, in sheer frustration and desperation, the All India Congress Committee met at Bombay on August 8, 1942 and at midnight passed the famous Quit India Resolution. Gandhi, in his characteristic way, gave a slogan of 'Do or Die'.

It was unfortunate that the Congress leadership headed by Gandhi, Nehru and Patel had not prepared any blue-print and programme for those who were expected to 'Do or Die'. They had ridiculed Subhas Bose in 1939, when he urged them to issue a six-month ultimatum to British and launch a struggle. In three years the Government of India was fully prepared to face the challenge of Gandhi and Congress. They had already marched the tried freedom fighters to Deoli Camp in the heart of Rajasthan desert. The entry of America in War had provided the British with enormous resources to suppress the unplanned Indian uprising. Early in the morning the vigilant British authorities struck and arrested Gandhi, and all the members of the Working Committee, in Bombay except Rajendra Prasad who could not attend the A.I.C.C. session due to indisposition.

Though I was a member of All India Congress Committee, I did not attend the session but watched the proceedings from a distance in disguise. I found the tired old men on Congress platform who had appeared to be making all efforts to have a reasonable compromise with their masters. The night of August 8, I spent at the house of Abbas, an old friend who was on night shift at 'Bombay Chronicle'. He came back in early morning to inform me that the telephone connection all over Bombay have been disconnected and leaders have been arrested and apparently being marched to Bombay Victoria Terminus. I rushed to Railway station where huge crowds of on-lookers were watching. Gandhi and the Congress giants being led like sheep to a waiting train for an unknown destination. In the crowd, I noticed Lohia and Aruna Asaf Ali and we decided to meet them in the afternoon at a building known as Son Mahal near Gowalia tank where Lohia was staying.

At 10 a.m. that day, Nehru was to address students rally at Chowpaty. I rushed towards the venue and found the entire place cordoned off by police and paramilitary force. I sat down in a nearby Irani tea house and sent a message to the leader of the students, who were assembling there to implement the slogan of Gandhi 'Do or die' and break the cordon. This was a signal of revolt throughout the city. The industrial metropolis of India was afire. Gandhi and members of the Working Committee never calculated that the Government of India, under the direction of Winston Churchill will take such a drastic step. In fact, Gandhi was planning to go to Delhi and to ask the Viceroy with folded hands and bended knees to accept the Congress demand to quit India. His and Working Committee members' arrest must have come as a great shock to Gandhi who was eager to compromise with the British provided they offered a face saving device.

The Congress organisation was declared illegal, and most of the Congressmen were arrested within a week of the A.I.C.C. session of Bombay. Some of them who were not arrested are reported to have telephoned to authorities to be taken into custody for they were afraid that they would be hauled up for fomenting violence.

Most of the Congressmen who later cashed their suffering and sacrifices collected garlands and quietly went to jails. It was left to the students and handful of leaders of the Congress Socialist Party and Forward Block who managed to avoid their arrest.

The role of orthodox Congressmen in the so-called August Revolution was very marginal, though after the Independence they were the greatest beneficiaries. Gandhi and Congress Working Committee had nothing to do with the uprising of August 1942. It is revealed from a letter, which he wrote five days after his arrest, dissociating himself from the movement in which, he said "Violence was never contemplated at any stage. A definition for what could be included, in non-violence action has been interpreted in action". Again, on September 24, 1942, he wrote to Home Secretary of Government of India and said, "In spite of all that has been said, to the contrary, I claim that Congress policy still remains unequivocally non-violent."

However, in spite of Gandhi, and the Congress Working Committee, the impatient masses took law in their own hands; the Forward Bloc and Socialist Party leaders from Bombay managed to send messages to their student cadres to take up the lead.

The students of Banaras Hindu University in spite of obstructions put by police, abetted by Sir Radhakrishnan, the Vice-Chancellor, who later on was rewarded for his services to the British, by being elected President of Republic of India fanned themselves in Eastern U.P and Bihar; for weeks, the administration in Ballia in U.P. was completely paralysed, the District Magistrate and police chief ran away and parallel Government functioned under a kisan leader Chitu Pandey, till the British army came to relieve the siege and butchered men, women and children.

In Allahabad, the students marched towards the city after a meeting in the University campus and they were fired upon by the police and the army, one of them died on the spot, and many of them were seriously injured. Some students headed by H.N. Bahuguna who later on held high office under the Congress and Opposition went underground and worked in various University towns till they were arrested. The only member of Nehru household, who joined the demonstration, was Chandralekha Pandit, eldest daughter of Vijayalakshmi Pandit, was arrested.

Mrs. Indira Gandhi, was also arrested and imprisoned for a brief period, for she was being suspected to have harboured some underground workers in the servant quarters of her ancestral house Anand Bhavan. But only after few months, she was released on the recommendation of Col. Oberoi, Superintendent of Naini Jail, for being pregnant and, in Bombay, the present Prime Minister of India Rajiv was born.

The orthodox Congressmen were nowhere to be seen. Though Gandhi had shouted the slogan of 'Do or Die', he left no programme for his followers. It was left to socialist and forward blocists to mobilise the masses. However, the programme was announced by Subhas Bose, from Berlin Radio urging his countrymen to realise that Britain's difficulty was India's opportunity. He urged on his countrymen to disrupt the British line of communication to erect blockades on roads, remove railway lines, to disrupt telegraph and telephone wires, to blow up bridges. He appealed to the father of the nation to bless these efforts. But the father of the nation was planning a fast unto death to secure his release from Aga Khan palace, where he was detained with his wife, secretaries and close associates like Mira Ben, Miss Madliene Slade, the daughter of a British Admiral.

In this struggle many students laid down their lives; a young student hardly eighteen years old, Himu Khilani, was hanged in Sind for having removed a railway fish plate.

In the absence of an organisation, and proper leadership, the war time British power crushed the movement within few months, most of my comrades and friends were already arrested. I felt that I could not serve the country, by remaining in India and decided to go abroad to join Subhas Bose's force. A friend gave me a Pathan darban of Bombay flying club, who knew the North Western Frontier very well, belonging to one of the tribes. I accompanied him to Peshawar Banu and Kohat but found that after the escape of Subhas Bose the frontiers were so well guarded that it was impossible to crossover to Afghanistan. Disappointed by my efforts I came back to Bombay, after visiting Lahore and Rawalpindi and I planned to cross over to Burma which was occupied by the Japanese.

In Calcutta, I contacted Prof. Humayun Kabir who was assisting the underground workers by arranging shelter and funds for them. He was a member of Bengal Legislative Council and Muslim League Ministry opposed his arrest, for they did not want to give an impression that even Bengal Muslims were in revolt. But he was keenly watched by Intelligence Department, and it was a job to contact him in a discreet way.

When I told him my proposal, he put me in touch with Maulana Islamabadi, a legislator from Chittagong which touched Burma border. I accompanied him to Chittagong dressed like a Muslim peasant of East Bengal. He provided me with a guide who knew the terrain. By crossing a number of rivers on foot having covered more than sixty miles from Cox Bazar, I entered Arakan, a predominantly Muslim province of Burma. Having left me alone, the guide disappeared and being very tired I lay down in front of a closed shop. While I was fast asleep, the kick of a British woke me up. I was immediately taken into custody. In the beginning I behaved like a deaf and dumb man. In military lock up in Cox Bazar, I gave my name as Anil Chaudhary. I was interrogated by an army intelligence officer Col. Tyson, who threatened that as enemy agent, I might be shot dead.

However, on re-thinking, they sent me to Calcutta and handed over me to civil authorities. I was lodged in Lal Bazar, the Police Headquarters of Calcutta and later was taken to the court of Chief Presidency Magistrate, Mr. Ranjit Gupta. He called for my name Anil Choudhari, I did not respond. I was pushed forward by an Anglo-Indian sergeant and I shouted, "Your worship I have been wrongly arrested, I am not Anil Choudhary, I am Ansar Harvani". The Magistrate gave a smile and said I still remained as Anil Choudhary *alias* Ansar Harvani.

For almost a fortnight, I was kept at Lal Bazar and was daily taken to Lord Sinha Road; the headquarters of intelligence branch. I was closely interrogated that what I knew about the escape of Subhas Bose, and whereabouts of his associates. For three days and nights I was kept sitting without a wink of sleep with arc-light on my face but, fortunately, I did not break down.

Ultimately, they sent me to Alipore Central Jail, in judicial custody to stand a trial in Tollygunge Conspiracy case for obtaining arms and ammunitions from British soldiers with a view to overthrowing His Majesty's Government. When this case could not be sustained in the court of an Alipore Magistrate, I was served an order under Defence of India Rules to be detained for indefinite period. Thus, my life, as an underground soldier for liberation of my country, came to an end.

As I have already pointed out, Gandhiji and his faithfuls in the Congress Working Committee had sheepishly marched to the isolation of Aga Khan Palace and Ahmedabad to write their memoirs and to study *Bhagwad Gita,* the responsibility of leading the resistance movement, and implementing the slogan of 'Do or Die' was left to a handful of socialist forward blocists and student leaders, who had managed to avoid the arrest.

It is true that many of them had no training or background to work underground. Most of them in their early political career were taught that Swaraj can be obtained by playing spinning wheel, and propagating *Khadi.*

The communists who knew how to operate underground and to smuggle instruction even from behind the prison bars were busy to mobilise support for the British war efforts. Even a veteran socialist leader Jaya Prakash Narayan who was not trained in these practices was caught for smuggling a message through his wife from Deoli detention camp putting the police on track of many of underground workers.

May of them thought a little disguise would save them from police vigilance. H.V. Kamath who was staying with us and disguised himself as a Sadhu dressed up in saffron clothes with beard which he carried on till his death, was recognised at a Gita class in Bharatiya Vidya Bhavan and marched to prison. J.P. scaled the prison wall but by that time all the resistance was crushed by the mighty British force.

Chapter 7

SERVING THE JAIL SENTENCE

THOUGH I was baptised in the struggle for Indian Freedom in 1928, I was never sent to jail being too young during the successive movements launched by Congress under the leadership of Gandhi in 1930 and 1933. I was often arrested but was set free after strict warning by the police.

As I have written already, I was advised by Subhas Bose not to join the individual satyagraha launched by Gandhi in 1941. It was a symbolic movement where selected satyagrahis were made to inform the time and venue to British authorities as to where they were to recite a set of anti-war slogans or mantra. Gandhi had declared Nehru as his political successor, but he selected one of his unknown disciple, Vinoba, as a first satyagrahi to give it more of a moral than political complexion. Nehru, before he could follow Vinoba, had already been arrested in Gorakhpur for delivering a seditious speech and sentenced to four years' imprisonment, by Moss, a notorious District Magistrate.

Following Subhas Bose's instruction, I did not enlist myself as an individual satyagrahi, but the communist till then treated the war between two warring imperial powers were being arrested in large numbers. They started vilification campaign against me that I was avoiding arrest for I was a British informer.

However, in April 1941, I was arrested for delivering a speech on the occasion of Jallianwala Bagh Day. I was produced before Lord John , a young city magistrate of Lucknow who sent me to Lucknow District Jail. Later, after a trial in which I declared the magistrate as a representative of an usurper administration and refused to say anything in my defence, I was sentenced to one year rigorous imprisonment and two hundred rupees fine and, in default, to serve for six months more.

Though student leaders arrested before me were placed

either in 'A' or 'B' class which entitled them for better food, a cot to sleep, a mosquito net for protection, I was to get treatment as a 'C' class prisoner like an ordinary criminal.

I was supplied with two iron cups for drinking water, taking meals and using them for my bath buy a common water tap. I was supplied a coir mattress and coarse blanket for my bed. The food was uneatable which consisted of boiled *dal* full of stoned coarse rice and hard bread of mixture of wheat gram, tea was unknown to us. Since I was convicted with hard labour, grass was supplied to us to be made into rope. Since I had no training in this art, some fellow prisoners helped me to learn it. Most of my fellow prisoners were peasants from districts of Lucknow, Barabanki, Unnao and Kanpur. They were jolly-good fellows. In fact, they were real freedom fighters whom leaders staying in luxurious 'A' class cells treated as cannon fodder. I conducted their literacy classes and taught them Roman alphabet.

Under the jail manual, graduate convicts, even the ordinary criminals, were placed in the category 'B' class prisoner who were entitled to better food and treatment. I was advised by some sympathetic junior jail officials to put in an application for being treated as 'B' class prisoner but, in my idealism, I refused to do it. It appears that some wellmeaning friends approached the government and after few months, I was transferred to a nearby barrack, which housed 'A' and 'B' class prisoners.

The barrack housed some prisoners repatriated from Andaman, Chandan Singh Garhwali the leader of Garhwal Regiment, who had refused to fire on unarmed red shirt demonstrators in Kisakhani Bazar of Peshawar as 'A' class prisoners, Pandit Jawaharlal Nehru and his brother-in-law Ranjit Pandit. With Nehru as prisoner all of us were given VIP treatment. Col. Jafari, the Superintendent of Jail was a frequent visitor to find out about the comfort of Nehru and consequently of ours.

We were allowed indoor games, like chess and carrom and Nehru arranged to have a badminton court in the ward, where we played with him. Later, Nehru was transferred to cool climate of Almora and many of our facilities were consequently withdrawn.

After a few weeks' stay in Lucknow Jail, I was transferred to Banaras Central Jail. It housed most of the prominent Congress leaders of Eastern U.P. many of whom became Ministers in U.P. Government after the transfer of power. It was a very happy family life, and we had full opportunity to know the plus and minus points of those who were later on to rule over India. Some of them openly collaborated with jail authorities for petty advantages.

It may be noted that Gandhi, in the entire political career, managed to see that his followers were never made to serve the full term of their imprisonment. He always engineered some pretext to secure their early release. By the end of December, Gandhi called off his individual satyagraha, to have another round of talks of compromise with British Administration. He withdrew his individual satyagraha, and Nehru, and other satyagrahis were released though Nehru had not completed his sentence for four years.

Through some misunderstanding of U.P.Government, I was also a beneficiary of Gandhi's action, though I was to be proclaimed as an absconder after a few weeks of my freedom. After my arrest on Burma border and being kept in police headquarters of Lal Bazar in Calcutta, I was sent to Alipur jail as an undertrial prisoner. I was kept with Anglo-Indian prisoners who were lodged in European ward. However, I managed to make contact with other political prisoners in different wards. After I was released in Tollyganj conspiracy case, I was served with detention order and was allowed to live with other political prisoners. In Alipur, the overwhelming majority of prisoners belonged to leftist group, though there were few followers of Gandhi also.

The young prisoners taunted the Gandhiites for their cowardice. According to Gandhi, when one enters jail, one meets one's civic death and had to fully to cooperate with jail authorities. The young prisoners made fun of and ridiculed Gandhiites for their submissiveness to jail authorities.

One day I found a criminal carrying huge suit case balanced on his head. I was surprised that who it could be who was to join us, for most of the Bengal prisoners came from lower middle class and they could not afford a big and expensive suit case. Afterwards I found Prabodh Chandra who later on became Minister and Speaker in Punjab was brought from Multan Jail to join us.

The treatment to security prisoners in Bengal was excellent. We were provided enough provisions, fish, fowl, meat, eggs for our upkeep. I was elected as leader of prisoners belonging to Forward Bloc, who constituted the largest section of political prisoners. We arranged study circles, to discuss social, political and economic programmes. Most of the prisoners were fresh from schools and colleges and a very happy-go-lucky crowd.

On Christmas eve in 1943, some Japanese planes flew over Calcutta and dropped few bombs. We were locked in our cells but shouted *'Bande Mataram'* welcoming Japanese planes for we knew that they were the allies of Subhas Bose.

Next day, we could see from the second floor of our prison huge masses carrying boxes, bed rolls and other things evacuating Calcutta. The prosperous Indian population had already migrated to upcountry, leaving poor people to face the difficulties of war.

Our most pathetic experience was great Bengal famine. The famished people, used to assemble near jail walls, where we used to thrown out leftover food which they eagerly lifted to satisfy their hunger. I wrote an angry letter to Jinnah pointing out that thousands were dying in the streets of Calcutta; while his League Ministry headed by Sayeed Shurwardy was ruling. He wrote tome pointing out that I was carried away by the propaganda of Hindu Press and he has asked Hasa Isphani, one of his industrialist lieutenant to meet me. But Ishpani never came.

I sent a representative to Sir Tenent Slogan, an I.C.S. adviser to U.P. Government using most abusive language that I was languishing in a Jail far off from my home. He always cared to acknowledge my letter but U.P. Government considered me too dangerous to be kept in their jail. We were not allowed a radio set, but could have some newspaper approved by the Government. It was interesting that we got the news about the activities of Subhas Bose and his national army only from communist papers who highlighted them to paint him as a traitor and fifth columnist of the Germans and the Japanese.

In our neighbouring ward were lodged some of the Chittagong army raid prisoners repatriated from Andaman. Though all of them had joined communist party and subscribed to the thesis of people's war, they were not released. From across the wall, I used to have interesting debates with them though none of us could convert to their views. But it was a good pastime.

Unlike my earlier experience in jail with satyagrahis, the morals of young prisoners belonging to Forward Bloc, Revolutionary Socialist Party, Revolutionary Communist Party was very high indeed. None of them felt home-sick and most of them were confident of the victory of Indian National Army led by Subhas Bose.

There were few followers of Gandhi like Atulya Ghosh who then was an obscure district Congressman, later on, to become one of the most important money collectors of the Congress Party, Satish Das Gupta who dressed and behaved like Gandhi and assisted the jail authorities. They were looked down upon for their non-militant attitude.

During great Bengal Famine, we succeeded to persuade the jail authorities to pass on the cooked food through drain gate for the hungry loitering about the jail walls as according to Jail Manual, it could not pass through the regular jail gate. This action was disapproved by Gandhiites, who were told by Gandhi that after their imprisonment, they met their civic death.

I was in regular correspondence with U.P. Government for my transfer to some of the jails in my own some province. But, I always used to receive an acknowledgement from the P.A. of Sir Tenent Slogan who was adviser for Home Affairs to the Governor of U.P. In the meantime, I was visited by Mohammad Ali Bogra, Parliamentary Secretary to the Chief Minister of Bengal who later on became Prime Minister of Pakistan.

I knew him from my Aligarh days for his younger brothers were my friends and I often stayed at his house in Amir Ali Avenue during Christmas holidays. He asked me to join Maulana Azad who was transferred to Bankura from Ahmedabad Fort in preparation of his release. I readily agreed.

It was a rare experience to be in the company of this philosopher statesman and scholar who embodies all the qualities of a leader, prescribed by ancient Greek philosophers. He was lodged in the Patiala House of a local zamindar which was converted as a special jail. I was amazed by his scholarship.

One day I received a blue envelope, containing a hand written letter from Sir Tenent Slogan pointing out that he has retired from his service and was proceeding to Bombay to await for a boat to go home but, before his retirement, he had passed the order for my transfer to Bareilly Jail. This demonstrates the attitude of British bureaucrats who became humane the moment they were to shed their official responsibilities.

While in Alipore Jail, my cell was on upper floor wherefrom condemned cells and the courtyard where execution by hanging used to take place was visible. I saw a number of murderers being hanged before the dawn. It was a pathetic experience.

My most vivid memory is of Hari Prasad Mitra married to Bela, a favourite niece of Subhas Bose. He was condemned to death by a tribunal for being an enemy agent. Often Bela accompanied by Abdul Rehman Siddiqui, the Muslim League Mayor of Calcutta and a family friend used to visit her husband who was awaiting his execution. I used to be thrilled to watch young beautiful recently married young lady uttering words of consolation to her husband and often smiling. But the moment she left the death row, she used to collapse to be helped by Siddiqui to jail gate.

During my presence at least two valiant soldiers of the Indian National Army were executed chanting *"Jai Hind"*. It was from them for the first time that we come to know that Subhas Bose was addressed as Netaji, and had given a new national salutation *'Jai Hind'*, to replace a number of denominational ones.

From Alipore Jail, I was transferred to Bareilly Central Jail, where most of the Congress prisoners had already been released. I travelled, under a special police escort by Punjab Mail. By the same train in a first class compartment, was travelling Nawabzada Liaquat Ali Khan later who become the first Prime Minister of Pakistan. Though we were in opposite camps at every important wayside station, he would come to enquire if I needed anything. This was an old political culture which has disappeared in present day India and probably, in Pakistan, and Bangladesh as well.

Before my transfer, I had smuggled a letter to my family that I was travelling on such and such a date by Punjab Mail. To the surprise of police the entire family was at Lucknow station, where I saw for the first time my nephew Javed Akhtar well known film script writer whose mother was Safia my most favourite sister. She was married while I was still in jail. My mother was completely illiterate. But she was endowed with more practical sense than me. She advised me to leave Subhas and join Gandhi if I needed a better personal future.

While most of the Congressmen in Bareilly jail had already been released some of the prominent of them like S.K.D. Paliwal, President of P.C.C., Damodar Swarup Seth, an important socialist leader and Mahavir Tyagi later to become a Central Minister were still there.

Before I arrived in Bareilly, Nehru, Acharya Narender Dev and Pandit Pant had already been transferred to Bareilly from Ahmednagar. Pant managed to secure his release on the basis of a medical certificate for an operation which never took place. The other two national leaders were kept in a separate ward from us. However, a selected number of political prisoners including me through the courtesy of jail authorities were allowed to visit them for two hours every evening to give company to Nehru in his badminton game. I spent most of the precious time in talking to Acharya Narender Dev, one of the giants of Indian Socialist Movement.

I had known Nehru for long. But here I came in closer contact with him. I found him to be a snob and conceited about his academic achievements. He considered the fellow Congressmen as just cannon fodder in his struggle to come to power.

The Independence of India was on anvil. We often discussed the shape of things to come in Independent India. Nehru felt that the Congress could not offer a cadre for diplomatic services for they lacked the necessary refinement, good manners and upbringing and he would have to scout talents from University teachers. Apparently, he could not say to those who were still in jail that he would find them those Indian magistrates, who ordered *lathi* charges, shooting and imprisonment of Congressmen.

I was disillusioned with Nehru, whom I considered the next to Bose as ideal for emerging India. My apprehension came true on my release when he was more eager for compromise with the British than any of his colleagues.

Chapter 8

THE REAL LIBERATOR

I have already described my early associations with Nehru. Like most young men of my generation, I was deeply impressed by his fresh looks, his dynamic personality, his attachment to young Congress workers. I was thrilled by his small pamphlet 'Whither India?', which gave a new direction to India's struggle for freedom, in early thirties.

When I attended for the first time, the Congress Session held at Bombay in 1934, presided over by Rajendra Prasad, it was a Bible for young Congressmen. I attended an informal gathering of some militant Congressmen, prominent among them, were Acharya Narendra Dev, Sampurnanand, Yousaf Meher Ali, Jai Prakash Narain, M. R. Masani, and Achyut Patwardhan, it was enthusiastically discussed though Nehru himself was conspicuous by his absence.

Later at Patna, the Congress Socialist Party was formed. The Socialist Party declared its ideology as Marxist which would determine its programme so as to fulfil its task. At that time it made it clear that the Party as such did not represent any single class. On the contrary it would unite on its platform, all anti-imperialist elements to overthrow it and establish a real Swaraj. It acknowledged the National Congress as the rightful vehicle of the Indian people's freedom struggle and therefore to stay within it. Its task within the Congress would be to help to prepare the Congress for mass struggle. To ensure this, membership of the Congress was made obligatory for anyone who wished to join the party, which was now appropriately titled the Congress Socialist Party. The members were also enjoined to show respect to the national leaders and maintain good relations with them.

The elder leaders who called themselves 'Gandhiites' took the formation of the Socialist Party as a challenge to Gandhi's leadership and his ideas. They passed a resolution in two successive working committee meetings, dissociating the

Congress from class war, appropriation of private property and the like, as these posed a threat to non-violence.

Though Socialist Party was formed under the inspiration of Nehru, he never joined it formally. In fact Yousaf Meher Ali published a syllabus for the study of Socialist Studies, which on its cover page had the pictures of Marx, Lenin, and Nehru.

Why Nehru did not join the Socialist Party it has rightly been explained by Subhas Bose in his autobiography *Indian Struggle 1924 to 1934.* He says "there were two courses open to him, if he wanted to live in history either to accept the tenets of Gandhism and join the Gandhi Wing with the Congress Party, or to build up his own party in opposition to the Gandhi Wing. He could not do the former, because though he was personally loyal to the Mahatma, he did not accept all the tenets of Gandhism. On the other hand, he did not build up his own party because that would have offended the Gandhi Wing, and he has never in his whole life had the courage to do anything in opposition to the Mahatma". All that Nehru could do for the Congress Socialist Party was that when he presided over the Lucknow Session of the Congress in 1936, he could manage to persuade Gandhi for the inclusion of three Congress Socialist Party leaders, namely, Acharya Narendra Dev, Jai Prakash Narain and Achyut Patwardhan, in working committee in spite of the reluctance of latter's close associate Rajendra Prasad and Vallabhbhai Patel.

I have already described my association with Subhas Bose. Apparently Gandhi felt that during his long imprisonment and exile Subhas Bose might have been tamed. He was blessed with Congress Presidentship in 1938 for Haripura session of the Congress. Haripura represented one of the most momentous session since the suspension of the civil disobedience movement. It represented as much clash of ideas as the clash of personalities in the Congress. It marked the emergence of Subhas Chandra Bose to top leadership at a time when the Congress was drifting from weakness to weakness. Subhas represented Bengal. He had the blessings of Gandhi but not his confidence. He was too popular and too great a hero in his own right to be opposed by the old guard. Since the Lahore Congress, Subhas had been intermittently in jail. He was almost in exile in Europe for five years and a detenu since his return. He had been only recently released. His health shattered with a suspicion of tuberculosis. Subhas had succeeded Das as Mayor of the Calcutta Corporation and had done remarkably well. He believed in non-violence, but than that he liked big rallies, parades processions, salutes, with himself standing by, as 'Commander'. Subhas was often suspected by the Government of having a secret hand in the underground activities of Bengali youths. He was supposed to be the brain behind the terrorists. This was partially true. When he was detained in Kurseong, his brother had arranged to send a few 'pills' for improving his health. Intelligence experts suspected these might be 'bullets or bombs'. A watch was kept, when the parcel arrived it contained only a dozen *rasgullas.* The police felt like fools.

Subhas Bose soon felt disillusioned with Nehru's role in the Working Committee. He even began to kickback. His unkindest cut was that Nehru had been behaving like a 'stooge' of the 'old guard'. Subhas wanted a clear showdown with Vallabhbhai and others. Subhas had prepared a master plan which he confidentially unfolded to Nehru and to some of us. It was his firm view, based on information which he had been getting from Europe, that there would be an international crisis near about the spring of 1939, involving Great Britain. It may be even an international war. As a first step, Subhas was of the view that a one year ultimatum should be given to the British Government, either to appoint a Constituent Assembly to draft the Constitution of a free India or to be prepared for the resumption of civil disobedience. They should jointly persuade Gandhi to prepare the ground for this resumption and take charge of the operations. Meanwhile, from among the radical elements, youth leagues, Kisan and Mazdoor Sabhas etc., daring young men should be secretly recruited for acts of planned sabotage, to paralyze communications, by cutting off telephone and telegraph wires, disrupting railway lines and blowing up bridges. Intense secret propaganda should be carried out for insurgents and guerilla force should be created to act at appropriate time to fight the British might.

One of the actions of Subhas Bose that might have created suspicion on Gandhi was his appointment of a Planning Committee with one of the most eminent economists Prof. K.T. Shah as Chairman and H.V. Kamath who had recently resigned from ICS as Secretary. The concept of planning was the brainchild of Bose though Nehru took full credit for it. Incidentally, Prof. K.T. Shah stood as the opposition candidate against Rajendra Prasad in 1952, for Presidentship of India.

The year 1939, started in India with violent controversy about the continuance of Subhas Bose as President of the Congress. The election was to be held on January 29, 1939.

The name of Pattabhi Sitaramayya was mentioned. Subhas Bose, the retiring President, announced his decision to contest. Some leading members of the Working Committee issued a statement from Bardoli questioning the validity of the reasons for the contest given in the statement of the Congress President. Pattabhi Sitaramayya announced his candidature. Statements by Subhas Bose, Sardar Patel and Jawaharlal Nehru also followed in quick succession.

On January 29, delegates met in different states to elect the President. The result was that Bose won by 1,580 votes to 1,375 for Pattabhi Sitaramayya.

Unfortunately, this did not settle the issue. On January 31, Mahatma Gandhi issued a statement from Bardoli declaring that "the defeat is more of mine than his (Pattabhi Sitaramayya's)". The result of the election had made it plain to Gandhi that 'the delegates do not approve his principles and policies, for which he stood. It was now for Subhas Babu to choose his homogeneous Cabinet and implement his programme", Gandhi observed "after all, Subhas Babu is not an enemy of his country.'

M.R. Masani, the then General Secretary of C.S.P. records in his memoirs: "This statement had all the overtones of a threat of non-cooperation much as those with which the British authorities has been familiar. Subhas Bose, recognising this, tried to avert a showdown when, in a statement on February 3, he expressed his grief that Gandhiji should have taken the result of the elections as 'a personal defeat'. He declared that it could always be his aim to win the confidence of Gandhiji and added: "It will be a tragic thing for me if I succeed in winning the confidence of other people but fail to win the confidence of India's greatest man." He added: "Let us make it quite clear that there would be no break with the past in the Parliamentary or extra-Parliamentary sphere."

It was hoped that the ground for a reconciliation would be prepared at the meeting that was scheduled between Gandhi and Subhas Babu on February 15. It lasted three hours but was obviously unsuccessful. It was announced that the Working Committee would meet in Wardha on February 22, Subhas Bose could not attend the meeting as he was seriously ill. On that day, Patel and eleven others informed the President of their decision to resign.

They declared "We feel that the time has come when country should have a clearcut policy not based on compromise between different incompatible groups of the Congress. It is but right, therefore, that you should select a homogeneous Cabinet representing the views of the majority".

Nehru also resigned separately. These resignations left Subhas Bose and his brother Sarat Chandra Bose as the only surviving members of the Working Committee.

It now became clear to the supporters of Subhas Bose that they, had, in fact, challenged Gandhi's leadership when they had voted for him and this appeared to have a demoralising effect on some of the delegates. Both sides claimed that they wanted unity, but there was none. The Congress met at Tripuri village in Central Provinces. I witnessed the pathetic scene that when Subhas Bose accompanied by his two devoted nieces was brought on a stretcher to the pandal of the Subjects Committee of the Congress, he was running high temperature and wet towel was being removed at a few minutes' interval. Kripalani jeered that a theatre party has arrived from Calcutta.

All the members of the Working Committee with the exception of Nehru refused to sit on dais and occupied their seats among ordinary members of A.I.C.C. Subhas Bose in a feeble voice begged them to come to dais. After some hesitation, headed by Azad, they trooped to their usual seats on the dais.

The Congress Ministry was in power in C.P. The Congress leadership suspected Subhas of pretending to be ill. The C.P. Prime Minister and Home Minister, D.P. Misra deputed their British Director of Health Services to examine him, who, much to their discomfiture, confirmed that Subhas Bose was really ill.

While Tripuri session was in progress, Gandhi was undertaking his usual fast unto death for some petty action of Dewan of a petty State in Rajkot. This drew the usual sympathy of delegates to him.

When the AICC met in the evening, Subhas Bose could not come under medical advice. The meeting was presided over by M. Azad, the seniormost former President of the Congress. It was really a stormy meeting. After two days of intense deliberation, Pandit Pant moved the crucial Resolution:

> "The Congress declares its firm adherence to the fundamental policies of the Congress which governed its programmes in the past twenty years under the guidance of Mahatma Gandhi and is definitely of the opinion that there should be no break in these policies, and that these should continue to govern the Congress programmes in the future.

> "In view of the critical situation that may develop during the coming year and, in view of the fact that Mahatma Gandhi alone can lead the Congress and the country to victory, during such a crisis, the Congress regards it imperative that the Executive Authority of the Congress should command his implicit confidence and request the President to nominate the Working Committee for the ensuing year *in accordance with* the wishes of Gandhi."

K. F. Narriman moved an amendment to Pant's motion stating that the Working Commitee should be appointed in *consultation* with Mahatma Gandhi and not with the approval of Mahatma Gandhi, as had been suggested in the resolution. J.P. was called upon to make a statement on behalf of the Congress Socialist Party. The previous days and weeks had been a period of agonising re-appraisal for the C.S.P. during the year since the Patna Session of the C.S.P. the party had to define its attitude towards the cleavages that developed within the Congress movement. The C.S.P. was faced with a real dilemma. On the one had, they were the Gandhians or the 'Right Wing', who still had a majority in the Working Committee but they had lost the first round in the fight when Subhas Bose was re-elected Congress President against a Gandhian candidate. Subhas Babu, however, found that he was not able to nominate his Working Committee on the eve of the Tripuri session because of the fact that Gandhians refused to cooperate with him except on their own terms. As it happened the Congress Socialist Party, caught between the Gandhians on the one side and what was described as the 'Left Bloc' consisting of Bose's followers, who had at some stage acquired the name of the 'Forward Bloc' and the 'Communist', on the other.

The Congress Socialist Party was divided. On the one hand, J.P. and Marxist in the party wanted to align with the 'Left Bloc' against Gandhians, on the other hand, Achyut Patwardhan, Ram Manohar Lohia, Ashoka Mehta and Masani were against this. Masani records further in his memoirs:

> "At Tripuri, before we could take our stand we had a series of talks with Subhas Babu and with Nehru. Subhas, who was a down to earth politician, clearly wanted his own Cabinet and his friends, who would include the Congress Socialist Party, to be in a majority in the Working Committee. He wanted us to cooperate.

> "Jawaharlal Nehru, on the other hand, said nothing to contribute or advise. He was as vague as ever. When faced with a difficult choice, he would be non-aligned. Subhas Babu was quite cynical towards such an attitude and told us that Nehru was an opportunist who thought about his own position first and then about everything else."

The Resolution of the Gandhians, placed before the session by Govind Ballabh Pant, put the Congress Socialist Party squarely on the spot, if the Congress Socialist Party voted with Subhas Babu and the Communist, it was likely that the Gandhian Resolution would be defeated; in which case, the Gandhians would be driven out of the Congress which would then, for all practical purposes, be controlled by Subhas Bose and the Communists. So far as I am concerned, this was an unthinkable proposition and many of my colleagues shared that view, on the other hand, if we supported the Gandhians, Subhas Bose would be thrown out of the Presidentship. Jaya Prakash was not prepared for this; nor did he want to antagonise Subhas Bose and the Communists, because he believed in the concept of the 'Left Bloc of Progressive Forces'.

So, as happens so often in policies, we compromised and decided that the Congress Socialist Party should abstain from voting in the final division.

It was against this background that Jaya Prakash stated "Our party, voted for Mr. Subhas Bose, but, from the very beginning, we had made it clear that our vote did not mean a settling of the issues between the Rightists and the Leftists."

Maulana Azad then put the various amendments to vote. The tension became tremendous as the time for voting approached. It strained the loyalty of many of the members of the Congress Socialist Party, most of the members of the Party who were present abstained from voting. The amendments were declared lost by majority on show of hand amidst cries of 'Mahatma Gandhi Ki Jai' (Victory to Mahatma Gandhi). Pandit Pant's resolution was carried. The dye was cast. It led to the resignation of Subhas a little later.

I have already mentioned his escape from his wellguarded house 38A, Elgin Road, Calcutta under disguise. The saga of his travel to Germany *via* Afghanistan is too well known and need no repetition.

His heroic travel by a submarine *via* Cape of Good Hope to Far East, his mobilisation of businessman, peasants and workers in French Indo-China now known as Vietnam and Kampuchea, East Indies now known as Indonesia, Malaya now known as Malaysia and neighbouring Burma, was one of the highlights of his achievements.

His formation of provisional Free Indian Government described as 'Arzi Hukumat Hind', and as Supreme Commander-in-chief mobilising Indian War prisoners in Indian National Army, were the greatest landmark, in India's Struggle for Freedom.

Even Gandhi who was responsible for ousting him from the Indian National Congress and forcing him to leave India to carry on the mission of his life, could not remain unmoved.

Maulana Azad in his memoirs 'India Wins Freedom' has recorded the following:

> "In discussion with him, I felt that he was becoming more and more doubtful of an allied victory. I also saw that Subhas Bose's escape to Germany had made great impression on Gandhiji. He had not formerly approved many of Bose's actions but now I found a change in his outlook. Many of his remarks convinced me that he admired the courage and resourcefulness Subhas Bose had displayed in making his escape from India. His admiration for Subhas Bose unconsciously coloured his view about the whole war situation against the British in East Asia had to be continued."

While inaugurating Free India's Provisional Government, Subhas Bose declared:

> "This will have a twofold effect in that it will influence the cause of India and it will also help to purge our countrymen at home of the defeatist mentality which is the result of successful enemy propaganda. Secondly, it would tend us to secure the support of friendly powers, to continue the armed struggle we must keep our confidence in our final victory."

It was with his invincible spirit that Bose opposed Wavell's offer and criticised those Congress leaders who were considering it because of their pessimism and defeatism.

"I have no doubt in my mind that under normal circumstances, nobody belonging to the Congress would have even looked at Lord Wavell's offer... The Congress stands for complete independence. Lord Wavell's offer, as has been rightly pointed out by Mahatma Gandhi, does not even mention the word 'Independence'... Nevertheless, the fact that some Congressmen and leaders are actually considering the British offer is because a wave of defeatism has swept over India since the Anglo-American success in Europe and in Burma. In a fit of pessimism and defeatism some Congressmen are forgetting their lifelong principles and are now reconsidering the offer which they rejected in 1942." These repeated attacks of Bose helped in no small measure in bringing about the failure of the Simla Conference.

The war was coming to a close with decisive allied victory in almost all fronts. Bose was forced to leave Burma with a heavy heart, his faith in the destiny of India remaining as ever before: His last order of the day as Supreme C-in-C of Azad Hind Fauj was, "I am leaving Burma with a very heavy heart. We have lost the first round of our fight for independence; but we have lost only the first round. There are many more." He spoke out his heart, when he concluded.

"The only reward that we desire for our efforts, for our suffering and for our sacrifice is the freedom of our motherland. There are many among us who would like to retire from the political field once India is free."

He ended his message with the following words:

"Father of our nation in this holy war of India's liberation, we asked for your blessing and good wishes."

The revolutionary spirit of Bose was never depressed even after the surrender of Japan. After hearing the stunning news, he first broke into a smile and said, according to those who were with him.

"So, that is that now, what next?"

"Japan's surrender was not India's surrender. Japan's surrender was not the surrender of the liberation forces fighting for India's Freedom. We would not admit defeat." Bose had himself said about the invincible spirit of a true revolutionary.

"A true revolutionary is one who never acknowledges defeat, who never feels depressed or disheartened. A true revolutionary believes in the justice of his cause and is confident that his cause is about to prevail in the long run." Bose knew that a war of liberation demanded great sacrifice, courage and patience. Even after decisive Anglo-American Victory in Europe and the surrender of Japan, he had no intention to give up the fight. He said, in his last message "In spite of our losing, the first round, I see no reason for losing heart."

Bose asked his soldiers not to be disheartened. He was conscious that 38 crores of people living in India were looking to him and the INA as to what would be their next step:

> "Be, therefore, true to India. Let not your faith in India's destiny be shaken. There are many roads to Delhi. And Delhi is still our goal. The sacrifices of your immortal comrades and yourselves will certainly bring us victory. There is no power on earth which can keep India in bondage. India will certainly be free and, that too, soon, *Jai Hind*."

This was the special order of the day on August 17, 1945 seven days after the surrender of Japan. The same day in the same invincible spirit, in a message, he asked the Indians in East Asia not to be disheartened in their temporary defeat. He asked them not to lose faith in the destiny of India.

Bose could, no longer, remain in East Asia. Gen. Isoda sent for him on August 20, 1945. He had made up his mind to go to Russia to seek Russian help. He thought that a conflict between the Soviet people and the Anglo-Americans was inevitable. He was sure that Soviet Russia would prove to be a greater menace to Anglo-American Imperialism that Germany was:

"The provisional Government of Azad Hind will continue to follow international developments with the closest interest and endeavour to take the fullest advantage of them. The fundamental principles of our foreign policy has been and will be: 'Britain's enemy is India's friend'."

He told the Japanese:

> "I wish to go to Russia with some of my Cabinet Members. I will go alone, if I have to. I would like the Japanese Government to see that my Cabinet Members can follow me later."

The Imperial General Headquarters rejected this proposal of Bose. But, Field Marshal, Terachchi fully appreciated Bose's point of view and decided to help him on his own responsibility he arranged for Bose to fly by a special aeroplane to Shinkyo Manchuria and was for transportation in Saigon. Bose's plan was to surrender to the Russian Army after reaching Manchuria and then to try to seek Soviet help to fight the British. He was to fly to Dairen first *via* Taipei. This illfated plane in which Bose travelled, crashed in Paidei on August 18, 1945, on its way to Dairen, resulting in his death. Bose had insisted upon taking with him all the members of his Cabinet but this could not be possible due to lack of accommodation in the aeroplane. He had asked Colonel Habibur Rahman alone to accompany him.

Even at the time of his death, the idea of the liberation of his motherland was foremost in his mind. His death occurred at 9.00 P.M. on August 19, 1945 and the following were his last words to the ADC, Col. Habibur Rehman.

> "Habib, my end is coming very soon. I have fought all my life for my country's freedom. I am dying for my country's freedom. Go and tell my countrymen to continue the fight for India's freedom. India will be free, and before long."

The trial of Shah Nawaz Khan, Prem Saighal and Dhillon in the historic Red Fort, the venue of the trial of last Mughul King, Bahadur Shah Zafar who was exiled to Burma, generated more enthusiasm in India than even the 'Quit India Resolution' and Gandhi's call to 'Do or die' on the August 1942. Unlike Congress, Subhas succeeded in demonstrating that he could mobilise Hindus, Muslims and Sikhs for the common cause for liberation of India.

Even after his unfortunate death, he did not give peace to the British and his adversaries in Congress. The Congress once again has formed Government in the Provinces when the rating of Indian Navy revolted, much to the discomfiture of Sardar Patel, who was Home Member of Viceroy's Executive Council.

Lord Wavell apprehended, though wrongly, that the Congress may use the general discontent, and the Indian National Army, to encourage mutiny in the armed forces which sustained the British rule over India since 1857. He warned His Majesty's Government of his feelings and in support of his suspicion, *Wavell* referred to his interview with Nehru: "In order to make sure that there was no misunderstanding, I saw Nehru on 3rd November and pointed out to him the danger of the course he and other leaders were advocating. He made it clear that violence was never in their mind, and, shortly after our interview, delivered an inflammatory speech of the usual kind. I believe that the Congress are counting on the I.N.A. as the spearhead of their revolt; they would stubborn the Indian Army if they could, and they hope that their threat will impair the loyalty and efficiency of the Police. They have been encouraged by event in French Indo-China and Indonesia which they are watching carefully and a good deal may depend upon what happens there and in Syria and Palestine".

The ratings of the Royal Indian Navy in Bombay went on strike on 10 February complaining against hardship regarding pay and food and racial discrimination. They numbered above 3,000 from slopes, mine sweepers and shore establishments and marched into the city in a procession. Some British soldiers in uniform were chased and belaboured by them. On the 20th, the Naval Officers ordered them to return to their barracks and the order was complied with by most of them. However, about 40 of them refused to obey and were arrested. But even those who had returned to their barracks continued on the strike. On the 21st some of the ratings tried to take possession of the armoury inside the Castle Barrack, and assailed their officers. British troops were ordered to take the place of Indian troops, who were suspected of sympathy with the ratings. There was a six-hour battle between the troops and the ratings and then ceasefire was signalled.

Meanwhile, over a thousand men of the RIAF camps near Bombay had gone on strike in sympathy with the ratings. The strike of the ratings quickly spread to many other ports such as Calcutta, Vizagapatnam, Madras and, above all, Karachi where incidents as mutinies as those in Bombay, occurred. The situation was brought under control only when Vallabhbhai Patel was approached by the leading ratings and he advised them to surrender after having been assured by the Commander-in-Chief that no victimization would be resorted to by the officers of the Navy.

D.P. Misra, a former Chief Minister of M.P. and a close associate of Patel records in his memoirs:

> "That dissatisfaction in the Indian Armed Forces was not confined to the RIN ratings and the RIAF, and that men serving in every wing were yearning for the freedom of their motherland, became evident when Indian sepoys from the Indian signal corps and Indian electrical and mechanical engineering depots in Jabalpur, numbering about 200 struck work on 22 February, and disobeying the orders of their officers, marched in a peaceful procession through the town. They had a meeting and complained against low pay, poor ration, unsatisfactory housing and demobilization system. They expressed

> sympathy with strike of the Naval ratings and demanded to release the men of the Indian National Army. Their leaders made a fiery speech in the course of which, he said:
>
> 'Although we all were born as slaves, we do not want to die as slaves'. On hearing of the strike, I, along with some congressmen, proceeded to their meeting place and persuaded them to return to their lines. They consented and after taking food, supplied by the public, saluted the portrait of Subhas Chandra Bose and returned to their lines.
>
> Instead of welcoming the cooperation extended by Congressmen iin accordance with Vallabhbhai Patel's promise to Lord Wavell, General Francis Tuker, GOC, Eastern Command said: "The local (Jubbalpur) Congress leaders seemed to have advised them to return to their lines and they took the advice. Congress appeared by now to have been a little awed by the Frankenstein Monster it had created. "The target of Tuker's criticism was in fact Vallabhbhai, who helped to end the agitation of naval ratings in Bombay."

Gandhi toc was not unaware of the new spirit inspiring the Indian Army. While he was staying in Bombay, almost every day, groups of Indian soldiers came to have his darshan. Once he was told by them: "There was a time when we were not allowed to read any civil newspaper. And now we go and tell our officers that we are going to see our greatest leader and no one dares to stop us. Gandhi replied: "I know there is a new ferment and a new awakening among all the army ranks today. Not a little of the credit for this happy change belongs to Netaji Bose." Thereupon the soldiers shouted *"Jai Hind"* and *"Netaji Ki Jai"*. I am told that even Gandhi, who had ousted Bose from Congress could not remain unmoved by his great contribution to India's liberation. I had just reached Bombay, and many students were busy in providing relief to striking rating. Morarjee Desai who later became the Prime Minister and many students were arrested and sent to jail as Patel had promised to Viceroy that any revolt of the armed forces would be ruthlessly crushed with the help of civilian police; and support of Congressmen.

Though Patel had promised to ratings that there would be no victimisation if they went back to barracks, but most of them were deprived of their pensions, and dismissed.

Nehru had donned a Barrister's gown to defend INA officers but in spite of this theoretical gestures, the INA officers with long service and soldiers were summarily dismissed and deprived of their pension and other benefits.

The fate of Muslim soldiers of INA in Pakistan was still worse. They were treated as traitors for on behest of Subhas Bose, they had pledged to hoist tricolour flag on the Red Fort of Delhi and had adopted *'Jai Hind* as their salutation.

The Congress rulers instead of expressing their gratitude, did their best to remove the memory of Subhas. It was left to Janta Government after the death of Nehru to find a place of his portrait in Central Hall of the Parliament and it was only when Congress lost the control of Delhi Municipal Corporation that his statue was installed in a park in front of Red Fort. It was again Shiv Sena Mayor of Bombay who sanctioned a site on Chowpaty sand where Netaji statue has been installed on 23rd Januar , 1989.

Chapter 9

THE BEGINNING OF CONFLICT

RECENTLY published thirty pages of Azad's book *India Wins Freedom* have brought to limelight the contribution of League and Congress conflict over the formation of the Government under Government of India Act, 1935 in 1937 in U.P. to partition of India.

In fact, it was in 1916 on the eve of Montague and Chelmsford Reforms that at Lucknow, Tilak on behalf of the Congress and Jinnah as President of the All India Muslim League signed the famous Lucknow Pact which conceded the Muslims the right of separate electorate thus laying the foundation of Muslim separatism.

Following the split in 1928, when Jinnah decided to join hands with the Congress in the boycott of Simon Commission, it was reduced to a paper and sign board organisation.

Jinnah in disgust had migrated to London to practice before Privy Council. However, he came back in 1935 and called a session of the All India Muslim League, presided over by Syed Wazir Hasan of Lucknow who for decades was the General Secretary of Muslim League. These were the days when Jinnah was interested to cooperate with the Congress in fighting the provincial elections under Government of India Act, 1935,

In September 1936, on my invitation he came to Lucknow to preside over the All India Students Conference which was inaugrated by Jawaharlal Nehru. It was the last time that the two shared the same platform.

During his stay at Lucknow, he met Chowdhury Khaliquz-Zaman, Nawab Mohammad Ismail and some other nationalist Muslims and urged them to reorganise the Muslim League to fight the coming general elections.

In the meantime, Sir Malcolm Hailey who was Governor of Punjab and later of U.P. inspired Muslim landlords and Hindu businessmen to form their own party to fight Gandhi and Jinnah.

In Punjab the Unionist Party emerged out under the leadership of Sir Sikander Hayat Khan, Sir Chotu Ram and Sir Gokul Chand Narang in U.P., a National Agriculturist Party was formed, by Nawab Sir Ahmed Syed Khan of Chhatari and Sir U.P. Srivastava.

The Congress in U.P. was not confident to achieve the absolute majority in assembly. It lacked finances as well as dedicated Muslim workers to fight the powerful taluqdars, businessmen, money lenders and bankers in Muslim constituencies. It persuaded Khaliquz-Zaman, a prominent Congressman, Hafiz Ibrahim, a former Swarajist legislator, and some others to contest on the Muslim League ticket. There was a definite undertaking between Pandit Pant, the leader of Swarajist Party, Mohanlal Saksena, the President of U.P.C.C. that the League will not set up its nominees against Muslim Congress candidates in eighteen Muslim Constituencies and in remaining Congress will give full support to the Leaguers.

It is worthy to note that all the eighteen Muslim Congressmen including Mr. Rafi Ahmed Kidwai were defeated and with the exception of seven seats all of the Muslims' seats were won by the leaguers defeating the nominees of National Agriculturist Party.

In brief, I may describe Khaliquz-Zaman's background. He was one of the prominent leaders of the Non-cooperation and Khilafat movement. As Congress Chairman of Lucknow Municipality, he had supplied free electricity and water connection to the Congress session in 1936, presided over by Jawaharlal Nehru at Lucknow. He was one of the right hand man of a former Congress President, Dr. M.A. Ansari.

UNEXPECTED VICTORY

Though Congress failed in Muslim constituencies, it managed to get unexpected absolute majority in general constituencies. Even after this massive victory, the Congress was undecided about the acceptance of office under Government of India Act, 1935. In six of the provinces, where Congress declined to accept offices the Governor set up interim Government in U.P. Nawab of Chhatari formed the Government and sought the support of Khaliquz-Zaman and league, which was declined with contempt.

In the mean time a vacancy occurred in Baharaich, the league withdrew its nominees Ali Kasan Khan Dewan of Nanapara Estate and allowed Rafi Kidwai to get elected unopposed.

After a few months' hesitation, convention of the elected Congress members of Legislative Assemblies and members of A.I.C.C. met at Delhi where in spite of opposition of Congress, socialists and other members like Vijaya Lakshmi Pandit, C. Rajagopalachari, Satyamurti and Pant persuaded the congressmen to accept the office, provided an assurance came from the Viceroy that the Governors will not use their veto power.

In due course an assurance was given that the Governors will enter in an unwritten gentleman's agreement not to use their veto power and Congress Working Committee gave green signal to the leaders of the Congress parties in the provinces where it had gained absolute majority to accept office.

Within days of the Working Committee's resolution, the leaders of the Congress parties in the six Congress majority provinces were invited to form Cabinets. Congress ministries were formed in Bombay, Madras, U.P., Bihar, C.P. and Orissa. Soon after the accession of a group of eight non-Congress members in the Frontier Province to cooperate with the Congress and acceptance of Congress discipline gave the Congress an absolute majority there, leading to the formation of a Congress Ministry there also. In Bengal, the Congress was the largest single party in the legislature but as it was not in absolute majority, it did not enter the Government. This story I will narrate in the next chapter.

Nehru had taken full part in the Working Committee's discussion and had along with Pant, had long talks with Gandhi. After the decision on office acceptance, he said, "Acceptance of office does not mean total acceptance of the slave constitution. We have taken a new step involving new responsibilities and some risk. But if we are true to our objectives and are ever vigilant, we shall overcome these risks and gain strength and power from this step also, eternal vigilance is the price of liberty".

EMBITTERED TIES

The U.P. Congress Ministry was not yet complete when the question of a Congress-League coalition in U.P. and elsewhere if possible, came up and while it caused a misunderstanding about missed chances, it embittered relations between the Congress and the League further. The first hint of a possible coalition came in a letter from Nehru to Pant on 30 March, 1937, when Pant was still residing at Safdarjung Road in New

Delhi. "I have just received a letter from an old Muslim friend whose opinion I value, in the course of this letter he said that 'a scheme is being hatched with the help of Pantji and Mohanlal to bring about a coalition between the Congress and League parties in the assembly."

"As I told you on the telephone last night I have telegraphed to Vallabhbhai suggesting to him that a meeting of the Parliamentary sub-Committee be held there about the 7th April. Abul Kalam is keen on this and I think on the whole it will be a good thing to have the meeting. But we must have a Working Committee also before long."

Pant and Mohanlal Saksena not expecting their own party to take office in the near future approached Khaliquz-Zaman to reinforce his decision not to join the interim Government and pressed him to return to the Congress. To keep an eye on the negotiations, Jinnah went to Lucknow and insisted on separate identities of the two organisations. The Congress could not agree. But when it was clear that the Congress would take office, Khaliquz-Zaman again suggested a coalition and even informed Azad that the League would accept any terms if he and Ismail Khan were included in the Ministry. Azad was attracted by the coalition idea if the League would cease to exist as a separate group in U.P. and Bihar and with Muslim representation in all the provincial ministries. He held consultations with Nehru, Pant, Kripalani and Narendra Dev and it was decided to offer ministerships to Khaliquz-Zaman and Ismail Khan in return for acceptance of the Congress programme.

Nehru related the course of these events in a letter to Rajendra Prasad on 21st July, 1937.

> "Towards the end of June and little before the Working Committee meeting in U.P. Muslim leaders, Khaliquz-Zaman and Nawab Ismail Khan, made an approach towards the Congress. This had obviously some connection with the possibility of ministries. They pointed out that in last March their Parliamentary Board had offered co-operation to the U.P. Congress Party on the basis of the 'Wardha Programme' as laid down by the Working Committee resolution on the Congress Party. You will remember the Working Committee resolution in the Congress policy in the legislatures passed at the Wardha meeting prior to the convention. It was not clear whether the Mulsim League Board accepted the whole resolution

or only the particular items of the legislature programme. If the former, when they accepted the Congress policy 100 per cent including independence, fighting the act, the Constituent Assembly etc. I knew nothing about all this nor did Maulana, still it was vaguely hinted at Wardha early this month by Pantji. But it was all very vague and I did not like the look of this angling for ministries.

"When Maulana Abul Kalam went to Lucknow from Wardha he saw Khaliquz who told him that he was practically prepared to give him a blank cheque provided two of their members were included in the Ministry, himself and Nawab Ismail Khan the President of the U.P. Board, Maulana looked at all this with suspicion but he felt attracted by the possibility of the whole Muslim League ceasing to exist as a separate group and being practically absorbed by the Congress.

"He and Pant came to Allahabad and we discussed the matter at great length. I disliked (we all did) this bargaining for seats in the Ministry. We disliked taking in two persons who from the Congress point of view, were weak. We feared reaction among Congressmen in general and Congress Muslims in particular who would have been irritated at their being excluded in preference to those who had been fighting the Congress. What of those who had severed their connection with the League and joined us? What of those Muslims of ours who had stood by the Congress during all these years? What of the Jamiat which was supporting us and opposing the League?

"All this and more we considered and hesitated. And yet the alternative was worth having if it could be secured. This was the winding up of the League group in U.P. and its absorption in the Congress.

"After much discussion in which two other members of the U.P. Congress joined (Kripalani and Narendra Dev) we came to the conclusion that we should offer stringent conditions to the U.P. Muslims League group and if they accepted them in toto then we would agree to two ministers from their group. Besides them one minister would be Rafi Ahmed.

"We drew up these conditions. But we did not ask them to severe all connection with parent Muslim League. The position would have been a peculiar one involving a dual loyalty to some extent it could not last and we expected the U.P. League to break away from the parent League.

"Maulana and Pant went to Lucknow. There were talks with Khaliq who agreed with all the conditions except two the winding up of the Parliamentary Board and not to set up the separate candidates at by-elections. These were vital conditions. Khaliq said that he personally would agree but he had not authority to do so. In effect, he pointed out, this might happen anyhow. Therefore, Maulana said he would not give a full answer and came to Allahabad.

"Ultimately we sent word that we regretted we could not alter our previous conditions at all; if they were to accept in toto we would agree, nôt otherwise. We had no authority to go beyond this without consulting the Working Committee. So the matter dropped and Maulana Azad went off Bombay, Khaliq said he was unable to agree.

"Today khaliq made another approach..... I referred him to Pantji but didnot encourage him at all.... Maulana Azad is keen on Hafiz Ibrahim being taken into the cabinet. He is a good and competent man and used to belong to the Swaraj Party. He might be described as a moderate Congressman. This composite accord is an authentic account.

It is significant that Nehru in his letter to Rajendra had admitted that the Congress should offer stringent terms to UP Muslim League group and if they accepted theml, the hand then alone they could be admitted as ministers in proposed ministry, the note which was later sent by Nehru, was drifted by Dr. K. M. Ashraf and had support of Rafi Ahmed Kidwai who considered Khaliquz-Zaman as his rival in U.P. politics because latter was better known and more popular than him — Azad suggested some amendments and it was handed over to Khaliq, the leader/Muslim League group in U.P. It would be good to supplement this account with the account given by Khaliquz-Zaman in his book "Pathway to Pakistan".

"Pandit Govind Pant, who was a forceful and eloquent speaker, perhaps the best in the Indian legislature was elected and again chosen as the leader of the U.P. Government.

> "Rafi Ahmed Kidwai brought me a message from Pant that on his way to Wardha he would stay in Lucknow to meet me for a talk. Pandit Pant, when he met me in the morning, asked me how many seats in the cabinet I would demand in case of coalition between the Congress and the League I replied: "Three in nine and two in six, that is, one third of the total strength of the cabinet, whatever it may be. Then he asked me whether he would have any

> voice in the selection of the Muslim League mnisters, I replied, "As much voice as I should have in your election". Then came the question. "Please be practical and don't go in for more show and public applause. "I said on July 5, 1937. The Congress agreed to accept office and Azad came to Lucknow on July 12.
>
> "Azad returned to Lucknow on July 15. This time he came with Pant; Azad handed overto me a two-page note which I was supposed to sign as a price for Muslim League coalition with Congress this was immediately rejected. I said, "You want me to sign the death warrant of the Muslim League Parliamentary Board as well as the Muslim League organisation, which I am representing here. I cannot sign this document".

On July 27, 1938, Khaliquz Zaman and Nawab Khan went to Pant residence and handed him the document delivered to them by Azad, and informed him that when the Assembly session started they will sit in opposition. M.A. Jinnah always suspected Congress under Gandhi's leadership/found an unwilling ally in Khaliquz-Zaman. Being a literate and constitutionalist he had no experience of agitational politics.

In December 1937, a session of All India Muslim League was held at Lucknow with Jinnah as President and Khaliquz-Zaman as Chairman of Reception Committee. It was at this session that the League adopted a flag and a Constitution on the lines of Congress and was transfomed into a mass organisation of Indian Muslims.

The uncompromising attitude of Congress led by Nehru gave a handle to Jinnah to rouse the Muslim frenzy in Congress governed provinces with total consequences.

It may be noted that in Bombaywhere no Muslim was selected on Congress ticket Yashin Nuri, a Leaguer was included in the Cabinet. The same was repeated in Central Provinces where Yusuf Sharf was appointed as a Minister.

After the partition of India Jinnah advised the Muslim League members belonging to India to join the Constituent Assembly to watch the interests of Muslims. Though most of them migrated to Pakistan to grab the valuable properties of those Hindus and Sikhs who were foerced to leave on the point of gun and dagger. Nawab Ismail Khan continued to attend the Constituent Assembly.

The entire family of Nawab Ismail Khan including two of his sons belonging to I.C.S. became Secretaries in Central

Government of Pakistan, but he continued to live in his ancestral home in Meerut where he was buried by the side of his grandfather Nawab Mustafa Khan Sharifta, who was hanged by the British in 1857.

Khaliquz-Zaman after delivering a speech in Constituent Assembly on the advice of Gandhi and Nehru went to Pakistan on a goodwill mission. But after Gandhi's assassination he never came back to Lucknow as an Indian citizen where he presided over Municipal Board for fifteen years as a Congressman.

PARTING OF THE WAYS

Following the rebellion of August 1942, most of the Congressmen and other anti-imperialist elements in Indian Public Life were marched to jail. The Muslim League headed by M.A. Jinnah had a field day to propogate mostly imaginary and some real grievances of the Indian Muslims during the short lived government in eight of the proinces.

The British authorities and their heavily war time subside press gave him full and free publicity. Jinnah who had his own personal grievances against Gandhi had full opportunity to create a frenzy among the Muslim masses.

It may be noted that Jinnah had started his political career as an ardent nationalist and Congressman. Mrs Naidu, the poitess politician had described him as the Ambassador of Hindu Muslim unity. During 1936, he had given me an autographed photograph with inscription "work for Hindu Muslim unity".

The break between Jinnah came about just after letter's arrival from South Africa on Indian scene. On his arrival the Gujarati Samaj of Bombay arranged a reception in his honour to be presided over by Jinnah. While replying to welcome address Gandhi described Jinnah as a fellow Muslim Gujarati, description of Muslim upset Jinnah, who till then never considered himself any thing but a Gujarati or an Indian.

But the greatest discomfiture Jinnah faced was at Nagpore Session of the Congress when he refused to address him as a Mahatma. He was hooted down by the Congress delegates majority of whom were long flowing bearded Mullas of the Khilafat movement. Jinnah walked out of the Congress never to come back again.

Chapter 10

DAWN OF A NEW ERA

ON release from Jail, I was accorded a heroic reception. While we were still in Jail, I was elected as the President of All India Youth League, an organisation floated by Subhas Bose in early twenties and later christened as 'Navjawan Bharat Sabha' by Shaheed Bhagat Singh.

My disclosure to the press that a number of valiant soldiers of Indian National Army were secretly hanged in Alipore Jail in Calcutta before my own eyes was flashed in all national newspapers with screaming headlines. The country was surcharged with emotion at the heroic deeds of Subhas and his legendary 'Azad Hind Fauj'. While I was still in jail, the British had released the Congress leaders and lifted the ban from the Congress organisation. In my absence, the All India Congress Committee met in Bombay, at the same venue where they had passed the so-called 'Quit India resolution', and I read with surprise and pride that when Sarat Bose, the elder brother of Subhas Bose, who was expelled from the Congress for indiscipline on his entry did not only get standing ovation from the members of A.I.C.C. but was also embraced by Sardar Vallabhbhai Patel, who was reported to have shed tears.

The British had staged a trial of three I.N.A officers namely Shahnawaz, a Muslim, Prem Saighal, a Hindu and Dhillon, a Sikh at the historic Red Fort where Subhas Bose had pledged to hoist tri-colour flag demonstrating that how he had integrated the three communities to fight the might of the empire.

I took an extensive tour of the country to highlight the brave deeds of I.N.A. soldiers and their officers. The entire country was disillusioned by the complete failure of illconceived and directionless 'Quit India' call given by Gandhi. The name of Subhas Bose and his army was the only source of encouragement, and inspiration to desperate Indian masses.

His heroic deeds in South East Asia had given a message of hope and courage to Indian people.

While the court martial trial of INA officers at the historic Red Fort of Delhi was widely reported, the Congress leadership was busy negotiating with Field Marshal Wavell for a peaceful settlement. Gandhi was busy corresponding with Jinnah, and knocking at his doors at Mount Pleasant Road, Malabar Hill, Bombay only to be snubbed and humiliated repeatedly.

The three INA officers were ultimately sentenced to life imprisonment by the Judge Advocate of Court Martial. On Auchinlekh as Commander-in-Chief's recommendation Marshal Wavell, Viceroy and Governor-General of India released them using his power of clemency. Thus the two British Field Marshals, who had already retreated from North Africa in the face of German Penzer division had to repeat their performance in the face of strong public opinion in India.

The Congress which had earlier disowned Subhas Bose and his Azad Hind Fauj, took full advantage of it in its election campaign under the Government of India Act, 1935. They took full credit for having secured the release of INA prisoners. Hari Das Mitter, the husband of Subhas Bose's niece whom I had left in the death row of Alipore Jail was released on Gandhi's intervention who thanked Lord Wavell for this act of mercy.

While the country was seething with post-war discontent and was ripe for an uprising supported by the Indian Armed Forces, Congress leadership was alarmed that this would disturb the social *status quo*.

The British administration was tired and bankrupt after the war. They had lost all confidence in the Indian Army and Navy and Air Force. They were anxious to pull their youth power from garrisons in India to man the factories in Lancashire, Liverpool and Burmingham. But, they were also aware that the Congress leadership was equally tired. Many of them including the members of the Congress Working Committee, had spent the longest term of their imprisonment in their life during 1942. Earlier, Gandhi used to send them to jail as Satyagrahis and managed to secure their release by withdrawing his movement on some flimsy ground or the other and none of them including the tallest of them had served their full term of imprisonment. In 1941, the District Magistrate of Gorakhpur had sentenced Nehru to four years of rigorous imprisonment but, only after few months, he was released because Gandhi suspended his individual Satyagraha movement to resume negotiations with the rulers for some compromise.

All efforts to mobilise the masses were discouraged by the Congress leadership who were commuting between Gandhi's headquarters in Wardha and Summer Capital of British in Simla Hills.

During the war Indian businessman had field day. While Britain was being bombed, the Indian businessmen living in the safety of Bombay, Calcutta and Ahmedabad were minting money. Even the petty shopkeepers were taking full advantage of wartime shortages The blackmarketing and hoarding and profiteering was rampant. There was a boom in business.

The country was thrilled, when Nehru, after his release, declared "black marketeers and profiteers have flourished at the cost of the nation. All such persons will be hanged from the nearest lane post, when Congress comes to power." What brave words are these?

I, along with the millions of my countrymen, anxiously awaited for the dawn of new era. I having been born a Muslim by accident of birth, was once again encouraged when Gandhi declared "So long as I am alive, I will never agree to the partition of India."

But, I never imagined that I will live for more than four decades to witness both of these lofty and noble declarations of Nehru and Gandhi to be dishonoured much to the distress of myself and my countrymen.

Chapter 11

PARTING OF THE WAYS

WHILE in Jail, I had realised that the Muslim League aided by the British was making a great headway. The Muslims living in the provinces, where they were in minority, were swept away by the League campaign that freedom of India would mean the domination of Hindus and the only alternative for them was to have a home land.

I have already described my meeting with Jinnah in early thirties, when he had come back from his self-imposed exile in England to lead the Indian Muslims. It was the last occasion in 1936 that I managed to get him and Nehru on the same platform in Lucknow to launch the All India Students' Federation. Jinnah once described as the Ambassador of Hindu-Muslim Unity was trans-formed into a new Jinnah.

Jinnah was one of the greatest egoist born in Indian sub-continent. He nursed personal grievances against Gandhi since that caught the imagination of his followers. Though Gandhi made repeated attempts to cajole Jinnah, but all his efforts were in vain. It was Gandhi, who addressing a letter to Jinnah, and enclosing the clipping of his mouthpiece 'Harijan', began by writing Dear Quaid-e-Azam. Replying to him Jinnah in a letter on January 21, 1940, wrote it was indeed noble of you to join in the silent prayer Long Live Quaid-e-Azam".

It will be an interesting revelation that while writing this letter, Gandhi is reported to have asked one of the Muslim woman inmates of his Ashram to let him know the Urdu word of Great leader. In her innocence she told him 'Quaid-e-Azam' though in Arab and Muslim world, the word 'Quaid' was never used for leader.

Those were the days of Fuehrer and ill-Deuce for Hitler and Mussolini. Gandhi's bestowing this title Quaid-e-Azam on Jinnah made him as arrogant as Hitler and Mussolini. And 'Quaid-e-Azam Zindabad was taken up by the Muslims who were mesmerised by the League campaign.

In Bengal the Krishnapersa Party headed by Fazul-ul-Haq had gained a majority of the seats reserved for the Muslims. But, that was not sufficient for forming a Ministry by itself. On account of the electoral system, a ministry in Bengal could be formed only by a coalition. Many members of the party were nationalists and therefore inclined towards the Congress. So, that at first Fazl-ul-Haq showed a broadbased ministry of all Bengalis. This overture was not accepted by the Congress High Command. Thus it happened that Faz-ul-Haq turned to the other Muslim Party and formed a Coalition Ministry with the Muslim League.

The refusal to permit Sarat Bose, Leader of Congress Party, to join hand with Fazl-ul-haq was a serious mistake. Not to accept office in the province in which the Congress had a majority in the legislatures could not do any permanent harm. And only three months later that happened. But the lost opportunity did not come again to Bengal. Yet in regard to Assam, the Congress did make an exception. It allowed the Congress there to join with other parties after Subhas Bose was elected as Congress President at Haripur. But there can be no doubt that there was indifference to Bengal in the Congress, if not some real antibathy, which in spite of being only latent influenced policies. I can attribute that to the character of Bengali nationalism, which was wholly non-Gandhian in its historic form, had that character persisted in spite of the Bengali Hindus to his way of thinking and feeling. Later however, I had opportunities for discovering at all events suspecting a rather dubious motive behind the treatments of Bengal by the Congress.

After continuing in powerless opposition for about a year, Sarat Bose tried in the later summer of 1938 to bring down the Muslim Ministry by moving a motion of no confidence. He hoped to persuade some dissatisfied Muslims and also the Scheduled Caste Hindus, who were supporting the ministry, to vote with him.

In 1938, Bose Brothers were to try to break up the ministry by inducing the most influential Hindu Minister in it to resign. He was Nalini Ranjan Sarkar, the Finance Minister, who, if he resigned, could carry some Hindus with him and force Haq to resign. For this move Subhas Bose discussed the question with Gandhi many times, and came away with the impression that Gandhi supported the move. But immediately after Subhas Bose had his last talk with Gandhi in December 1938, he got a letter from him which showed that, so far from being in favour of tappling Huq ministry, Gandhi was quite decidedly against it. This shocked Subhas Bose and correspondence followed, which was acrimonious on the part of Bose and very blunt on the part of Gandhi.

I came to know that what happened was this. Shortly after Subhas Bose had his last talk with Gandhi, Nalini Ranjan Sarkar, who had got wind of the scheme of Bose, went to see Gandhi at his Ashram in wardha, with Ghanshyamdas Birla, the great Marwari financial magnate whose influence over Gandhian his unstinted provider of money was decisive. Thus Nalini Sarkar showed very great astuteness in engaging this advocate with Gandhi, who wrote to Subhas Bose about what happened at the meeting. The letter was sent to the hand of Birla and was not dated. But Subhas Bose replied to it on Dec. 24 1938. I quote relevant passage of the letters:

"My dear Subhas Babu: (this was very formal which he never did in the ordinary way).

> I must dictate this letter as I am wilfully blind. Whilst I am dictating this, Maulana Sahib, Nalini Babu and Ghanshyamdas are listening We had an exhaustive discussion over the Bengal Ministry. I am more than ever convinced that we should not aim at ousting the Ministry. We shall gain nothing by a reshuffle; and, probably we shall lose much by including Congressmen in he ministry. I feel, therefore that the best way of securing comparative purity of administration and a continuation of a settled programme and policy would be to aim at having all the reforms we desire, carried out by the present ministry. Nalini Babu should come out, as he says he would, on a real issue being raised and the decision being taken by the Ministry against the interests of the country. His retirement from the ministry would then be dignified and wholly justified"

Nalini Sarkar would like to keep his office and Birla had his motive of which I shall say something later on. Subhas Bose was naturally very much upset by this letter and he replied in fairly strong languages on 24 Dec. 1938.

"My dear Mahatmaji,

> "The letter which Sjt. G.D. Birla brought from Wardha came as a profound shock to me. I remember to have discussed the Bengal situation with you time and again.

> Both of us have the clear impression that you have always agreed with the idea of a coalition ministry in Bengal'. (He meant a coalition between the Congress and Krishak Praja Party.) I do not know what has happened since I left Wardha."

It is obvious that G.D. Birla who had business interest with League Ministry through two Iranian brothers Hasan Isphani and Ahmed Isphani and did not trust Bose brothers had influenced Gandhi. If league would not have been in power, there would have not been great Calcutta killings which unnerved the congressmen and they championed the partition of Bengal. It may be remembered that partition of Bengal in 1905 by Curzon gave birth to the militant National Movement in India.

Having spent four years in a Bengal jail, I found fellow political prisoners with the exception of few, suspicious of Gandhi's attitude towards Bengal. They never had accepted his absolute leadership, like the people living in other provinces of India.

I have dealt with Bengal affair in a little detail for it is very relevant to the events that led to the partition of India and later to Bangladesh war in which Mrs. Gandhi poured all Indian resources of men and money, only to have another Islamic Republic of Banqladesh on our eastern frontier quite hostile to us.

The League had appointed a Commitee, under the Chairmanship of Raja Mohammad Mehdi of *Pirpur* to enquire about the alleged atrocities on Muslims in Congress governed States. It published a report known as 'Pirpur Report' describing the real and mostly imaginary grievances of the Muslims in Congress ruled States. The Muslims by and large took the findings of this Report as Gospel truth.

The final drama was enacted in Mach 1940, at the bank of Ravi, where Jawaharlal Nehru has taken the pledge for Independence of India. The league met in Dec. 1940, and passed a resolution for Partition of India. The Resolution at no point used the word of Pakistan, but the Congress press described as demand for Pakistan.

Having earned the title of Quaid-e-Azam and christening of his demand as creation of Pakistan, by Congress there was no going back for Jinnah.

Following the Quit India Resolutions most of us who could have in our own humble way counteracted his campaigns were marched to jail. Jinnah and his League had free field for his campaign. The technical know how was provided by the cadres of the Communist Party of India, who described the league as a patriotic organisation and its demand as the right of self-determination by Muslim nationalists.

On his release from Aga Khan palace, in Poona, Gandhi kept on carrying futile correspondence with Jinnah. He repeatedly knocked at his door at Mount Pleasant Road of Malabar Hill in Bombay only to be insulted and humiliated.

After the members of the Congress Working Committee were released from jail, they started commuting from Wardha to Simla to convince Lord Wavell the Viceroy that they could solve the communal problem.

As pointed out earlier, Britishers had lost all faith in Indian personnel of their armed forces as a result of massive response to the Indian National Army organised by Subhas Bose, and by the revolt of Naval personnel in Bombay and Karachi and other sea ports. They were in hurry to pull out the British personnel of the Army to run their shattered industries. The anxiety of the Congress to share power and Jinnah's insistence on having his share of flesh got even on the nerves of hardened soldier, Field Marshall Wavell.

In sheer disgust, Prime Minister Attlee, announced his willingness to permit Indians to form a Constituent Assembly to be elected by provincial assemblies, elected on the basis of separate electorate, with restricted franchise of only six per cent of adult voters, and to form an interim government composed of Viceroy's Executive Council, to be selected by the Congress and the Muslim League within the framework of Government of India Act, 1935. The tired Congress leadership, eagerly welcomed this magnanimous gesture. But Jinnah had his own reservations.

On March 4, 1946, a Cabinet Mission headed by Lord Pethrick Lawrence, Secretary of State for India, with Sir Stafford Cripps and some other senior British ministers arrived in Simla. They had prolonged discussions with Gandhi, the Congress President Azad and Jinnah and his supporters. The Congress paraded the Akalis as their allies, before the Mission.

After a long stay in India, the Mission went back to London. After two months of intensive analysis, the Mission concluded in its report released on May 16, 1946 that India should not be partitioned. The Mission showed that more than forty per cent of the population in the six provinces claimed by the Muslim League was non-Muslims, while twenty million Muslims would still remain in India. Thus, the creation of Pakistan would not solve communal and minority problem. Moreover, partition would entail serious disruption of the administrative, economic, military, transportation by India. The Mission also noted the problems posed by having the two sections of Pakistan separated by 1,000 miles of foreign territory. Even a smaller Pakistan, possible if the Punjab and Bengal were themselves partitioned, was rejected because any boundary would unnaturally divide linguistic and cultural units and leave sizeable numbers of Sikhs and Hindus in both countries.

While rejecting complete partition, the Mission nevertheless acknowledged "the very real Muslim apprehension that their culture and political and social life might become submerged in a purely unitary India, in which the Hindus with their greatly superior numbers must be a dominating element".

Therefore, a compromise was proposed by which India's provinces would be grouped into three sections, corresponding to the two Muslim majority areas in the North-West and North-East with the remainder forming the third group. Each group would borm its own constitution and enjoy autonomy in all matters except foreign affairs, defence and communications which would remain with the Union of India at the centre. In seeking to preserve India's unity while adequately safeguarding Muslims interest, the plan sparked a complex round of debate, misrepresentations, accusations and denials the end-results of which were the total collapse of the Mission Plan.

Jinnah held serious reservations concerning the plan. Since it (Cabinet Mission Plan) rejected the idea of a Sovereign Muslim State and realisation of Pakistan and because the plan gave the entire Punjab and Bengal provinces to the Muslim majority groups. Gandhi too entertained misgivings about the proposals since pro-Congress North-West Frontier and pre-dominently non-Muslim Assam provinces were both assigned to Muslim majority groups.

At a press conference in Bombay on July 10, Nehru declared that the Congress would not be bound by any British imposed settlement and claimed that his party would change the plan at will by virtue of its majority in the Constituent Assembly. Nehru's remarks gave a handle to Jinnah to describe that Congress was untrustworthy and that the British would capitulate Muslim safeguards to appease Congress intransigence, he called for drastic measure. On July 29, the League passed a Resolution calling for 'Direct Action' throughout India inspiring Jinnah to indulge in the rhetoric of violence. He told his followers: "This day we bid goodbye to constitutional methods . . . . we have also forged a pistol and are in a position to use it".

Communal relations grew increasingly ugly. In his 'Id' message to Muslims in August, Jinnah condemned the Viceroy and the British Government for surrendering to the 'Fascist Caste Hindu Congress'. Venomous pamphlets circulated. On August 16, the day appointed for direct action, riots broke out in Calcutta. Four days of violence left about 5,000 dead and as many as 25,000 wounded.

In June 1946, the election for A.I.C.C. which had not been held for the last seven years due to Congress being banned and congressmen being imprisoned was held. I was elected with the highest number of votes from U.P.

The newly elected Congress Committee met at Cawasji Jahangir Hall in Bombay on July 6, amidst great enthusiasm. The first task of committee was to elect a new Congress President.

At Simla, M. Azad, Congress President had approached Jinnah for an interview. Jinnah announced in the press that Azad was mere a show boy of the Congress and he would not meet him. Since Congress needed a Hindu President to negotiate with Jinnah, the architect of Indian secularism Pandit Jawaharlal Nehru was unanimously elected to replace M. Azad.

I was in high spirits, when M. Azad called Gandhi, to address the members of A.I.C.C. I raised a point of order that since he was not even a primary member of the Congress how could he address the A.I.C.C.? My objection was politely brushed aside by M. Azad though I shocked quite a big section of his devoted members of the AICC.

After Gandhi's address, the Chair was taken up by Nehru. The main resolution was adopted with the approval of the Working Committee's negotiations with the Government.

A number of amendments moved by Jaya Prakash Narayan and others were overruled by Nehru. However, my amendment was accepted but while I was in the midst of my speech, the President overruled it. I thanked the President for he gave me an opportunity to make frontal attack on the Congress Leadership.

I quote from Indian Register, 1946:

> "Pandit Nehru read out a number of amendments given notice of by members. He said all of them were irrelevant and ruled them out of order. He then called upon those

> who had sought to have amendment to speak on the Resolution.
>
> Mr. Ansar Harvani who wanted to move an amendment seeking total rejection and started debate by attacking the Working Committee's decision calling upon the A.I.C.C. to reject the British Government's proposal. Mr. Harvani said that the Constituent Assembly envisaged in the British plan was not going to be on the basis of adult franchise but on restricted franchise based on separate electorates. Such a Constituent Assembly could not bring the freedom for which the Congress had been fighting during the last 25 years. If the proposals were accepted, the Congress would be playing into the hands of British Imperialism. The proposed Constituent Assembly was a far cry from the 'Do or Die' slogan of 1924."

Though the Cabinet proposals were rejected by the Muslim League, they participated when the provincial assemblies met to elect the members for proposed Constituent Assembly. Since the Muslim members of provincial assemblies were to elect Muslim members only and non-Muslim members, non-Muslims only the overwhelming number of Muslim Leaguers were elected. The British India was allotted 296 seats. He provincial assemblies elected 205 non-Muslims, mostly, Congressmen and some British stooges picked up by Nehru. The Muslims elected 73 members all Leaguers with the exception of 7 and among them only three were Congressmen, M. Azad and Khan Abdul Ghaffar Khan were elected from N.W.F.P. and Kidwai from U.P.

Chapter 12

TASTE OF POWER

ABOUT the composition of interim Government, the league had its own reservations. A hectic correspondence between the Hindu President of the Indian National Congress and Muslim President of the Muslim League resulted into a complete stalemate.

However, on August 12, 1946, in sheer disgust, Lord Wavell, as Viceroy and Governor-General of India, issued a command from Viceregal Lodge, declaring that His Majesty the King and Emperor of India had been pleased to appoint Pandit Jawaharlal Nehru, Sardar Vallabhbhai Patel and some other Congress nominees as Members of Viceroy's Executive Council.

Since League refused to recommend nominees, on the recommendation of the Congress, two Muslim non-entities, Syed Ali-Zaheer, a Lucknow lawyer and Sir Dr. Shifat Ahmed Khan of Allahabad University were also included in the Council. Nehru assumed the title of the Vice-President of Viceroy's Executive Council, though there was no such provision in Government of India Act, under which this Council was constituted. Once Nehru described it as a Cabinet and Jinnah quipped you cannot call a donkey an elephant.

The A.I.C.C. met at Delhi on September 23, to endorse this decision of the Congress leadership. The Socialist and Forward Bloc, members of A.I.C.C. were very much agitated on this surrender of Congress leadership. Nehru who presided in a long speech justified their action.

When I was called upon to speak, I pointed out that I hung my head in shame, for I thought that the Congress President, will be the President of the first Socialist Republic of India, but what I find is that he is the Vice-President of Viceroy's Executive Council.

Once again I quote from Indian Register 1946:

"The Congress President ruled out of order an

> amendment moved by Mr. Ansar Harvani, which directed the interim Government to press for the immediate declaration of India's complete Independence; immediate withdrawal of all foreign troops, abolition of the Viceroyalty and the immediate election of Sovereign Constituent Assembly on the basis of universal adult suffrage to draft the Constitution of a Free and Sovereign India."

Pandit Nehru also ruled out of order another amendment of Mr. Achyut Patwardhan of C.S.P. which *inter alia,* directed the interim Government "to create conditions, by such means as removal of British troops as to endow the Constitution making body with Sovereignty" and thereby to transcend the limitations imposed by the British Cabinet Mission's proposals and further to transform the Interim Government into an instrument of sovereign power.

While most part of the walled city of Delhi reeled under curfew, the inmates of Ashrams walked in the spacious colonial bungalows, with acres of lawns and gardens formerly occupied by the knighted members of the Viceroy's Council. Nehru's dream to handle the Foreign Department of India was realised; he needed the help of an expert and his choice fell on Sir Girija Shankar Bajpai, who was selected by the British to carry on anti-Indian propaganda in U.S.A. to convince the devotees of Lady of Liberty that Indians were not fit to govern themselves without the help of their British masters.

He started selecting personnel for proposed Indian Foreign Service, and his eyes fell on scion of Indian princely order. When in my own humble way, I pointed its absurdity, Nehru remarked that they had "better education and breeding".

I retorted that after Russian revolution, Lenin selected working-class and peasant boys who proved to be very good diplomats; he was annoyed and not convinced.

Gandhi and Nehru in the meantime kept on urging Jinnah to permit his boys to enter Viceroy's Executive Council. I was in Delhi and I met Prof. Z.A. Bukhari the Chief of Indian Broadcasting System, and he told me that the Muslim bureaucrats like Iskandar Mirza, Ghulam Mohammad and Choudhari Mohammad Ali were pressing Jinnah to lift his ban.

However, pressed by Muslim personnel of Central Government Secretariat, Jinnah agreed to allow the Muslim League to join the Viceroy's Executive Council.

Now controversy started that which of the important portfolios would go to League nominees. Nehru would not give up External Affairs, Sardar Patel had tasted the glamour and power of Home Department and hence would insist on it. The Defence was under the charge of the nominee of Akalis who were faithful allies of Congress, Sardar Baldev Singh who represented the Sikh community described as the sword arm of British Empire.

According to Maulana Azad, Rafi Ahmed Kidwai, who was a free style wrestler of the Congress suggested that the League should be offered Finance, where their failure was certain.

The League initially was reluctant to accept this offer. But, two of the wizards of the Finance Department of Government of India, Ghulam Mohammad and Ch. Mohammad Ali gave it moral courage to accept the challenge.

On October 15, His Majesty was once again pleased to appoint Nawabzada Liaquat Ali Khan as the Finance Member of Viceroy's Executive Council. While the two Muslim nominees of the Congress were made to step down, Sarat Bose, the older brother of Subhas Bose and leader of Congress Party in Central Legislative Assembly elected in 1946 election was also given a marching order by the Congress to accommodate the League nominees.

The novice Congress leadership intoxicated with newly acquired power had not bargained, for the disaster that they had invited for them by handing over the finance of India to the Muslim League.

Nevertheless, the reconstituted Council took office on 26th November. In the early December, Wavell, accompanied by Nehru, Jinnah, Liaquat Ali, Baldev Singh, flew to London to resolve the deadlock over the differing interpretations of the Cabinet Mission regarding the setting up of the Constituent Assembly. But, the effort proved futile. The Assembly met on 9th December without the League members and adjourned till 20th January.

The Cabinet, meanwhile, functioned uneasily. Nehru originally felt that all members of the Cabinet should first meet informally in his room and take decisions on the items of the agenda so that the Cabinet meeting under Wavell would become a mere formality. However, an unconscious act of Nehru disrupted this plan. Instead of writing personally to Liaquat Ali to attend the first informal meeting, he asked his personal secretary to send the invitation. This roused the league leaders' ire and, in retaliation to this affront they started meeting separately.

Sir Archibald Rowlands served as Jinnah's economic

adviser. It was he who advised Liaquat to frame his budget as Finance Minister in the interim Government. This budget forced the dismemberment of India, more than the lawlessness engineered by the League. The budget was so framed as to derive a wedge between Nehru and Patel, on the one hand and industrial concerns, which were mostly run by non-Muslims on the other. Liaquat put forward proposals to wipe off war profits which it was believed had Nehru's approval. He recommended a ninety per cent levy on capital gains. This hit the Hindus more than it injured the Muslims. The latter were economically still pretty backward. The proposals were cunningly camouflaged in socialistic language. Several Congress Socialists felt agitated when Liaquat's budget so completely astounded and shocked rich persons of the Congress that they brought all their pressure to bear on leaders to break off from the interim Government, divide India if need be, but have nothing to do with men like Liaquat and Jinnah, who were taking advantage of the socialist bias of the Congress to exploit it for a communal advantage to the Muslims.

When the proposals came to light, there was a feeling of total discomfiture, Nehru had, no doubt, asked Dr. Mathai earlier to scrutinise the Finance Minister's budget speech. But Mathai was unable to discover anything objectionable in the absence of the offending tax proposals. Some in the Cabinet felt that the proposals should not be approved. But, by then, it was too late to apply the brakes. The Viceroy moreover would not permit any frantic last-minute revision and urged Nehru to let Liaquat Ali go ahead. There would be ample opportunity later to make amends, he argued.

The crucial difference between the two wings in the interim Government had in truth come into the open earlier. Both sides voted en bloc and Liaquat Ali, determined to disrupt the Government from within adopted invariably an obstructive stance. What made matters worse was that Wavell, who had begun extremely well, was showing signs of partiality for the League and acting largely on advice of pro-League officers. The Congress found this intolerable and discreetly conveyed to White Hall, the need for Wavell's recall.

The leading figure had never seen such high living in all their previous life. For them, the prospect of leaving it even for some type of struggle must have seemed heart breaking. This could be inferred from the conduct of the leading man among them, i.e., Sardar Vallabhbhai Patel.

As soon as he moved into 1, Aurangzeb Road, he ordered

luxurious furniture from Brooks, the expensive English furniture dealer in New Delhi, and without calling for tenders, as Government rules required. He also ordered expensive carpets. The bills went to the Government department concerned.

However, when the League entered the interim Government and its members took over the financial affairs of the Government, they discovered Patel's taste for luxurious living and leaked the information to their newspaper 'Dawn'. It published the news in brief, taunting the Congress on its past insistence on austerity, which had prompted its ruling that no Congress Minister could draw a salary larger than five hundred rupees a month. Now, the paper said, the new carpets of Patel's house alone were going to cost a fortune. A categorical statement that the report was false was issued on behalf of him. But it did not proceed from one of his English permanent secretaries Bazman. The next day, 'Dawn' published the full series of notes to prove that its story was absolutely true. Then another statement was issued that the orders were private and the bills had gone wrongly to the Government. I came to know later who finally footed these bills.

Patel had lost all patience with the interim Government. J.N. Shani a freedom fighter and important journalist records in his memoirs 'Lid Off', "Sardar Vallabhbhai Patel and his supporters in Congress had by now got reconciled to Jinnah's demand for Pakistan." Vallabhbhai according to Dr. Khan Sahib, Prime Minister of N.W.F.P., was believed to have said at this time that "Let Jinnah have it. Let him take with him all the Muslim goondas, pimps and prostitutes." When I met Dr. Khan Sahib, Shani records he was terribly upset.

The interim Government would indeed have broken up but for a momentous development. On 20th February, Attlee announced in London, Britain's firm intention to leave India by June 1948. That was accompanied by the further announcement that Lord Mountbatten had been chosen to succeed Wavell as Viceroy. The feeling that India's moment of destiny was, within the sight served to keep the Cabinet from falling apart. It was imperative to have a national Government functioning in Delhi until the final transfer of powers was accomplished.

Chapter 13

INDIA PARTITIONED

ON March 22, 1947, Lord Mountbatten, grandson of Queen Victoria, the 'First Empress' of India, accompanied by his charming wife Edwina arrived in India.

In 1946, Nehru found the time to pay a visit to Singapore and Malaya. At Singapore, Rear Admiral Mountbatten was in command. Nehru was to unveil a memorial to the Indian National Army, some of its officers and men were still being held as prisoners of war. Nehru was then President of the Congress, and was shortly to be invited to head the interim Government. Wavell had sent advance words secretly to Mountbatten accordingly.

Mountbatten had been on tour till the actual day of Nehru's arrival. The British authorities disliked Nehru's idea of unveiling a memorial to men who had "deserted the King's forces!" They were reluctant to receive him. Mountbatten, on arrival, overruled the boycott and threatened to send him his own car to receive Nehru. He also ordered that Indians residing in outlying areas were to join the reception to their great leader.

The British in Rangoon had been pigheaded, they refused permission to Nehru's plane to land on its way to Singapore. Nehru baffled them by making what seemed to a "forced landing" in a field near the airport, thanks to the daring of an adventurous pilot, Biju Patnaik, later the Chief Minister of Orissa and Union Minister. While the landing was "forced" to all appearances, more than a few thousand Indians had "mysteriously assembled" near the field to receive him. This delayed Nehru's arrival in Singapore by a few hours. Nehru did not know that Mountbatten had arranged for him to meet some high-ranking officials and civilians. He drove straight from the airport to Government House where Mountbatten and other dignitaries were waiting.

It was an informal stage affair, as a sort of late lunch and early tea. Nehru forgot all about I.N.A. memorial. In fact, after his departure, it was blown up by a British canon.

Next on schedule was a drive through the streets where Indians, Malaysians and Chinese were all lined up to cheer Nehru. Nehru was agreeably surprised when Mountbatten directed him to an open carriage and sitting side by side, drove him through the cheering, festive crowd to an Indian soldiers' canteen. Here he was to meet some of the Indian officers and soldiers who fought against I.N.A. headed by Subhas Bose. Lady Mountbatten had been taking keen interest in the welfare of refugees lodged at YMCA hostel. There was a big rush as Nehru and Mountbatten entered the main reception room. They found Edwina missing. They both got on chairs anxiously trying to scan the milling crowd. As Nehru started pushing some people in the front row he saw a petite woman crawling out of the crowd. The lady re-arranged her dress as if nothing had happened and greeted him with a cheerful, terribly winsome smile. Nehru later learned that while Edwina Mountbatten had been there waiting for him and her husband to arrive, the crowd had made a mad rush knocking her down, till she just managed to crawl out of the melee. It was the most unusual introduction for both, unforgettable and touching. The visit would have remained Nehru's fond remembrances if events had not occurred later to revive this friendship and bring all three of them together in the centre of India stage, in the final drama of India's struggle for Freedom

Having dismissed Wavell, Attlee summoned Mountbatten to take over the Viceroyalty with a clear mandate that power was to be transferred to one or more than one successor government or governments, as the case may be, before June 1948. The Cabinet Mission Plan still held the field. Churchill almost prophetically but approximately described his new command 'Operation Scuttle'. So it was Mountbatten who was sent 'ostensibly', to preserve and save the unity of India if he could. Failing which, though this was not stated in his mandate, to scuttle the ship, divide the country, leave the salvage operations to others and come home. He carried out 'Operation Scuttle', in the shortest possible period, with utmost tact, of which only a naval commander of great resourcefulness, was capable.

The Mountbattens were great extroverts. The arrival of the Mountbattens was heralded with a lot of pre-arranged fanfare. The departure of the Wavell was an unusually tame affair. In fact, it had been conventional for the coming Viceroy and the parting Viceroy to say farewell without meeting. Wavell was made to stay on. He stayed over till the Mountbattens arrived. He received the Mountbattens and then attended a dinner to bid farewell to himself. Next morning, on the 23rd of March, the Wavells quietly left. A gun salute welcomed the Mountbattens who were sworn in. There was something theatrical about the ceremony. The pomp and splendour with which they surrounded themselves seemed like a Hollywood presentation of royalty. They both played the part with consummate perfection. The Durbar Hall which earlier used to be modestly lit, even though the chandelliers were expensive and aplenty, was in a blaze of lights. The 'throne' seats had been raised by a couple of feet. The blue and the gold in the tapestry were emphasized by hidden lights playing on the Viceroy and the Vicereine. A mammoth red velvet screen hung in the background with the Mountbatten crest.

Aides, in the uniform lined up on both sides of the 'throne', on one to the right sat Nehru and the Congress members of the interim Government. On the left, Liaquat Ali Khan and his League colleagues. The Mountbattens wore spotless naval white with sashes in royal blue, and rows of medals of great distinction. Everything was colourful; they both looked under the false light, terribly young, so magnificently dolled-up that one would have mistaken it as a minor royal coronation or a delayed royal wedding.

They were like two actors constantly engaged in playing a chosen part. They played their parts with consummate perfection. I can only say that very few escaped the Mountbatten spell among those they had decided to work upon. After describing his staff companions, Pyarelal writes: "Last but not least, a 'secret weapon' of no small strategic value in Lord Mountbatten, Edwina, a heroine, in her own right...who by her unfailing tact, warm womanly sympathy and fine discrimination provided just what her impetuous husband needed most. Abul Kalam Azad was even more suggestive of the role of Lady Mountbatten. "Jawaharlal Nehru was also greatly impressed by Lord Mountbatten", he wrote, "but perhaps even greater was the influence of Lady Mountbatten. She is not only extremely intelligent, but has a most attractive and friendly temperament. It should be said to the credit of Nehru that while on occasions he was deeply influenced by her .

On June 2, Lord Mountbatten disclosed his plan to partition India, to Congress and Muslim League leadership. The Congress accepted the plan on the spot, on their return Kripalani as Congress President sent their acceptance in writing.

Jinnah expressed his inability to commit unless he had consulted his Council. The next day when they again met, Jinnah only nodded his head when he was asked about his acceptance.

On June 3, the fate of sub-continent was decided and the plan was announced. Indian sub-continent was divided on religious lines making a geographical mockery.

I have earlier mentioned that I knew the first Prime Minister of Pakistan, Nawab Liaquat Ali Khan, from my Aligarh days and in spite of our political differences, he had a soft corner for me. When he visited New Delhi in 1950 to parley with his counterpart, the Indian Prime Minister, Nehru to sign what came to be known as Nehru-Liaquat Pact, I buttoneholed him and asked him that while accepting Mountbatten Plan did Jinnah and his League consider the fate of Muslims who were to be left behind in India after partition as hostages.

He took me into confidence and told me not to disclose the story even to my wife. He said on the evening of the fateful day, he received a phone call from Jinnah to rush to his York Place residence immediately. He accompanied by Raja Mohammadabad was asked by Quaid-e-Azam's Secretary, to go to first floor. On the verandah, he noticed a glass of whisky and an ash tray full of cigarette butts and Jinnah walking up and down to the terrace. He was shocked because he had never noticed his leader touching liquor before sun was down.

Jinnah was in an agitated mood, he disclosed to him, that an hour earlier, he was asked to rush to Viceregal Lodge for a cup of tea with Mountbattens. On reaching there the couple apologised to him for the short notice and after a few minutes' silence, Mountbatten said that he knew that if he did not accept the plan immediately, he would hand over the power to Congress and in future Jinnah could deal with them.

On giving some thought that if all power to Congress was transferred unconditionally, he would have to go sack and ashes rubbing his nose on the floor before that 'Wrecked Bania', meaning Gandhi who will command police, army and the state force, in that situation, he had no alternative but to give his consent.

I was at Nainital, when I heard the announcement on the All India Radio, that the plan had been accepted by the Congress as well as the League. I was shocked and dismayed for all my life work was destroyed by the aging and tired leaders. The Muslims in Congress had faced the worst type of persecution from their co-religionists. While Hindu congressmen on their release from jail were garlanded, Muslims were treated as traitors by most of their co-religionists.

In a state of shock, I left my hotel room, to find some solitude on the Nainital lake. On my way, I met Khaliquz-Zaman, Z.H.Lari, Begum Aizaz Rasul the top leaders of the League. Obviously they were jubilant and mocked at my discomfiture. I asked them what next, they laughed and said that Congress would have to give full guarantee for the protection of Muslims in India in return of protection of non-Muslims minority in Pakistan. I remarked as you were leaving us as hostages and left with tears in my eyes.

Since U.P. Legislative Assembly was in session, almost all of the Muslim League leaders, and Congress leaders, of U.P. were at Nainital. While Muslim Leaguers were jubilant, the congressmen were dismayed and had a sense of defeat. The sympathies of the most of Muslim bureaucrats were with league, and foolishly they thought the imaginary discrimination against them would be a thing of the past.

Almost every Congress leader and Hindu bureaucrat, I met felt that this division of the sub-continent was a temporary phase and Pakistan not being viable ultimately will rejoin their motherland. The complacency was noticeable ever among the top Congress leaders which I was to find, when I reached Delhi on June 6 to attend the A.I.C.C. meeting which was to meet on June 14-15 to endorse the Working Committee decision accepting what was described as Mountbatten Plan dividing the Indian sub-continent in three parts. India, West Pakistan and East Pakistan at a distance of 1,500 miles from one another.

On reaching Delhi, I, with some friends, met Sarat Bose who was still the leader of Congress Legislative Party, in Central Assembly.

He was heartbroken. He pointed out that all his attempt to salvage the situation had failed. He had persuaded Shaheed Suhrawardy, the League Supremo of Bengal to have a sovereign Bengal, in which Muslims would have only two per cent majority. But Patel had roped in Shyama Prasad Mukherjee the President of Hindu Maha Sabha by offering him a seat in Dominion Cabinet, who would not allow a state even with a slender majority of Muslims.

The powerful newspaper *Amrit Bazar Patrika* which had violently fought against partition of Bengal by Curzon in 1905 completely forgetting that its past also opposed Sarat Bose and Suhrawardy.

On the evening of June 13, some of us headed by Sarat

Bose went to Gandhi who was staying in Bhangi colony to remind him that he had promised that the vivisection of India would be on his dead body. We found him in a dejected mood and came back with the impression that we had his blessing, if we opposed it in A.I.C.C. which was slated to meet on June 14.

On our return, we moved among A.I.C.C. members who were staying at different places to mobilise them for a battle which we knew we had lost. the Muslim members in general and the followers of Khan Abdul Ghaffar Khan who was to spend thirty years of his life in Pakistan either in jail or in exile were crestfallen and agitated.

Though I had not much faith in Gandhi, but I felt that he could create a miracle by coming to our side. On June 14, the A.I.C.C. met at Constitution House on Curzon Road now Kasturba Gandhi Marg presided over by Acharya Kripalani. Almost all of us expected Gandhi to give us a lead. He came for short time accompanied by his usual entourage of young Ashramite ladies. In feeble and unconvincing way, he delivered his sermon much to our dismay and disappointment.

He said, "Who will listen to my pleading? But the President said that I should at least show my face here. Hence, I have come to show my face and speak a few words".

"You will not doubtless agree that no one could be so much hurt by the division of the country as I am", he said, "and I don't think that anyone can be more unhappy today as I am. But what was to happen has happened. The Working Committee, he reminded them, acted on behalf of the Congress. If you reject it the world will call you irresponsible, the leaders had accepted the partition because there was no other way. They now see it clearly that the country is already divided in two camps".

"The decision that has been arrived at", he told the members in plain words, "has been reached with our complicity yet you complain of the Working Committee which has men of such great a calibre. It was easy to criticise the leaders, he said, but the critics should think out what they would do if they were in the leader's place, I criticise them, of course, but afterwards what? Shall I assume the burdens that they are carrying? Shall become a Nehru or a Sardar or a Rajendra Prasad? Even if you should put me in their place, I do not know that what I should be able to do".

He, therefore, advised "you have a perfect right to do so if you feel that you have the strength" he told the members. "But I do not find that strength in us today. If you had it, I would also be with you and if I felt strong young myself I would, alone, take up the flag of revolt. But today, I do not see the condition of doing so".

He, therefore, advised them to accept the resolution without changing it in any way and set their minds to what was to be done in the future. We have to draw something good out of this bad thing, he said, I am not the one to be upset by defeat..... We should draw out gold and diamonds even from mud.

Pandit Nehru, the Register recorded, was outspoken. "India's heart has been broken, he said, but her essential unity has not been destroyed. We will repair the broken heart. It can be only on the basis of a programme for a partition".

Sardar Patel was even more outspoken. During these nine months in office, Sardar Patel said, he had completely disillusioned him of the supposed merits of the state paper. He had noticed that Muslim officials right from the top down to *chaprasis* except for a few honourable exceptions, were all for the Muslim League. There should be no mistake about it. Mutual recriminations and allegations were the order of the day. The May 16 plan was gone and he was glad. That plan left much room for conflict and bickerings. The Congress was opposed to Pakistan but yet the resolution before the House accepted partition. Whether the A.I.C.C. liked it or not, there was already Pakistan in action both in Punjab and in Bengal. In the circumstances, he would prefer the real Pakistan because then they would have some sense of responsibility.

Pandit Gobind Ballabh Pant, who always, piloted the controversial Resolution of the Working Committee, as he did at Tripura which resulted into expulsion of Subhas Bose from Congress and later his great escape from India moved the Resolution to ratify the decision of the Working Committee.

I vehemently opposed the resolution. I warned the Congress leaders, that they were playing with fire. The partition of India would hardly solve the communal problem. It will result in more bloodshed and affliction of the people. I particularly warned them that Pakistan would be a pistol in the heart of India, and in future those who would accept it would rue their decision.

Among others who opposed the resolution were Purushottam Das Tandon, Speaker of U.P. Assembly, Maulana Hafizul Rehman, leader of Jamaet Ule-ma and Gopal Singh Quami, a Sikh leader.

The Congress Socialist Party as usual was divided. While Jaya Prakash Narayan was opposed to resolution, Dr. Ram Manohar Lohia who was completely under the influence of

Gandhi and Nehru advised in his speech at the A.I.C.C. to remain neutral.

He pointed out that while the resolution was bad, they themselves were responsible for acceptance of 3rd June plan. They could not blame the leaders, as they themselves were weak and the leaders therefore were forced to accept the Government proposal. He demanded that the Socialists could not vote for or against the resolution.

The resolution was eventually put to vote. The Socialists and Gandhi's supporters of Bengal, Punjab and Sind remained neutral. It is a significant that in spite of the blessings of Gandhi, 157 votes were cast in favour and we could mobilise only 29 votes against, most of us especially, Muslim congress-men were shocked by the surrender of Gandhi and his power thirsty lieutenants. It was particularly dismayed that even Maulana Azad took the partition as temporary phase and was deluded by the optimism of his, tired, exhausted and beaten colleagues who had no stomach for further struggle.

It was obvious from the speech of Sardar Patel, that his Muslim League colleagues in Interim Government had exhausted their patience. All that they wanted now was to get over it at all costs, and to put a brave face while doing it.

Sardar Patel was more forthright, when he expressed his intolerance to have at least three provinces with Muslim majority within united India. He felt that their exit would give him a free hand to carve out a Hindu empire.

The Congress as well as League had accepted the partition. The Akalis and Hindu Maha Sabha had become subsidiary parties to the Congress and were led by its decision. The voice of some of us was a cry in wilderness.

The Congress had missed the bus, to preserve India's unity, due to Nehru whose remarks provoked the league to withdraw its support to Cabinet Mission plan. I myself felt that transfer of power could have been postponed for getting along with unity of India. But, Patel who controlled the Congress Party with the support of men like Shyama Prasad Mukherjee, who belonged to Hindu Maha Sabha, a chauvinist Hindu organisation, wanted the Muslims to get out so that they could be master of their own home without further delay.

Apparently, Nehru rationalised his support to partition of India, as he was afraid of a civil war. He, a student of world history, failed to realise that the casualties and destruction following the civil war in America after independence and in most recent times in Soviet Union have been too insignificant than that followed the partition of Indian sub-continent.

In mid-June, the Indian National Congress led by Gandhi, Father of the Nation, Nehru the darling of Indian youth and Sardar Patel, the iron man, put their seal on partition of India creating two dominions of India and Pakistan. They had not the vision that we would face three wars, incessant arms race, declaration of Pakistani Premier Zulfiquar Ali Bhutto that they would continue to fight India for a thousand years.

However, the great ego of Jinnah whose only life's ambition was to humiliate Gandhi was satisfied, and the tired and demoralised Congress leaders were to be installed as the rulers of divided India.

Chapter 14

TRYST WITH DESTINY

AT midnight on August 14, Jawaharlal Nehru accompanied by his colleagues marched on red carpet to be sworn in as the first Prime Minister of Dominion of India.

The moment was marked by a stirring ceremony in the Central Hall of what was then India's Constituent Assembly. An imposing circular, sandstone building built for the use of Legislative Assembly of the Raj in the Indo-Baroque style of Sir Edwin Lutyens, it now houses the Parliament of Independent India.

The chimes of midnight were greeted by fanfare of conchshells and then a female coir sang the Sanskrit National Anthem 'Vande Mataram' (I bow to thee, my motherland). The point of the ceremony was a lyrical speech by Independent India's first Prime Minister, Jawaharlal Nehru. "Long years ago", he began 'we made a tryst with destiny' and now the time has come when we shall redeem our pledge, not wholly or in full measure, but very substantially at the stroke of the midnight hour, when the world sleeps, India will awake to life and freedom".

Nehru's Independence day speech has gone down in history as a masterpiece of political rhetoric. The price of Independence had been the partition of the sub-continent into two new States. The Muslim-majority areas of British India were to form the Islamic State of Pakistan; the rest would continue to be India. Partition was intended to avert the threat of civil war between Hindus and Muslims. But its architects failed to anticipate the shape of things to come.

The occasion has been described by Indians as 'Independence Day', to British Parliament under Independence of India Act, 1947, it was transference of power, to me it was distribution of heritage to two feuding children by a *'Mai Bap'*, father and mother government.

Both of them in India and Pakistan inherited the British

system of Government with the steel frame of civil service based on 'dealing clerks' the mercenary army with British uniforms and decorations bestowed by His Majesty the King Emperor, for loyal service to the Crown, the police which was used to suppress the struggle for India's Freedom.

To me it was a change of bureaucracy from white to brown, though Pakistan retained many white civilians, India also for some time had a British Commander-in-Chief in Auchinlek.

India as well as Pakistan inherited the same laws and regulations, the same system of education, the same laws of land revenue and taxation.

While the entire country was rejoicing and the people in India were dancing and singing in the streets, there was no warmth or glow of freedom in my heart.

On the night of August 14, when Nehru had his tryst with destiny, I was in Lucknow. After performing my professional duties at Patrika office, I went to a lady friend of mine belonging to a high Christian family. She was preparing herself for a ball organised in a white men's club of Mohammad Bagh, where the departing British Masters had to toast their Indian collaborators for their liberation.

Obviously, she was shocked to see me dejected and pensive on such an occasion, when according to her, I must have redeemed my dreams. It was natural that none who had not fought for freedom and integrity of this country could understand me.

Later, I went for the first time in my life to U.P. Government House to report the swearing-in-ceremony of my adopted mother, Sarojini Naidu.

It was an interesting sight for me to see, Mrs. Naidu to enter Darbar Hall, followed by silver mace carrying chobdras dressed in Bengal lancers dress accompanied by a horde of ADCs dressed in British Military uniforms decorated with medals that they had earned for their gallantry against Indian National Army in Burma and Malaysia.

The erstwhile British stooges who were special invitees were taken unawares. Not knowing the shape of things to come they had rushed to Khadi Bhandar and purchased unbleached dhotis and Gandhi caps, and in that dress, they appeared a pathetic and comic figure. Till then, they did not know that their new masters would see that in new set-up they were dressed up in well tailored *chust* pyjamas, as smart as British breeches, and black sherwani not less elegant than the previous frock and tail coats.

I had known Mrs. Naidu since my *Bombay Chronicle* days. She was one of the most remarkable and admirable women of the twentieth century. A great conversationalist, her wit and humour was joy for everyone who came in contact with her. After the formal ceremonies were over, and those present were presented to her, by her senior A.D.C. who had a long list of invitees and was making frequent mistake in announcing the names, my turn came, and Mrs. Naidu shouted "He is a 'naughty boy' but as Governor, I will tame him", this remark generated great laughter.

After that, the Lucknow Government House became my second home and almost every evening I spent there as one of Mrs. Naidu's courtiers.

Mrs. Sarojini Naidu, had full command over English, and Urdu languages. Though a Bengali by origin married to an Andhra doctor, she was born and brought up in the court of His Exalted Highness, the Nizam of Hyderabad the last relic of Mughal culture. She was a remarkable woman, steeped in the composite culture of India. She was a broad and a cosmopolitan outlook, and in her in presence one felt oneself a real Indian.

As the constitutional head of the province, she had enough leisure, which she spent in the company of young men and women interested not only in politics but art, literature and poetry.

In the evenings, she would sit on a huge chair surrounded by her young admirers, and often would hear her Prime Minister Govind Ballabh Pant being ushered in and whisper "a big bore has arrived".

She used to invite girls from respectable families, and to the horror of colonial *Khidmatgars* and *bawarchis*, she would take them to Government house kitchen and help them to prepare her favourite Moghul dishes.

She knew that I was a bachelor, and after Independence, the days of my hectic life of going underground and marching to jail were over. She arranged my marriage to a lovely girl belonging to one of the noblest aristocratic families of the province and I had to agree to her choice.

In spite of my protest, she insisted that in my marriage all Moghul rituals, mostly based on Hindu traditions should be observed. She came to my house and received by my bride with fanfare usual in feudal and aristocratic Muslim families.

She was keeping indifferent health. She was shocked at the assassination of Gandhi, whom she affectionately described, as her Micky Mouse.

She arranged a Mushaira to hear the compositions of Hindi and Urdu poets on the death of Father of the Nation in Government House. She was too ill to be present, but her sick bed was placed from where she could listen to her favourite poets. She was especially impressed by the poem of my brother Majaz and invited him to her sick bed side to congratulate him.

After a few months early in the morning, I received a message from her daughter, Padmaja Naidu, who later on became the Governor of West Bengal, that she had died. Padmaja entrusted me with the task of arranging her funeral, and informing her friends. By next morning, Pandit Jawaharlal Nehru, Rajaji and Maulana Azad arrived and her body was put to flame on the bank of Gomti with full military and state honours.

On August 14, while New Delhi, Lucknow and other provincial capitals were illuminated, the cities of Lahore and Amritsar were in total darkness. In the streets of Bombay and Patna, the jubilant masses were dancing for redeeming the tryst with destiny while the people of West as well as East Punjab were witnessing the dance of death.

The largest exodus in the human history was taking place from both the sides of Radcliffe Line. Within a few days of Independence, the National Capital New Delhi was experiencing the worst type of human butchery.

At a distance of only a few miles, from high dome of Parliament, where Nehru had delivered his classic oration, manhood was being butchered, womanhood was being dishonoured and innocent newly born children being consigned to flames.

The Hindu and Sikh refugees from Pakistan were marching desperately to kill Muslims in India and to find a roof on their head.

The province of Uttar Pradesh bordered the Delhi city, and it was feared that the fire would engulf the cities like Kanpur and Lucknow. Fortunately, Kanpur had a very young and dynamic District Magistrate as named Kishan Chand, and later on, became Lt. Governor of Delhi during emergency and had to commit suicide to atone the sins of Indira Gandhi and her rising son Sanjay. He made herculean effort to maintain law and order.

Rafi Ahmed Kidwai was the Home Minister, and he showed remarkable courage and vision in facing the situation. But later on he had to pay for it.

The communalist Congress MLAs of U.P. led by Charan Singh who became for a brief period Prime Minister of India, carried on a campaign that a Muslim Home Minister is security risk, and on advice of Sardar Patel, the first policeman of U.P. was kicked up to be first postman of India as Nehru inducted him as Communication Minister in his Government.

It must be said to the credit of Pandit Nehru that he was anxious to see that U.P. does not meet the fate of East Punjab. The refugees were marching to Hardwar, Dehradun, and other borders. He did not fully trust the official machinery and wanted Congressmen to be mobilised for this task.

A team composed of Mahavir Tyagi, Govind Sahai, and myself was sent to tour these areas to assess the situation and to guide and monitor the administrative measure.

Hardwar and its neighbourhood were the most affected areas. Mahavir Tyagi who belonged to Dehradun, performed heroic deeds in saving the life of Muslims. The frightened Muslim women and children, had taken shelter in a building belonging to prosperous Muslims, on hearing the news that the Hindu Sikh refugees uprooted in Pakistan, were going to burn that building, he announced on a loud speaker that he was there to be burnt along with the Muslim women and children.

On hearing his voice local population rallied and surrounded that building and saved the lives of innocent Muslim women and children, who were left behind in India by the architect of Pakistan.

I myself with my friend, Govind Sahai who was Parliamentary Secretary in Pant Ministry went to most of the districts of western U.P. seeing that the district authorities are making adequate efforts to save the lives of Muslims.

Our worst experience was in Jawalpore a suburb of Hardwar where almost the entire Muslim population was slaughtered. In barracks, recently vacated by armed forces, the refugees were lodged. Many of them had lost their kith and kin in Punjab now in Pakistan. Many of them got there in wretched condition, after days and nights of misery and terror. Some of them arrived mutilated; many of women had their breast cut off by the Muslim gangs as they left home. On arrival of safety refugees would have discernible relief on their faces, of safety sprouted from their very skins. In two or three days they would become conscious of their discomforts; in a week some of them might even start joining groups out for revenge on the opposite religion at this end.

In those days, I visited Delhi also, where Nehru had his tryst with destiny. The Sikh and Hindu refugees were busy settling their accounts with innocent men and women, and children. It was to the credit of Nehru that a band of devoted congressmen and women were busy defusing the situation. The Muslims were being evacuated to Old Fort, built by Sher Shah Suri, and to Humayun Tomb to be transported to Jinnah's promised land. The prosperous Muslim along with their families even with their courtesans, were availing facilities of air transport, while the rest were being sent by trains to be slaughtered on their way.

It was a pathetic sight to see the Muslims, women, children being escorted by armed personnel to these camps. I was reminded that only a few months earlier, while going to attend the Jubilee Celebrations of Jamia Milia Islamia in Okhla, I had seen the same crowd marching and shouting 'Pakistan Zindabad', 'Quaid-e-Azam Zindabad'.

The Muslim League campaign had even unnerved some of the nationalist Muslims. Dr. Zakir Husain, who later on, became the President of India, had invited Jinnah as the chief guest on this occasion. Though Jinnah in his speech expressed his distrust of him and almost snubbed him.

I was reminded that as Vice-Chancellor of Jamia Milia Dr. Husain provided Jinnah and Liaquat Ali Khan seats on the dais, while Maulana Azad one of the founder had to take seat among the audience amidst jeers and cat calls of the teachers and students of Jamia Milia.

Now the lives and properties of Jamia itself were threatened and it goes to the credit of Nehru and Azad that today it is a prosperous and growing educational institution.

One of my worst experience was a visit to Victoria, Zana Hospital in Jaimal Masjid, which was attacked and newly born children were dragged from maternity wards and torn to pieces. I hung my head in shame when a British subaltern who was present told me that he never saw such scences even in Nazi Germany.

One day while returning from Safdarjung Airport, with my friend of student movement days, a Sikh, Mohan Singh Sawhney we passed by a jeep with Sikh Army officer, they shouted 'Jai Hind' and declared that they had transformed Ali Ganj into Kishan Ganj. Ali Ganj was a small village near present day Jorbagh. We rushed there and found the entire population of men and women and children gunned down.

On our way back, we rushed to York Road, the residence of Nehru, the Prime Minister of India, and informed him what we had heard and seen.

He was greatly moved, and for sometime was dazed. Later he asked his Secretary, M.O. Mathai, to inform the Governor-General that he was on his way to Viceregal Lodge, yet to be christened as Rashtrapati Bhavan. It was on the advice of the Governor-General that the Gorkha and South Indian troops were obtained to restore some type of law and order in national capital.

I went to Lucknow completely demoralised with all that I had witnessed. I could never even visualise that such heavy price, Indian sub-continent would have to pay to satisfy Nehru's desire to get power and Jinnah's ego to have a Pakistan.

All these killings, arsons, continued unabated for almost a year and half. It was on January 30, that I was in Hazarat Ganj the market place of Lucknow, that Mr. Adam, Librarian of U.P. Legislative Assembly came to me very much agitated and informed me that he had heard the announcement on Radio that Gandhi had been assassinated. I did not believe him and immediately rang the office of Associated Press of India, now Press Trust of India and the news was confirmed.

Though I have never been a great admirer of Gandhi, but I burst into tears and felt that he had said that vivisection of India would be on his dead body, but vivisection was followed by his dead body.

I rushed to *Amrit Bazar Patrika* and giving the reaction of Lucknow citizens said 'Gandhi had been crucified at the altar of partition of India'.

Gandhi was immobile, otherwise I felt he would have walked out of his own funeral with more than a million people watching. The last remains of the apostle of non-violence was mounted on a gun carriage. These were followed by the Vice-regal bodyguards with lances balancing in the sun, three thousand armed men drawn from the services closed up the ranks. Everything against which he has struggled when he lived everything for which he seemed to have died, lay crumbled at his feet.

In spite of the fact that the Union Jack, was hauled down from the Lucknow Government House, and U.P. Secretariat on the morning of August 15, 1947, it kept on flying on the ruins of residency, which became famous during the heroic seige by freedom fighters in 1857. It may be noted that in whole of British Empire where the sun never set, this was the only building where it was not hauled down even in the night.

On my protest, it was pointed out that at the time of transfer of power, it was agreed that the British monuments and graves would be looked after by a Commission under the control of British High Commissioner and Lucknow Residency was a British monument. As the leader of the Forward Bloc, I threatened to march there with my volunteers, to haul it down, and to hoist national flag. Pandit Pant deputed one of his Ministers, K.D. Malaviya to persuade me not to do it.

However, when I was found adamant the British Commission looking after British monuments and graves, was persuaded to agree to haul down the Union Jack, but till today, the tri-colour flag has not been raised there to fulfil the ambition of those Indians who laid down their lives during its siege in 1957.

Chapter 15

OUTCASTE CONGRESSMEN

IT was unfortunate that the Muslims who joined the Indian National Congress and fought for India's independence were always given a separate identity by the Congress leadership even from Gandhian era. They were desciibed as Nationalist Muslims. Gandhi's support to Khilafat Movement had brought a huge army of Muslims in Congress-fold but most of them deserted the ship after Kamal Ata Turk abolished Khilafat, and Gandhi withdrew his Non-Cooperation Movement following Chauri Chaura incident.

But many of them particularly Ahrars of Punjab, and the products of Muslim seminary of Deoband continued to support the Congress and its programme.

The Khudai Khidmutgars led by legendary Pathan leader Khan Abdul Ghaffar Khan stood by the Congress till the end to be betrayed by Congress leadership to enter into an agreement with the Muslim League, and to accept the partition of sub-continent.

As long as Congress was fighting the Muslim League the Muslim congressmen who were described as Nationalist Muslims were often pampered to their own embarrassment by the central as well as local Congress leaders. But after the transfer of power, it appears Congress had no use for them. Since all the Muslims were spread all over India, the electoral compulsion forced the Congress to find new allies.

Some of the Muslim Congressmen joined the mainstream of hangers on and sycophants, and were provided with some seats in legislatures as well as in Government.

But, many veterans — most noteworthy among them was Dr. Saifuddin Kitchlu — did not join their rank and were completely neglected by Congress.

It may be relevant to recall that it was on the arrest of Dr. Kitchlu, the protest meeting was held in Jalianwala Bagh which was beginning of the demise of British Rule in India.

When, India was partitioned and Dr. Kitchlu was the President of the Punjab Provincial Congress Committee, even he could not face the wrath of Hindus and Sikhs following the incident on the other side of the sub-continent. He was forced by his friends to flee from his beloved home Amritsar, leaving huge landed properties to take shelter in safety of Delhi.

Since he was an independent man, he was completely neglected, though much less important people were given various assignments in free India. He had to die leading a pathetic life.

The products of Deoband were kept in Congress organisation and some time were offered some patronage over the cost of purely secular minded Muslim Congressmen, for it was felt that they could cash for the Congress in electoral bank due to their obstructionist attitude to modernise Indian Muslims.

It was unfortunate that Congressmen belonging to Muslim community were not treated as Congressmen; they were categorised as Muslims Congressmen or Nationalist Muslims. After the transfer of power from British hands to Indians, the same attitude continued. Though under the new Constitution, the separate electorate for Muslims was abolished, but for all practical purposes, they fixed up Muslim quota in States as well as Central Legislatures, while nominating their candidates.

In the first General Election, even the top Congress leaders belonging to Muslim community were set up from the constituencies which had predominantly Muslim population. The classic example is that of Maulana Azad a top national leader, who could have contested from any constituency in India and would have won. He belonged to Delhi due to his family connections and to Calcutta as a result of his domicile. But, he was set up from erstwhile princely state of Rampur which has almost fortyfive per cent Muslims electorate. Later on, he decided not to contest from Rampur; in 1957, a search was made to find out a constituency with predominant muslim population, and, a safe seat was found for him in Gurgaon in the neighbourhood of Delhi which claims substantial Muslim population.

The fact is that with his prestige and personality Maulana Azad could have easily been returned from any constituency in India but, even twice elected Congress President, and one of the topmost Congress leaders was treated only as a Muslim by his colleagues headed by Nehru.

The Congress leadership at the centre as well as in States entrusted the selection of Muslim candidates to some of the

Muslim Congress leaders with disastrous results. Most of them who were entrusted with this task wanted to demonstrate unwanted generosity to those Muslim Leaguers who had abused them, arranged demonstrations and social boycott of them.

The best beneficiary of this generosity were in Bihar at the hands of Dr. Syed Mehmood, the veteran Congress leader. In Bihar, there were scores of Muslim Congressmen who had courted arrest, faced the social boycott by the Muslim Leaguers, but in preference to them, Dr. Syed Mehmood selected Ghulam Imam the leader of National Guard, a para-military force of Muslim League whose dubious role has been described even by Pyarelal in *Last days of Gandhi* and Mazhar Imam, and Nawab Tajmul Hussain, who, for their personal reasons, had not migrated to Pakistan after having given all support to league.

In U.P. Rafi Ahmed Kidwai and Hafiz Ibrahim both of them had acquired the taste of sycophancy, and who could have been better sychophants than the erstwhile Leaguers who had perfected this art at the courts of British Deputy Commissioners and Governors.

In 1952, Begum Aizaz Rasul, former president of women section of All India Muslim League headed by Jinnah; Akhtar Hussain, a staunch Muslim Leaguer, Nawab of Chatari, a former Member of Viceroy's Executive Council, were preferred to me and a dozen of devoted highly educated Muslim congressmen.

I have already mentioned that I jumped into the national movement at comparatively an early age. I had some humble contributions in building up a powerful anti-imperialist student movement. In the cause of India's independence, I undertook the rigours of an underground worker. I was the last political prisoner to be released from U.P. jail at the event of transfer of power to India.

But, after Independence, the Congress leadership had no use for me. I had earned their displeasure for having opposed their plan to divide India. Even after Independence, I kept on attacking them for their pro-feudal and pro-capitalist policies at various meetings of A.I.C.C. of which I was elected a Member at a very early age.

At Jaipur session, of the Congress, Shankar Rao one of its General Secretaries, moved a resolution urging the Congress rank and file to keep high moral standard in public life. I moved an amendment that the word of top Congress leadership should also be added with rank and file.

While my amendment was under discussion, Patel and Nehru left the venue of the meeting to attend a ceremony in connection with an exhibition.

In their absence, I asked for division on my amendment which was passed. Nehru and Patel were furious on this development. Next morning when A.I.C.C. met again they asked for the issue to be re-opened. I approached the Congress President, Pattabhi Sitaramaiah pointing out its absurdity. He shrugged his shoulder and told me frankly that Sardar wanted it; Nehru wanted it who he was to reject their request?

Later at almost every occasion of A.I.C.C. I moved amendments to Congress Constitution to include socialism as its objective, but in view of the opposition of Congress leadership, I could not get it implemented.

In 1948, when the Congress leadership banned the dual membership and socialists led by J.P. and Acharya Narendra Dev had to part company with the Congress, I declined not to leave the mainstream of Indian politics which I considered Congress. However, I was never trusted by Congress leadership though they could not find any pretext to expel me for any act of discipline.

The U.P. Congress leadership headed by Pant and Kidwai was allergic to those connected with the student movement. While Bihar and many other States returned a number of student activists to State and Central Legislatures, there was definite discrimination against those who had joined the national movement through students' organisations.

Those freedom fighters, like Balram Singh, S.M. Jaffer, Chandramouli Awasthy who had gone to jail as students were not allowed by Congress leaders namely Pant and Kidwai to come near the legislature, though they continued in the Congress. However, after the death of Pant and Kidwai some of them came to State Legislature and Parliament and made a mark.

The story of the student activists who left the Congress was different. Narain Dutt Tiwary, the present Chief Minister of U.P., Raj Narain whom I have described earlier, Prabhu Narain Singh to name a few, defeated Congress nominees as the candidates of Socialist Party.

Unfortunately, I had earned the displeasure of Kidwai as well as Pant and they were determined not to admit me in legislature. I was working for National Herald, a paper owned by Nehru for all practical purposes. After the Congress Ministry resigned in 1939, Kidwai who was the main source of collection of finances, as revenue Minister from U.P. Taluqdars and Zamindars became ineffective. The newspaper was sinking due to lack of finances. Nehru never had any occasion to raise fund for any cause. It was done by other Congress leaders. Kidwai approached Subhas Bose to finance the paper.

Subhas Bose was Chairman of a Delhi based Insurance Company. Its Managing Director was Lala Shankarlal, a veteran Congress leader who was known to have financed a number of revolutionary and terrorist groups. He agreed to take it over and sent one of his lieutenant Abdullah Atawal to take charge of it.

On hearing these developments, I approached Subhas Bose and warned him that with his finance only Nehru's image would be built. On last minute he backed out.

For sabotaging this scheme, Kidwai never forgave me. On my release from jail, I wrote a number of articles for an Allahabad weekly exposing his close relations with landed aristocracy.

I had known Pant from early days and I have described in Chapter "My forays into Journalism", how unhappy he was with the exposure of rampant corruption in his Ministry. He did all that was possible to curtail my journalist activities.

I have already described that how he overruled my candidature for Constituent Assembly against a former Muslim League M.L.A. Choudhary Hyder Hussain. Later, when Khaliquz-Zaman resigned from U.P. Assembly, from Lucknow, the city Congress Committee of which I was Vice-President, unanimously recommended my name. Till then Election Commission was not formed and the Law Secretary of the State was Election Officer. In my own presence, Kidwai asked him to postpone the election to enable one of his nominees whose name was not on electoral to be included in rolls and it was done.

However, as a loyal Congressman, I proposed his name before the returning officer and faithfully campaigned for him.

The only Congress leader who had affection for me and had some regard for my talents as well as contribution to national movement was Maulana Abul Kalam Azad.

While Congress was selecting its candidates for the first General Election, I had approached the Central Parliamentary Board. Azad is reported to have strongly supported my candidature. Pant could not oppose it openly for Azad was too big a man for him. He assured Azad that my name should not be announced till he had persuaded some of his local colleagues to accept me. Azad considered it a firm assurance but I knew Pant's game. When I met him at Lucknow, he very politely told me that who could be better campaigner for the Congress than he and I should meet him after the dates of nominations are over.

However, to cut a long story short while selection for the second General Election in 1957 was discussed, Azad expressed his desire not to contest from Rampur. The Parliamentary Board unanimously endorsed his proposal to set me up from Rampur in his place but Pant's request was accepted to delay the announcement.

In the meantime, Hafiz Ibrahim who had developed a great friendship with Lt. General Raza Ali Khan, the erstwhile ruler of Rampur started running from pillar to post for the support of Raja Ahmed Mehidid whose father had produced the notorious Pirpur Report which paved the way for partition of the country.

Maulana Abul Kalam Azad declined to meet Nawab informing him that he does not discuss Congress affairs with non-congressmen. But, Hafiz Ibrahim was adamant.

One fine morning I met Sampurananand, the Chief Minister of U.P. at Pant's residence. He asked me whether I was a Sunni Muslim or Shia. I was furious and obviously embarassed and told him that I joined Congress as a very early stage and never realised whether I was Hindu, Muslim or Sikh, I considered myself just an Indian. He pointed out that he appreciated my feelings but he would like to know to what sect my father belonged. I had to confess that he was practising Sunni.

Sampurananand frankly told me that I could not be put up from Rampur since my father belonged to Sunni sect and Nawab could not be persuaded to support me. This will demonstrate that as early as 1957, Congress had succumbed not only to communal but caste and sectarian considerations due to electoral compulsions. They did not care for principles; their only consideration was to retain power by fair means or foul.

However, Azad was determined that this time I was not ditched. I got the most valuable support from Lal Bahadur whom I will describe later.

Lal Bahadur was to contest from Fatehpur in U.P. But, at the last minute, he shifted to Allahabad for Purushottam Das Tandon declined to contest on reasons of health.

I had lost all hopes of my nomination. I left Delhi for Lucknow just a day before nomination day. On the day when nominations were to be filed, I called on Sampurnanand and to my utter surprise he asked me to proceed to Fatehpur to file my nomination. He lent me a car of U.P. Congress Committee. Had it failed for few minutes, I would not have reached Fatehpur in time to file my nomination. As luck would have it just half an hour before the closing time, I reached district court and filed nomination.

As a student activist and Congress worker, I had visited almost every district of U.P. but Fatehpur was too significant a district and I had visited it briefly for some time in the thirties. When I reached there not even the town or any part of the district had electricity. There were only two high schools in the district.

The local Congress leaders were hostile and they considered me an intruder. They carried on a campaign that I was not son of the soil and after I was elected the electorate would never see my face.

I was opposed by two of the top most members of the Bar. One of them was the nominee of the Socialist Party and the other was a candidate of Hindu chauvinist Party Jan Sangh.

I had neither men or financial power. However, I managed to secure the support of some young Congressmen. With them I toured the entire length and breadth of the constituency, introducing myself as a close associate of Subhas Bose. Some former I.N.A. soldiers were my main supporters. The local Congressmen saw my defeat as foregone conclusion. But, after the polling was over and counting took place, I defeated my rivals with a wide margin of votes.

I came back triumphant to be sworn in as member of Lok Sabha. My contribution to parliamentary debates and in various parliamentary committees earned me the respect of Congress as well as opposition benches.

Once again, I aspired to represent my constituency Fatehpur in 1962 which I had nursed to the best of my ability. But Dr. B.V.Keskwar who had been a Minister of Information and Broadcasting for ten years had become unpopular in his own constituency in Sultanpur felt that if an outsider like me could be elected from Fatehpur, he would have a cakewalk victory. He was one of the blue eyed boys. Nehru had looked after his publicity in Paris in pre-war days. The U.P. Congress leaders could not reject his request. He managed to the U.P. Congress Parliamentary Board to recommend his name and I was left high and dry. Though as a Member of Parliament I had rubbed S.K.Patil and Morarji on wrong side, yet both of them came to my support. I had crossed sword with Morarji Desai a number of times which I will describe later. But I cannot forget his words that such Congress should be burnt which might consider whether to give Harvani nomination or not.

However, my friend, Lal Bahadur came to my rescue once again and gave me a list of almost half a dozen seats which the Congress considered to be shaky. The beggar had no choice. I selected Bisauli in Budaun District in U.P. Here again I was faced with the hostility of the local Congress leadership. But, I neglected them and repeated the performance of Fatehpur and was elected with huge majority.

By 1967, when General Election was announced I had made a mark as successful parliamentarian. As long as Nehru was on the scene though I managed to be elected to some of the important parliamentary committees, he never sanctioned my nomination to any of parliamentary delegations to go abroad. It was Lal Bahadur Shastri who took me to Cairo to attend the Non-Aligned Conference. He again included me in a parliamentary delegation on the eve of Tashkent negotiations to go to Soviet Union.

When Indira Gandhi assumed office as Prime Minister of India, I remarked on the floor of the Lok Sabha that Nepolean III failed France but I am confident that Nehru III would not fail India. I often criticised her method of working

Apparently, Dr. Ram Manohar Lohia knew her better than me. He warned me that she would never trust and tolerate me. But till 1967, she was not strong enough to veto.

This was the first general election after Nehru's death. He acted as shock absorber between people and his Congress colleagues who were thoroughly discredited among the masses. Their corruption, maladministration and nepotism had created a wave of discontent throughout the country.

Most of the top leaders like Kamraj who were described by media as Black Stalin, S.K. Patil uncrowned King of Bombay, C.B. Gupta the Boss of U.P. Congress, Atulya Ghosh, Congress Treasurer and Financier were rejected by electorate.

I had to face a different and difficult situation. My M.L.A.s were thoroughly discredited and I had to carry the cross of five of my M.L.A. colleagues. Moreover, on the eve of election, a Federation of Muslim Communal and fundamentalist organisation was formed whose main aim was to humiliate Congress candidates. A few days earlier a procession of saffron clad Sadhus had marched. It had created communal tension in Delhi and the entire western U.P. The result was that the Congress lost all seats in capital except one with slender majority. The entire western U.P. was wiped out of Congress and I.N.A. hero Shahnawaz Khan, prominent Congress leaders like Mahavir Tyagi and Ajit Prasad Jain were defeated.

My defeat in Budaun in General Election of 1967 provided an opportunity to Indira Gandhi to seal the doors of Parliament to me. In subsequent Lok Sabha, Muslims who were of no consequence and behaved as deaf and dumb followers of her were preferred. None of them made any worthwhile parliamentary contribution.

While selecting candidates for Rajya Sabha, she preferred long bearded Mullas who were completely innocent of English and Hindi languages, spoken on the floor of the Parliament.

As I have described earlier, I joined the Congress at an early age but unlike many I did not desert it out of frustration. It was only when Indira Gandhi imposed Emergency with the support of her son Sanjay that I parted company with her Congress.

Chapter 16

DECLINE OF CONGRESS

I had joined Indian National Congress, as an ordinary volunteer. I could not be enrolled as a voter to elect various levels of Congress Committee till I became 18.

It was during my early Aligarh days that the realisation came to me that the Congress was not a unified party. It represented various anti-imperialist groups, the only common thing between them was the urge to get rid of foreign yoke.

The Aligarh district and town Congress committees like all over India were divided between 'rightists' and 'leftists', those who had unquestioned faith in Gandhi, regularly played *charka,* were described as 'rightists', and those who wanted to combine their struggle against imperialism with a fight with local landlords, who exploited the peasants, forced them to undertake labour without any payment, and made them to pay various illegal taxes were known as 'leftists'.

I allied myself with the leftist group, for I had no stomach for the tyranny of landlords, though I myself belonged to one of their family. However, it was much later that I read socialist and Marxist literatures and had developed somewhat mature ideas about anti-imperialist struggle of Indian people.

Till 1948, Congress was composed of all those elements who pledged support to Indian struggle for freedom. Congress constitution laid down that one could not be enrolled as its member unless one was a habitual wearer of *Khadi* and many of them adopted Gandhi cap, as their headgear but, to many of us, it was just a uniform of freedom fighters as described by Subhas Bose.

I have already mentioned following the Quit India Movement in 1942, the Congress was declared by the British authorities as an illegal body, and its offices were sealed. It was only in 1945 that the ban was lifted. The first task when All India Congress Committee met at Bombay in 1945 was rightly to expel the Communist members from the Congress for having opposed the call of Gandhi to 'Do or Die', in spite of their long explanation by P.C. Joshi, the General Secretary of the Communist Party of India.

However, it may be noted that even at that time, Congress leadership adopted double standards, for no notice was taken of the activities of C. Rajagopalachari, whom, long ago, Gandhi had described as his conscience keeper. Though he defied the Congress decision and his support was taken more seriously by the British authorities than that of Communists. Ultimately, he was included in Dominion Government, drafted to the Government House, Calcutta previously occupied by Hastings and Clive, as Governor, and was later to become the first Indian Governor-General of India.

In 1937, when under Government of India Act, 1935 Congress agreed to accept office, and having won absolute majority in seven provinces, the top Congress leaders were not tempted to accept office, in those provinces where they could form Government with the support of friendly parties.

They were happy to function as 'Congress High Command' monitoring and guiding the performance of the Congress ministers. However, Subhas Bose, when elected as Congress President, who did not enjoy the confidence of either Gandhi or Patel, managed to install the Congress Government in the eighth province of Assam, where Congress Party was not elected with absolute majority.

But, after the war, the situation changed. The lure of office was too great and all the top leaders of the Congress, Nehru, Patel, Rajendra Prasad and Azad were sworn in as Ministers of Dominion of India.

Gandhi tried to save the Congress from falling on evil days. When Congress leaders were about to enter the Interim Government in 1946, he expressed the view that the top-notch Congress leadership should keep out of the Government. Writes Pyarelal, "Gandhiji proposed that front-rank Congress leadership should lay upon itself a self-denying ordinance, keep out of the Government and entrust the running of the Government to second-line fighters, who would act under their experienced supervision and guidance. It would enable the Congress High Command to take a detached view of governmental activity and to supplement it by organising popular initiative on a basis of self-help so that the work of nation-building could proceed apace without much cost to the exchequer untrammelled by the vagaries of the corrupt, wasteful and slow-moving bureaucratic machine office would be shorn of much of its glamour; power would not carry extravagantly high emoluments, control would vest in those who had proved their sincerity by their self-sacrifices in the service of the people and renunciation, and the powers and functions of the State would shrink as the people developed initiative, voluntarily discipline and a non-violent organisation. Thus would true democracy come to birth".

But, members of the Congress High Command thought otherwise, and therefore they could not resist the lure of power. In November 1947 Gandhi made another attempt. On the eve of meeting of A.I.C.C., he suggested to the members of the 'High Command', that the political goal of the Congress having been achieved with the attainment of independence, the Congress should voluntarily liquidate itself. Says Pyarelal, "The proposal did not commend itself to the members of the Working Committee because without the Congress machinery to back, they cannot face the election".

Ever since Congress became a mass organisation in 1920, it had a regular constitution, though it was often amended to satisfy the whims of Gandhi. Almost every year, except when the Government declared it as an illegal organisation, the Congress sessions were held; its President was not chosen but duly elected by delegates.

It used to have elected bodies from town, city, and district level to the provincial and national levels. But, things changed after the top leaders of the Congress assumed offices in the Government. The climax came when on the proposal of Patel, the Congress constitution was amended banning the membership of any other party. They abolished dual membership.

The Congress Socialist headed by Jaya Prakash Narayan, and Acharya Narendra Dev after serving Congress for decades had to re-enter the legislature on their own label.

Among them the most outstanding personality was Acharya Narendra Dev who represented the district of Faizabad, where the birth place of Lord Rama is believed to be situated.

The Congress set up a sadhu against him, and Pant, in his appeal, pointed out that how the people of Ayodhya, the birth place of Ram and Laxman can vote for an atheist? The orthodox Hindus were organised against this great scholar and ardent socialist and an architect of secularism, and he was routed.

Earlier, the All India Congress Committee used to meet regularly and have debate and discussion on every issue.

Since Gandhiites were in majority, they used to have their way, but by and large, it functioned in a democratic manner.

Patel who controlled the Gandhiites was keen to have some semblance of the organisation. In 1950, he proposed the name of Purushottam Das Tandon for Congress Presidentship. Nehru was allergic to him and decided to oppose him. Nehru had never even contested nor conducted the Congress elections. He always occupied the Congress Chair with the blessings of his mentor Gandhi, much to the disappointment of Patel. Though he had Kidwai to campaign for him but he was no match to Patel.

Determined to teach a lesson to Nehru after the death of Gandhi, Patel used all the weapons in his armoury to see that Tandon was elected.

The election of Tandon alarmed Nehru. He refused to join his Working Committee. But, Patel soon died and Nehru decided to oust Tandon from Congress. In the absence of Patel, Tandon felt isolated and helpless and in sheer frustration, tendered his resignation. As in the past, in times of crisis in the Congress, it was Pant who had moved resolutions for the acceptance of resignations of unwanted Presidents, particularly, at the time of Subhas Bose's resignation, and Pant, on his entry into the Hall, was greeted with many as hangman, and "Welcome to our Mahabrahman".

On the eve of Tandon's election a suggestion was made that Nehru should accept Congress Presidentship. But in a statement Nehru had stated, "I definitely think that it is a wrong thing practically and even otherwise for the Prime Minister to be the Congress President" and "it would not be proper to combine the office (of Congress President) with that of Prime Minister". But he first had Tandon's resignation accepted and then had himself elected Congress President with the help of a huge majority which he had managed to secure by means of his influence and prestige as the head of the Government, in the absence of Patel.

In fact, the office of the Congress President was already downgraded, when Nehru and Patel carried on the negotiations with Mountbatten over the head of the duly elected Congress President, Kripalani who resigned to record his protest.

After Tandon's resignation in spite of his earlier decision Nehru kept on wearing double crown of Prime Minister and Congress President for almost five years.

However, in 1956, he picked up an unknown, politician who, for some time, had acted as Chief Minister of Saurashtra, an amalgamation of score of tiny principalities (Saurashtra later was to be merged with Gujarat) U.N. Dhebar.

His name came as a surprise to many of us. I had been associated with All India Congress Committee since 1939, and had religiously attended all its meetings except for one which was held in Bombay in 1945, when I was still lodged in jail. I had never even heard of or seen him. Apparently, belonging to a princely State, he knew that art of intrigues and sycophancy. When he formed his Working Committee, he included Indira Gandhi, flouting all the provisions of Congress constitution.

Indira Gandhi, unlike some other members of her family, like Vijaya Lakshmi Pandit, Ranjit Pandit and Uma Nehru, had never sought the election of either a primary, city, provincial or All India Congress Committee, I doubted if she was even a primary member of the Congress, her only qualification for this honour was that she happened to be the daughter of undisputed supremo of Congress, Jawaharlal Nehru.

In early 1959, when Dhebar laid down his office, he had persuaded the AICC to unanimously elect Indira Gandhi as Congress President.

The most outstanding contribution of Indira Gandhi as Congress President was that she allied with the Muslim League to overthrow the Communist Government in Kerala. It was for the first time that, in the history of communism, they had captured power through 'ballots' and not by 'bullets', in a small southern State, Kerala.

When All India Congress Committee met at Chandigarh, on September 27, 1952, I vehemently opposed this move. I reminded the member of A.I.C.C. that it was the Muslim League which was responsible for the death of millions of Hindus and Muslims and their unprecedented migration from one part of the country to the other.

The task of replying to me was entrusted to soft spoken Lal Bahadur Shastri, who, while appreciating my sentiments, pleaded 'special', circumstances.

Indira Gandhi was succeeded by N. Sanjiva Reddy. He had to resign his office as Chief Minister of Andhra after the Supreme Court of India had passed a stricture against him. Nehru, was anxious to provide him a job to keep him away from Andhra, and he was drafted to 7 Jantar Mantar Road, the Congress Headquarters as its President.

In due course, the mighty Indian National Congress founded by W.C. Banerji, Dadabhai Nauroji, nursed by Gandhi, C.R. Das, Motilal not to speak of young Nehru and Bose was reduced to the status of a non-official public relation Department of Congress Government.

In pre-independence days, the Congress offices, not only on national level but also on provincial level used to be centres of all political activities. The dedicated workers used to attend the offices to listen to the grievances of the people and used to take them up with authorities.

The All India Congress Committee had on its staff men like Dr. Ram Manohar Lohia, Dr. Z. Ahmed and Dr. B.V. Keskar.

But, in Nehru-era things completely changed. The Congress offices became active only on the eve of General Elections, when thousands of aspirants descended to plead for their nominations to Parliament and Assemblies and to cash the myth that the Congress was solely responsible for Freedom of India.

When the Constituent Assembly adopted the tri-colour flag, with Ashoka Chakra as national flag, a suggestion was made to change Congress flag. But, Nehru brushed aside this suggestion, and till today the tri-colour flag either with *charkha* or Hand continues to be the party flag, as if these who are no more in Congress did nothing to liberate this country. It aims to confine the masses of this country, who fought and died to uphold it.

The Congress Parliamentary Board in Centre as well as in States continue to be dominated by the ministers, who are more anxious to justify their performance than to be critical of them.

In due course, it had ceased to be a cadre-based party and was to be dominated by careerists, opportunists and corrupt politicians and sycophants of the ministers. It was left to Nehru's grandson, who as Prime Minister and Congress President lamented at its Century celebrations that it was dominated by power brokers.

The myth that the Congress was the liberator continued till 1967, when it lost power in most of the States and was finally exploded when it lost power in 1977 in New Delhi.

Chapter 17

BENEFICIARIES

WHO has been the greatest beneficiary of transfer of power and subsequently after Independence of India, is a question that has often been asked. My reply is that those who, in prime of their youth, sold their soul, for a handful of silver coins to serve the cause of British imperialism.

In the initial days of the Raj, the doors of superior services either in civil or military were closed to educated Indians. They were used as policemen to ensure the safety of British rule.

But, later, some Indians were allowed to enter Indian Civil Services, on the basis of their family connection, declaring that their families had rendered meritorious services in the mutiny of 1857.

In late twenties, the British Government agreed to admit a few young men every year in military academy of Sandhurst and to be trained to be able to attain for them His Majesty's Commission.

But, till 1946, no Indian Civil Service officers rose to be a Secretary in Government of India with the exception of Sir Girija Shankar Bajpai, even at the end of war, there were only two Sandhurst trained officers who could be selected to rise in army to the rank of Brigadiers.

But, they got a bumper opportunity after the British officers' refusal to work under the 'natives', and their decision to repatriate home with suitable and very generous compensations. However, few white men decided to serve in Jinnah's Pakistan.

In provinces like U.P., an I.C.S. officer of Indian origin though having received higher marks in competitive examination than his white contemporaries could never dream to be the District Magistrate of one of the important districts like Lucknow, Allahabad, Banaras or Kanpur.

They were posted to some small and insignificant districts. The same pattern was followed in the other provinces also.

After 1947, with the exit of British officers and exodus of Muslim officers to their promised land Pakistan, Indian Civil and Army officers had the field day. Over night they were promoted to be Secretaries in Central and Provincial Governments. The doors of the highest offices, so far, closed to them, were suddenly wide opened.

The junior police officers were promoted as high officers. In army, there was an unprecedented spree of promotions. However, some Muslim I.C.S. officers who, in their patriotism, refused to migrate to Pakistan could not be benefited by this windfall.

In U.P., at least three very senior I.C.S. officers namely, Hifazat Hussain, Siddiq Hassan and Husain Zaheer did not desert the land of their birth. Though much junior officers than them were inducted in Provincial and Central Secretariat, they had to cool their heels, district and divisional officers, for the Home Ministry would not trust any Muslim officer. However, after the death of Patel, this situation changed.

Sardar Patel, the Home Minister had deep distrust of every Muslim and is reported to have remarked that he knows only one nationalist Muslim and that was Jawaharlal Nehru. This attitude, was manifested in the case of promotion. To be fair to Nehru, he disagreed with his Deputy Prime Minister, but, never in his life, he had risked his position in the Congress hierarchy, to uphold his views and principles.

While transferring power to India, the departing British had seen that Nehru Government agreed to all contracts made by them were fully honoured. Therefore, even those officers who had mercilessly beaten Congressmen, joined in shooting them and burning the houses of freedom fighters were fully honoured and often rewarded.

After Gandhi's assassination, there were left two elder statesmen contemporary of his father for whom Nehru had great respect, namely, veteran Hindu leader, Pandit Madan Mohan Malviya and Sir Tej Bahadur Sapru, a moderate nationalist. He visited both of them for their blessings after he assumed the great office of Prime Minister of India. I was told by one of his aides who accompanied him that Malviya was in coma and with great difficulty, he was informed that Nehru had come to see him. For just a moment, he was revived of his consciousness and touching his hand, uttered only two words *"Apne Desh Main Apna Raj"*, and again went in coma.

Sapru was also paralytic and was lying in his bed and is reported to have told Nehru, that the Congressmen have been mere agitators, they had no administrative experience and advised him to rely on Sir Girija Shankar Bajpai, and a number of former Dewans of princely states like Sir Gopalaswami Iyengar, Sir V.T. Krishnamachari and others. Obviously, Nehru was pleased with this advice and as future events would show, he very much depended on their 'mature' opinions.

In 1945, just after the conclusion of war, United Nations met at San Francisco to give it an organisational shape. India being a member of the United Nations, under the decision of Viceroy of India sent its own delegation, which was headed by Sir Feroze Khan Noon, the Defence Member of Viceroy's Executive Council. Some patriotic Indians headed by Dr Syed Hussain were already busy counteracting the campaign launched by Sir Girija Shankar Bajpai, as agent of Government of India against India's aspiration to be free. On their invitation, Mrs. Vijaya Lakshmi Pandit reached San Francisco and supported and financed by Sikh migrants in California purchased time on American Broadcasting System and, in the lobby of U.N., met other members to explain the exploitation and suffering of India, under the British rule.

When Nehru became Vice-President of Viceroy's Executive Council and was permitted to handle India's external affairs, His Majesty's Government agreed that he can select his team for the forthcoming U.N. Session to be held at Lake Success. Though the delegation was led by his sister, Vijaya Lakshmi Pandit, the names of other delegates came as a shock to us.

With the exception of Mrs. Pandit, the others were those who had actively worked against freedom movement of India. The prominent members were Sir Maharaj Singh, former Dewan of Bikaner, Sir V.T. Krishnamachari, who had served a Minister of autocratic Indian princes, Sardar Panicker, who just missed his knighthood but was known as loyal servant of Maharaja of Patiala, and a liaison man between princes and British political department, and His Highness Jam Saheb a member of British War Cabinet.

There was no dearth of patriotic Indians, but probably Nehru was afraid that they will not be very welcome to British delegation, which was to act as big brother at this Conference.

The claim of Dr Ram Manohar Lohia who was still the incharge of Foreign Affairs Department of A.I.C.C. was brushed aside. Even Dr. Syed Hussain, who, for two difficult decades, had carried the Congress flag in U.S.A. was not considered. I think this was the beginning of the break of cordial and affectionate relation between Lohia and Nehru. From this incidence their relations became strained. Dr Lohia was always considered a blue eyed boy of Nehru.

There were a number of former prominent British stooges who had not only abstained from supporting India's efforts to be free but had effectively and vehemently opposed it. Sir Girija Shankar Bajpai was the most outstanding of them. He belonged to Indian Civil Service. It was usual for its members to serve in the district and provinces for almost twenty years before being given an assignment in Central Government.

But, his ability, as well as loyalty, to the Crown was so outstanding that within a few years he was called to New Delhi to serve the Central Government. In the beginning, he was kept in non-sensitive departments like Health and Education, for Home, Defence and Political Departments were out of bounds for Indian Personnel, however, efficient they might be

When Americans entered War, there was a tremendous sympathy for India's aspiration among American people and American Press. It was difficult for the heirs of Lincoln and Jafferson and devotees of Statue of Liberty to appreciate the logic of millions of Indians being ruled by an islander who had nothing in common with them.

President Franklin Roosevelt was making frantic efforts to persuade Winston Churchill to seek the willing cooperation of Indian people and their leaders.

Winston Churchill could not think a better man than Bajpai to convince the Americans that Indians were unfit to rule themselves. Sir Girija Shankar Bajpai, arrived in Washington as Indian agent. The British Embassy organised his tour from coast to coast to convince Americans that the time was not yet ripe to free India from its bondage.

On his return to India, he had to face a hostile press and more hostile public opinion. I was present at the meeting of U.P. Provincial Congress Committee, when Nehru, in a long speech, described his abilities and assured us that he will serve his present masters with the same devotion as he did his previous masters. Most of us were not convinced, but obviously, were helpless.

Nehru inducted him in external affairs department as Officer on Special Duty and later on created a new post of Secretary General to External Affairs Ministry and entrusted him with the task to organise and to recruit the personnel for Indians diplomatic services.

I had watched the students of Lucknow being beaten by a Deputy Superintendent of Police Rai Bahadur Jamna Prasad

Tripathy. His victims had threatened him that they would settle accounts with him when India attained Independence. On one of my visits to Prime Minister's House, I faced him to find that he was selected as the Chief Security Officer of Nehru.

In U.P., there was one Indian police officer named Rai Bahadur Tika Ram. From subordinate position, he was promoted to be Deputy Superintendent of Police, for he had specialised in torturing revolutionaries after their arrest and forcing them to make confessions. In New Delhi, I found him as Deputy Director General of newly created Department of C.B.I. There are only a few examples of the immediate beneficiaries of India's Independence.

The erstwhile Muslim Leaguers whose role I have already described at length were also not forgotten. Many of them like Jinnah and Nawabzada Liaquat Ali Khan who most of their lives had lived in the Indian part of sub-continent migrated to Pakistan as conquerors to hold high offices. The others were lured by the prospect of acquiring valuable properties left by unfortunate Hindus and Sikhs, who were forced to leave the land of their birth at the point of gun, dagger and sword.

However, some of them remained in India for fear of losing their properties. But, the new Government was impressed by their sycophancy, which they had learnt at the court of British Governors and Deputy Commissioners. Overnight they were to be seen with Gandhi caps and well tailored Khadi *sherwanis*.

When Choudhari Khaliquz-Zaman who was initially reluctant to go to Pakistan, and even delivered a speech at the Constituent Assembly, pledging his support to Nehru, and his governments, on hearing that the well known Biscuit Factory of Manga Ram has been allotted to his younger brother, left India, under the pretext of going on a goodwill mission, never to come back and his seat from U.P. fell vacant.

Every Congressman, in U.P. speculated that as a devoted Congressman I will replace him. But, Pandit Pant had different ideas. There was one Choudhari Hyder Hussain, a lawyer by profession, and former League MLA, who had made it his routine to visit him every evening and touch his feet. He was selected in spite of the opposition of Purshottam Das Tandon. The dissatisfied Congressmen were told that Pant had obtained clearance from Nehru, and who dared to challenge it.

During the War the Britishers had set up an organisation known as 'National War Front'. Its main task was to carry on counter propaganda against national aspirations. It financed a number of newspapers to give news describing Gandhi and of course Bose as fifth columnists and traitors to the country of their birth.

The President of this organisation was Sir C.P.N. Singh a great favourite of Bihar Governor, Rutherford. It was expected that when India achieves Independence, he would be an outcaste.

But under Nehru he was ambassador to Nepal and Governor of Punjab. Even Nehru's daughter was so much impressed by his sycophancy that in his old age he was allowed to occupy the spacious government houses of Nainital and Lucknow as Governor of U.P.

The Secretary of this organisation was Rashid Ali Baig, who came from one of the aristocratic Muslim family of Bombay and married a charming young lady Tara, who deeply impressed Nehru. He was readily selected to Indian Foreign Service.

Frank Moraes, former editor of *Times of India* and a close friend of Baig writes in his memoirs.

> "Rashid was as close to Jinnah as a man twentyfive years his junior could be. He satisfied the older man's stipulations; he was educated, mentally alert, politically conscious and resourceful; and until he broke away on the issue of Pakistan in March 1948, was one of Jinnah's most trusted younger Lieutenants.
>
> "Over this period, I was in close touch with Rashid, and in my professional capacity, particularly, as a representative of the *London News Chronicle,* saw Jinnah fairly often, since in the late 1930s, he was understandably eager to have his public image projected abroad. I helped him in a small way, and must acknowledge that even later when he no longer needed me as a prop he remained accessible and friendly.
>
> "Apart from interview to foreign newspaper which he gave directly, Jinnah was sometimes invited to contribute articles to British and American journals. These were ghosted by Rashid, who sometimes showed me his draft which we went through with a fine comb. One of these was an article for Time and Tide written around October, 1939."

In 1952, first general elections were held, when India was declared a Republic within Commonwealth. Many of the former Muslim League members of Legislative Assemblies who, by force of their personal circumstances, had not migrated to Pakistan, were made Congress nominees, and Nehru campaigned for their election. The claim of Nationalists

Muslims, was brushed aside for it was felt that it could not influence the Muslim vote bank.

Later, Congress had to select its nominee for Council of State to be known as Rajya Sabha. The worst sufferers were the nationalist Muslims in U.P. and Bihar, the areas where Muslim leaders were most vocal in demand of the partition of the country.

From U.P., Congress selected Nawab Sir Ahmed Said Khan of Chhatari who, as Home Member of U.P. has sent senior as well as junior Nehru to jail in 1930 and 1932. Col. B.H. Zaidi a former Dewan of Rampur State and Choudhari Akhtar Husain one of the most vocal Muslim Leaguers, Begum Aizaj Rasul president of Women Wing of Jinnah League.

In this connection, I may mention that my sister Dr Hamda Salim was a lecturer in a Muslim College of Lucknow, of which Choudhari Akhtar Husain was a managing trustee. She was flatly told by him to resign because one of his brothers was Congressman and the other a revolutionary poet Majaz.

Within a few months, of assumption of office, the votaries of non-violence and austerity living had acquired the taste of sycophancy and who else could be better sycophant than the erstwhile Muslim Leaguers who had earned titles and positions from their British masters?

Much has been made about Patel's achievement to integrate princely States in India, by contemporary Short chroniclers'. But, my assessment though may appear unorthodox is completely different. The princely states were allowed to survive by the British as a model of maladministration and corruption and tyranny to convince the people living in British India, that they were really fortunate to have foreigners to bless their destiny.

Most of the Indian princes were drunkards; debauch and tyrant. They spent the hard earned money of their subjects on their whims and fancies. They discouraged education, and most of the princely States did not have even schools not to speak of colleges or universities.

They were rulers in name, the real authority was in the hands of British residents and political agents. Some of them had armies, whose officers, were either pimps or relations of concubines of the ruling princes. These armies were meant only for ceremonial purposes.

With the exit of British armed forces from India, they were completely helpless and unprotected. If Patel assisted by an officer Sir V.P. Menon, belonging to British Political Department would not have come to their rescue, they would have gone like Czar of Russia or Sultan of Ottoman Empire.

Patel provided them with fat privy purses to continue their life of luxury and leisure at the cost of Indian tax payers. They were given wide privileges to import luxurious goods like liquor, cigarettes, expensive cars even private aeroplanes without paying any custom duty. They freely sent their costly jewels to Tifny and other jewellers in Europe and America to be converted into cash and to be deposited in foreign banks.

At least three of them did not feel satisfied with the generosity of Patel and Government of free India. In Junagadh, the people rose under the leadership of Samal Das Gandhi, a nephew of Mahatma, and Nawab was driven away with his concubines and dogs to neighbouring Pakistan. His Exalted Highness Mr. Usman Ali Khan ruled over Hyderabad. It was a State bigger in size and the population than Germany and France. He had his own railway, currency and broadcasting station, besides a big army and a Jordanian mercenary General Eledroos as Commander-in-Chief.

For months and months, Government of India continued a stand-still agreement with him. When his Razakars started announcing, on Hyderabad Radio that the day was not far off when the Asfi Flag (Flag of Nizam) would be hoisted on Red Fort of Delhi even Patel lost his patience and sent his army to be described as police action and within a few hours, Nizam signed the Instrument of Accession receiving full generosity of Govt. of India, in the form of usual privy purses and privileges, and was appointed as Raj Pramukh.

The story of Kashmir is too well known to be recorded by me. But, credit of Kashmir integration goes to Jinnah and not to Patel. Had Jinnah, in his arrogance, not sent tribals supported by Pakistan army, who were more interested in raping Kashmiri women and looting their houses, the story might have been quite different.

Even after the princes acceded to India, they retained ceremonial offices of Raj Pramukh, equal to Governor. It was much later after the death of Patel that as a result of the recommendation of States Reorganisation Commission, this office was abolished.

But, Nehru found many of them suited to Diplomatic assignments. Maharaja of Jaipur was sent to Spain as India's Ambassador to play Polo, Maharaja of Patiala and Jam Saheb of Nawanagar represented India at U.N.O. Later, Maharaja of Patiala was Ambassador in Rome and at The Hague.

While the erstwhile British stooges, former Muslim Leaguers were benefited by the Independence of India, those thousands who had risked their lives to achieve it with the exception of few hundreds who managed to be selected by Congress as legislators and Ministers, faced starvation and humiliation. After twenty-five years of Independence it was left to Indira Gandhi, on the eve of declaration of State of Emergency to sanction them a pension, which is less than the pension received by the lowest of the Government employees.

Chapter 18

NEW MAHARAJAS

I watched with disappointment, and dismay the social transformation of those who had assumed power after the white man had shed his burden. Though they continued to profess to be followers of Gandhi, who lived mostly in huts and harijan colonies but, ultimately, died in the mansion of the biggest industrial house of Birlas. They still continued to profess simple living and high thinking. As a young boy, I had met Pandit Pant in his modest house at Cart Road, Nainital, a ghetto of poor hill men. In Lucknow, he occupied a huge colonial bungalow surrounded by an army of liveried foot men, with feudal splendour.

He would hold his darbar in the evening in his well furnished drawing room, where the senior civil servants, erstwhile British stooges and Muslim Leaguas would come to touch his feet or to prostrate before him.

His senior colleagues' performance was in no way better. Rafi Ahmed Kidwai, whose father was a tehsildar and came from a lower middle class family assumed the life style of a Nawab. He felt flattered when the Oudh taluqdars, who described themselves as Barons performed their sycophancy which they had learnt in the court of British officials and governors, I had seen him earlier dressed in unbleached coarse khadi, but now he appeared in the best tailored raw khadi silk or pashmina sherwani, dangling the most expensive Turkish or Egyptian cigarette, between his lips.

Sampurnanand, former school teacher who started his career as a socialist took pride that he served sixty- five dishes of vegetarian and sweet dishes to his guests on Hindu festival. His hobby was astronomy, and, for this purpose, he installed a very expensive German telescope on a hill side of Nainital to gaze at stars.

Hafiz Mohammed Ibrahim who was a petty lawyer in a tehsil town in Bijanore could not be left behind. He started to hold his darbars mostly of those Muslim Leaguers, who had not migrated to their promised land Pakistan, to save their properties from being taken over as evacuee property and non-discript, poets, while smoking a silver mouth hookka.

When I visited Delhi, I found the situation still worse, Nehru whom I had always seen in Dhoti Kurta, and often a jacket which came to be known by his name had complete sartorial change.

He started appearing in sherwani tailored by a well-known outfitter Mohmmed Umar, who was patronised by a number of ruling princes and in chust pyjama, but of course unlike present Congressmen he did not discard khadi and Gandhi cap.

Probably, inspired by Mughal Miniatures in which emperors carried a rose in their hand, he regularly displayed it in his button hole.

As Vice-President of Viceroy's Executive Council he stayed at York Road, but moved to the residence vacated by British Commander-in-Chief now known as Tin Murti House, Gandhi had suggested that the Viceregal lodge to be converted into a hospital. But, Nehru in his heart of hearts did not relish the proposal. He had dropped this proposal because, as he informed Gandhi, of "difficulty in finding suitable accommodation and making arrangements for changing over, when we are so busy." While making this excuse he seems to have forgotten that at a time when millions of refugees were changing over from one part of the sub-continent to the other, it would sound odd that he could not shift Mountabatten from one place to another. The real reason was that Nehru himself was thinking of shifting to some grand mansion, and after the demise of the Mahatma he did leave 17 York Road, and moved into what is now known as Tin Murti House, former residence of the British Commander-in-Chief of the Indian Army. Writes Taya Zinkin, a well known foreign journalist, "He harped constantly on the need to live simple, and chose for himself the most luxurious of all the residences the British built in Delhi, the residence of the Commander-in-Chief which, with its spacious grounds and comfortable rooms, was far more habitable than the gigantic viceregal mausoleum." But, in describing to keep the Governor-General in the Viceregal Lodge, Nehru had perhaps some thing more to the back of his mind. Writes Amiya and B.G. Roy, "It was unfortunate that when Nehru moved into Tin Murti House, he should have arranged that his kitchen, pantry and cellar should be treated as a part of the establishment first of the Governor-General and thereafter, of the President. He paid for whatever he and his own family members ate and drank, but at rates so low as to invite sharp criticism in Parliament. An important member explained the point of the critics: "I would not have grudged him his expenditure but for its pervasive effect on India's morality and economy. Everybody imitates him in his own small way. That is why his exhortations for avoidance of waste and corruption fall on deaf ears, when a man is himself the centre for such enormous pomp and luxury."

I had often visited Rajendra Prasad in Sadaquat Ashram at Patna, and found him sitting on a coarse hand woven blanket, with only one pillow to support him playing charkha and talking to his peasant colleagues and friends, but here I found him well shaved, very well dressed like Nehru in chust pyjama and sherwani surrounded by smartly dressed A.D.Cs belonging to army, navy and air force.

The House which he occupied was viceregal lodge was to be known as Rashtrapati Bhavan. Everything in the life of the president is on the same scale and panoply, as it was in the days of Curzon and Willingdon — Rashtrapati Bhawan was built when New Delhi replaced Old Delhi as the seat of Viceroy. It was formerly known as the Viceregal Lodge but was renamed Rashtrapati Bhawan in 1950 to Indianise the British name. It was designed by Sir Edwin Lutyens, in red and white sand stone and was occupied first by Lord Irwin in 1929. It was 630 feet wide and 530 feet deep, from east to west, and has an area of 210, 430 square feet. The place at Versailles is only 198, 300 square feet. The building stands in 330 rooms, 227 columns, 35 loggias and 1.5 miles of corridors, and the gardens (called the Moghul Gardens) cover 12 acres. There are a swimming pool, a cinema, a golf course, hockey, football and cricket grounds, tennis courts, a zoo and school. No wonder this is known as the President's Estate.

In addition, the President had for his use Rashtrapati Niwas at Simla (7050 ft) with 83 rooms and the Retreat at *Moshobra* (10626 ft) with 26 rooms and the Rastrapati Bolaram at Hyderabad with 19 rooms and the President has one Rolls Royce, 3 Mercedes Benz, 3 Cadillacs, 4 Chevrolets, one Vauxhall and a large number of small cars, jeeps, vans and ambulances. He has 2 state coaches, 2 victoria and 3 luggage brakes In addition, two battalions as body-guards, there are no less then 271 police officers of all ranks. There is a very well stocked library, a vast telephone exchange, billiard room and numerous other amenities. As super deluxe hotel with a staff of about 2500 persons for those who are lucky enough to occupy it.

Nehru could not avoid the company of Patel and Azad. But, in social life, he felt more at home with Sir Gopalaswami Iyengar, Sir Girija Shankar Bajpai, Sir Raghavan Pillai, Sardar Panicker, Sir V.T. Krishnamachari and a host of socialite ladies who pretended to be social workers.

This luxurious way of living was bound to affect thinking of India's new rulers. Pandit Jawaharlal Nehru who was now at the helm of affairs could have given a new direction. But, having lived for more than a quarter century in the midst of uncouth, unsophisticated Congress workers with rural and peasant background, he found himself back in the Anglicised way of life in which he was born, and brought up and educated. It was a relief for him from his previous drudgery being attended by those who had found favour with British aristocracy and being courted by those who constituted the cream of society in colonial days.

It was unfortunate that he could not resist the temptation of nepotism. Almost all available Nehrus, in particular and Kashmiri pandits in general, in Indian Civil Services suddenly were found to have a flair for diplomacy and with the recommendation of his new found adviser of Foreign Affairs in External Affairs, Sir Girija Shankar Bajpai were absorbed in diplomatic services. In return, Bajpai claimed that all of his three sons were born diplomats and recruited them in newly created Indian foreign services.

His close associate Rafi Ahmed Kidwai, was not to be left behind. He had no son, but he had three favourites cousins two of whom belonged to provincial civil service, the other was a Munsif in U.P. Judiciary, the third a junior and struggling journalist. All of them overnight became diplomats and at least two of them were sent as Indian Ambassadors to Saudi Arabia and Malaysia.

This style of living was bound to breed corruption and nepotism. As mentioned earlier, those poor nationalist Muslims who were persecuted by the Muslim Leaguers and jailed by the British were consigned to dust bin.

The Congress workers, who had really suffered and sacrificed were left to fend for themselves.

Chapter 19

"WE THE PEOPLE..."

WHILE the Cabinet Mission Plan was rejected by the Congress as well as the League, its proposal to grant a Constituent Assembly was readily accepted, without realising that what was going to be its representative character.

After the failure of the All Party Conference, where the Nehru Committee Report could not be accepted, the Congress at its Lahore session presided over by Jawaharlal Nehru, opted for a complete independence as its goal, giving up earlier demand of Dominion Status.

The failure of Satyagraha movement launched by the Congress in 1930, led to so-called Gandhi-Irwin Pact (1931), Congress agreed to attend the Second Round Table Conference at London in the hope to wrest at least some sort of Dominion Status.

Gandhi was the sole representative of the Congress, and was faced with Pandit Madan Mohan Malviya and his Hindu Maha Sabha on one side and the break-away section of Muslim League which had disowned Jinnah who had boycotted Simon Commission on the other. He miserably failed to arrive at a settlement of communal problem.

However, the British Prime Minister, Ramsay Macdonald agreed to give his award. He continued the right of separate electorates, to Muslims and also proposed separate electorate to depressed classes otherwise known as untouchables and to Sikhs in Punjab. The Congress was placed in a tight corner. It neither accepted nor rejected the communal award.

However, Gandhi could not reconcile himself to the grant of right of separate electorates to depressed classes. While staying in the marble palace of a socialite lady Thakersay at Poona he went on fast unto death. The British journalists described his fast at the marble palace like Jesus Christ going for crucifixion on a Rolls Royce. Dr Ambedkar got cold feet and agreed to have reservation of seats for depressed classes instead of separate electorates, and a pact was signed by him and Dr Ambedkar to be described as Poona Pact.

The communal award with this amendment was incorporated in Government of India Act, 1935. The Cabinet Mission envisaged a Constituent Assembly to be selected by the British Indian Provinces, by the Members of Assemblies elected on the basis of separate electorate.

The idea of Constituent Assembly for India was mooted by Subhas Bose, who urged the Congress to launch a struggle and to form parallel Government on all levels and to convene a Constituent Assembly to frame a Constitution for Free India. This caught the imagination of Congressmen. Apparently, they were inspired by the Constitution makers in America, who after the victory and conclusion of war of Independence had met in Philadelphia, and, under the guidance of Washington, Jafferson and Benjamin Franklin had adopted the Constitution with the words "We the People..."

In 1946 General Elections, in provinces like U.P., Bihar, Bengal, Madras and Bombay most of the seats reserved for the Muslims to be elected only by Muslim electorate were captured by the Muslim League. The result was that all the seats meant for Muslims were captured by the League leaving mere seven seats for Unionists, Independents and a solitary Congressman from U.P. The other Congress Muslims were Azad and Khan Abdul Ghaffar Khan from N.W.F.P.

Though the League participated in the election of Constituent Assembly, it boycotted its sitting when it was convened on December 9.

There has never been any prospect of success for the Constituent Assembly except on the basis of an agreed procedure. Should a Constitution come to be framed by a Constituent Assembly in which a large section of the Indian population had not been represented. His Majesty's Government could not of course contemplate forcing such a Constitution upon any unwilling parts of the country.

The Constituent Assembly met on December 9. The absence of the Muslim League representative was widely regretted, but there were no serious demonstrations anywhere against the meeting of the Assembly, in spite of the Muslim League's demand for its postponement. Sachhidanand Sinha, as the oldest member from the Chair until the Assembly elected a President. Later, Rajendra Prasad was unanimously elected as President. The most important and politically significant resolution, known as the 'Objective Resolution', was moved by Nehru. It envisaged the Indian Union as 'an independent Sovereign Republic' comprising autonomous units with residuary powers, wherein the ideals of social, political and economic democracy would be guaranteed to all sections of the people and adequate safeguards would be provided for minorities and backward communities and areas. Nehru described the resolution as "a declaration, a pledge and an undertaking before the world, a contract with millions of Indians and therefore in the nature of an oath which we mean to keep" His repeated statement that the House must rise above group or party politics was interpreted as a hint that, though the Assembly could not surrender on any fundamental matters, any reasonable grievance of the Muslim League would be satisfied. M. R. Jayakar moved an amendment suggesting that the discussion be postponed to a later date so as to enable representatives not only of the League, but of the Indian States, to participate in the Constituent Assembly. His suggestion, which was backed outside the House by Sir Sultan Ahmed (Constitutional Advisor to the Chamber of Princes) and the Dewans of Hyderabad, Travancore, Mysore and Bikaner, was ultimately accepted, in the hope, expressed by the President, that members of the League might attend by the time the resolution next came before the House. The Assembly was adjourned till January 20.

India was already divided into British India, and Princely India. While the People living in British India enjoyed some rights under Government of India Act, 1935, passed by British Parliament, the State people were still living under the autocratic and despotic rule of Indian princes.

The Constituent Assembly which, met in December only represented the elected members of British Indian Provincial Assemblies. The princes were still undecided about their future course of action. The Chamber of Princes had appointed a negotiation committee to ensure their continuance of their autocratic and despotic rule under new Indian Constitution.

Sardar K.M. Panicker was a very shrewd person. He started his life as a Congressman, later on became the first editor of the *Hindustan Times* when it was launched by the Akalis, and sold himself to Maharaja of Patiala to earn the title of Sardar.

Though he served Maharaja of Patiala as his political advisor, he essentially acted as a tout between the Political Department of Government of India, and the Indian princes, who were rulers in name, but really were ruled by the corrupt officials of the department.

On the eve of the negotiations of transfer of power, he was Dewan of Bikaner State. He was the first to read the writing on the walls and persuaded his Royal Master the Maharaja of Bikaner, to declare his willingness to join the Constituent Assembly.

The action of Maharaja Sardul Singh of Bikaner completely demoralised the other native princes. They were already in panic on the prospect of the British withdrawal and support, and felt the discretion to be better part of valour and many of them agreed to participate in Constituent Assembly.

It may be noted, that princely states like British India, had not even the nominal representative institutions to elect as members of the Constituent Assembly. Most of the princes nominated either themselves or some of their stooges to represent their States. Gandhi and Congress had always discouraged the State people's movements. However, Nehru and some other often gave their verbal and moral support to the aspirations of State people. Some of the Dewans of Princely States, who were later to play important role in Indian politics, persuaded their rulers to nominate some of the state people agitators to give it a representative character.

After June 3, the situation in India changed completely. It envisaged two Constituent Assemblies for the Dominions of India and Pakistan. Jinnah advised those Muslim members, who were elected from the areas which were to continue in Indian Dominion to join the Constituent Assembly to safeguard the interests of Muslim minority.

But most of the Muslim League members of Constituent Assembly from areas falling under dominion of India had different ideas. Some of them preferred to migrate to Pakistan to acquire valuable properties and business left by non-Muslim refugees. Some of them who could not leave India, just to save their own properties, like Nawab Tajnul Hussain of Bihar and Begum Aizaj Rasul of U.P. became sycophants of the new Congress rulers.

The Constituent Assembly was formed on the basis of state papers. It had yet to get final legal sanction from the British Government. It was only on July 4, when Clement Attlee the Prime Minister of Britain moved the Independence of India Bill in the House of Commons. It was passed by the House of Commons on July 15, and House of Lords the following day.

It became an Act of British Parliament, when it was assented by our Royal Master, in the following words "Be it enacted by King's most Excellent Majesty, by and with the advice by Lords of spiritual, and temporal and commons in the Parliament by the authority of the same."

The Constituent Assembly of India thus received legitimacy by Independence of India Act, 1947 passed by the British Parliament and assented to by the Majesty King George VI. The most relevant and current criticism of the proposal of Constituent Assembly was made by no other than Winston Churchill, who a number of times had refused to give any concession to Gandhi or the Congress.

He condemned the Constituent Assembly as having been elected on an inadequate and unrepresentative franchise. "The Government formed by the party leaders, meant that India would be delivered to politicians, who have no claim to represent the mass of the people. In handing over Government of India to so-called politicians, we are handing over to men of straw, whose in few years no trace will remain."

While representation to some of the freedom fighters in Constituent Assembly could not be avoided as the liberation of India was still a recent event. Nehru and Patel brought as many former British stooges as possible. There were galaxy of British Knights like Sir Gopalaswami Iyengar, Sir Alladi Krishnaswami Iyer, Sir J.P. Srivastava, Sir Ramaswamy Mudaliar and Dr Sir Radha Krishnan to name a few to frame Indian Constitution.

The Drafting Committee was headed by the eminent jurist Dr B.R. Ambedkar, but it did not include any grassroots political worker. Among its members were Sir N. Gopalaswamy Iyengar, V.T. Krishnamachari, Sir Madhav Rao to give it a political colour, K.M. Munshi was also included though he had avoided going to jail in 1942.

I feel that the Constituent Assembly which framed the Constitution to be promulgated on January 26, 1950, was the handiwork of British imperialist and the Indian Constitution was passed by an Assembly which was least representative of Indian people.

In fact, while adopting national flag, one of the members had the audacity to suggest that on its corner should be Union Jack, as India was a Dominion within British Commonwealth of Nations.

However, when it was transferred into provisional Parliament, the members were made to take the following oath:

> "I etc. do swear true faith and allegiance to the Constitution of India, and I will be faithful to His Majesty, his heirs and successors, according to law".

Chapter 20

INDIA GOES TO POLL

1951: India was having her first General Election. The Constitution declared India a Federal Republic and was formally adopted by the Constituent Assembly on January 26, 1950. Attempts had been made by legal and constitutional pandits then crowding the Constituent Assembly to provide for all kinds of eventualities. Every adult citizen was entitled to a vote. One hundred and seventy million men and women were enfranchised to vote in the first general elections. To make it convenient and intelligible for the illiterates to exercise their vote, the Election Commissioner had asked different parties to select their separate symbols. These symbols were printed against the name of every candidate. The voter had merely to put a cross against the symbol of his or her preference. The symbol of one party was an earthen lamp, of another the bicycle, of a third a hut, of a fourth the umbrella and so on.

No fewer than a dozen symbols had been adopted for as many parties, big and small. A pair of bullocks yoked to a plough represented the Congress. The Congress cleverly had adopted tri-colour Flag as its party flag. The only difference between the National Flag and the Congress flag was that while the former had Ashoka Chakra the latter had Charkha in the centre.

A development on the eve of the election is worthy of. mention. Rafi Ahmed Kidwai, who owed unquestioned loyalty to the Nehru and his family had resigned from Central Cabinet. He rallied round him all those who were dissatisfied with Patel to form Kisan Praja Party. Among national leaders to join this party were Acharya J.B. Kripalani who had earlier resigned from the Congress Presidentship and T. Prakasam who was ousted from the Chief Ministership of Madras.

They openly declared that they had formed the party to strengthen the hands of Nehru. But the death of Patel completely changed the situation.

Earlier Nehru was the darling of the nation but Patel controlled the Congress Party. But, now Nehru became Congress supremo. After ousting Tandon from Congress Presidentship, he adorned the double crown of the Prime Minister of India and the President of the Indian National Congress.

Kidwai made a hasty retreat and was re-admitted in the Congress by Nehru. He was commissioned to oust Patel loyalists. But most of Patel supporters had tasted power, and they could not live without it. Almost everyone of them overnight became Nehru loyalist and the only casualty was D.P. Misra, the Home Minister of Central Provinces.

Having seen the glamour of power of the Ministers and legislators thousands of aspirants for Congress ticket arrived in New Delhi, and the scene at 7 Jantar Mantar Road the headquarter of the Congress was like a *mela*. The aspirants came with the charge sheets against their rivals describing sordid deeds of those, who only a few years earlier were known for suffering and sacrifices.

Pandit Pant, the Prime Minister of the most populous State of U.P. had come forward with the most controversial list to be cleared by the Congress High Command. Some of us were made to light midnight candles to prepare charge sheets of corruption, nepotism and maladministration against some of his ministers.

But Kidwai knew the mind of the boss more than many of us knew. The day the U.P. list was to be discussed he feigned illness and retired to the rest house in Okhla. In his absence he sent K.D. Malaviya one of his most trusted lieutenants to argue the case against them. Nehru was unhappy with the list. He is reported to have remarked that Pant had brought a list of thieves and dacoits.

Pant pointed out that his list consisted of those who were likely to win the election. If any changes were made Nehru should find out someone else to supervise the election. Apparently, Nehru got cold feet, and accepted Pant's recommendations. Later, he issued a public statement that after the elections, he will see that the Congress legislators behave properly.

To the ignorant and the illiterate, Nehru and the Congress were their liberator. The tricolour was the flag under which thousands had marched to jail, and many of them had faced bullets and lathi charges. The millions all over India knew little about the candidates. They voted for Gandhi and Nehru.

In prestigious New Delhi constituency, the electorate used their discretion, and Mrs Man Mohan Saighal a close relation of Nehru was defeated by the veteran freedom fighter Sucheta Kripalani who was returned as a Kisan Mazdoor Praja Party candidate. A well known journalist and close associate of Patel, Durga Das editor of powerful English daily *Hindustan Times*, who was refused Congress ticket by Nehru, and contested as an independent candidate could get only six hundred votes losing his deposit.

The first general election was more of a referendum for the popularity of Nehru than an election. He emerged triumphant. The big business was on the side of the Congress. They contributed huge amount of black money that they had earned during the war and post-war period.

In former princely states where Congress had no base most of the ruling princes with exception of few campaigned for the Congress candidates.

Though Nehru was triumphant, because all the States were captured by the Congress and in the Union Parliament it was returned with thumping majority but the foundation of money politics and cult of personality was laid. The socialists and the communists who had parted company with the Congress a few years earlier though managed to get some seats in Union Parliament as well as State assemblies, but by and large their performance against well financed Congress machinery was very poor. Even Dr Ambedkar the messiah of depressed classes was floored by a Congress non-entity.

Nehru had again and again before the election declared 'candidates chosen should not only possess integrity but be known to do so. They should also have certain ability and capacity'.

But in selection of its candidates Congress went more for their ability to bag votes than for their other qualifications. It was for the first time that the Congress considered the caste and communal consideration of a constituency for selection of its candidate.

Maulana Azad, who was the tallest among the Congress candidates, was of Delhi origin, and a Calcutta settler. But he was fielded from Rampur in U.P. with a heavy concentration of Muslims electorate. Similar considerations were made in selection of other candidates. It was the first general election under Nehru where the foundation of casteism was laid with disastrous results in future.

Chapter 21

IN PARLIAMENT

MY entry on the floor of Lok Sabha was not a novel experience for me. Though I was never elected to a legislature, I had almost twenty years' experience as a lobby correspondent.

I was fully aware of rules and regulations, traditions and parliamentary etiquette. Just after my election, I had tabled a resolution to free the All India Radio from State control.

I participated in most of the important, the crucial debates and my contribution was appreciated by the treasury as well as opposition benches.

Most of the Members of the Government as well as opposition were known to me. But, I felt more at home with the Opposition Members like Prof. Hiren Mukherji, Inderjit Gupta, Renu Chakravarty to name a few.

Jawaharlal Nehru was the leader of the House and held the Parliament in great respect. Having been a great admirer of the Westminster system, he gave full latitude even to the Members of his own party to point out the lapses of his colleagues in the Government.

On Congress benches the most vehement critic of his Government was his own son-in-law, Feroze Gandhi. Myself and Feroze often exchanged notes before taking an issue. Though he was a poor speaker, he always marshalled his facts with great care and pain.

T.T. Krishnamachari was a sales agent of a multi-national firm dealing with cosmetics. Nehru appointed him as the Minister of Commerce and Industries. Within a short tenure in that Ministry he issued liberal licence for import of tooth paste, lipsticks, rouge and face powder making a great dent in the foreign exchange earned by India during the war. Later he was shifted to Finance Ministry. He showed undue interest in one adventurist businessman Mundhra who later spent most of his life in jail.

Feroze got wind of this shady deal. He thoroughly studied

the case and on the floor of the House asked for a judicial enquiry. Nehru seeing the temper of the House had to agree to it.

The case was handed over to Justice M.C. Chagla, Chief Justice of Bombay High Court. Justice Chagla accused Finance Minister of indiscretion and Nehru bowed to verdict and issued marching order to T.T.K.

The opposition as well as the Left Wing of the Congress attacked his ministers, but kept Nehru above controversy. The situation, however, changed when through one of the by-elections, Dr Ram Manohar Lohia was returned to Lok Sabha. Once a blue eyed boy of Nehru he was now his bitterest critic. Once he accused him of nepotism pointing out that all the key positions in External Affairs were held by Kashmiris. I jumped and pointed out that the greatest beneficiary of Congress rule had been the community to which he belonged, the Marwaris.

I had known Lohia from his Allahabad days. Though in the House we sat on opposite benches, outside we were great friends. He held an acid tongue but had heart of gold. He was one of the most affectionate person whom I met during my public life.

My maiden speech in Parliament was on community programme. There was one S.K. Dey who was working for some electrical firm in Lahore. After partition, he came to India and cultivated the all powerful special assistance of Nehru M.O. Mathai. Nehru was very much impressed by him and when American offered help in rural development, he was appointed the Administrator of Community Development Programme. Later, he persuaded Nehru to establish a Ministry and appoint him as a Minister.

I had worked with him for a short time. He dined and wined during national movement but copied Nehru in his dress with a slanting khadi cap. Though there was dearth of those people, who had dedicated their lives to rural movement, but Nehru was impressed by him. However, later, he was exposed.

I had a brush with Nehru about Dr Dharma Teja. He was supposed to have doctorate in nuclear science. Nehru was much impressed by him. He launched a huge shipping company and purchased a number of ships without investing any money of his own with Government of India as a guarantor.

I came to know this shady deal and approached Nehru to warn him. But, instead of listening to me, he delivered a lecture that here was a businessman steeped in science and technology unlike traditional Marwari businessmen and how I dared not to challenge his credentials.

Later, he ran away to a South American Banana Republic and was detected in London where he had come to settle some accounts and was extradited to India to spend few years in Tihar Jail for fraud and cheating. It was whispered in New Delhi social circles that Nehru was much impressed by Mrs Teja, a Punjabi beauty.

Keshava Deva Malaviya, was Minister of Natural Resources in Nehru Government. I knew him as an underground worker during Quit India Movement of 1942, later, he was inducted in U.P. Government as Minister for Industries and Development. He was progressive and leftist in his views.

After the Second World War, the German Industries were shattered. The German engineers were mostly migrating to U.S.A. and some of them had come to seek their fortune in India.

Malviya hired an engineer from well known electronic plant of Simens and persuaded U.P. Government to set up a precision instrument factory in Lucknow. It was probably the first public undertaking in India.

In Delhi, his proposal to nationalise oil industry created greatest resentment among oil giants like Burma Shell, Caltex and Standard Vacuum. His proposal to prospect oil in India was ridiculed as a wild dream.

The vested interests was after his blood. They had already managed to finish the Iranian Prime Minister Mossadeq who proposed to nationalise oil companies in his country. An opportunity came to them when during one of the routine raids on the premises of the residence of Serajjuddin well known philanthropist and mine owner of East India was raided. It was found in a diary, with a remark the Rupees Five Thousand were paid to one of Malviya's emissary.

The Opposition particularly Socialist Party which hated him for his pro-communist leanings raised a storm in Lok Sabha. Malviya offered himself for judicial enquiry and later resigned from the Cabinet.

I was also involved in Serajjuddin affair in some way. He was a nationalist Muslim and had faced Muslim League frenzy. He gave financial help to Muslim freedom fighters in Eastern India.

He approached me with the complaint that he was being harassed by Income Tax authorities. I passed on his complaint to Morarji the Finance Minister. On his suggestion, in his office,

Author (on extreme left) with his closest friend, K.A. Abbas (on the extreme right).

Author's wife, Mrs Gauher Ara, with Dr. Rajendra Prasad, President of India.

6. Jinnah's League Membership Form, 1913

Date Lucknow. 10th Oct 1913

Application for Membership under Section 4 of the Constitution and Rules of the All-India Muslim League.

THE HONORARY SECRETARY,

All-India Muslim League,

LUCKNOW.

DEAR SIR,

I desire to be elected a member of the All-India Muslim League, and in case I am elected I hereby declare that I shall adhere to the objects and Rules of the League as mentioned in its Constitution.

(Sd) M. A. Jinnah
Malabar Hill
Bombay

Proposed by : Mohammad Ali

Seconded by : ....Wazir Hasan

Muslim League was founded in Dhaka (Dacca) in 1907. Jinnah joined it only in 1913. His name was proposed by Maulana Mohammad Ali, one of the closest associates of Gandhi in Khilafat Non-Cooperation Movement.

Author following Jawaharlal Nehru to attend a meeting in 1937.

(top) Author with Mrs Indira Gandhi, his wife, and daughters. (bottom) Author with an African leader.

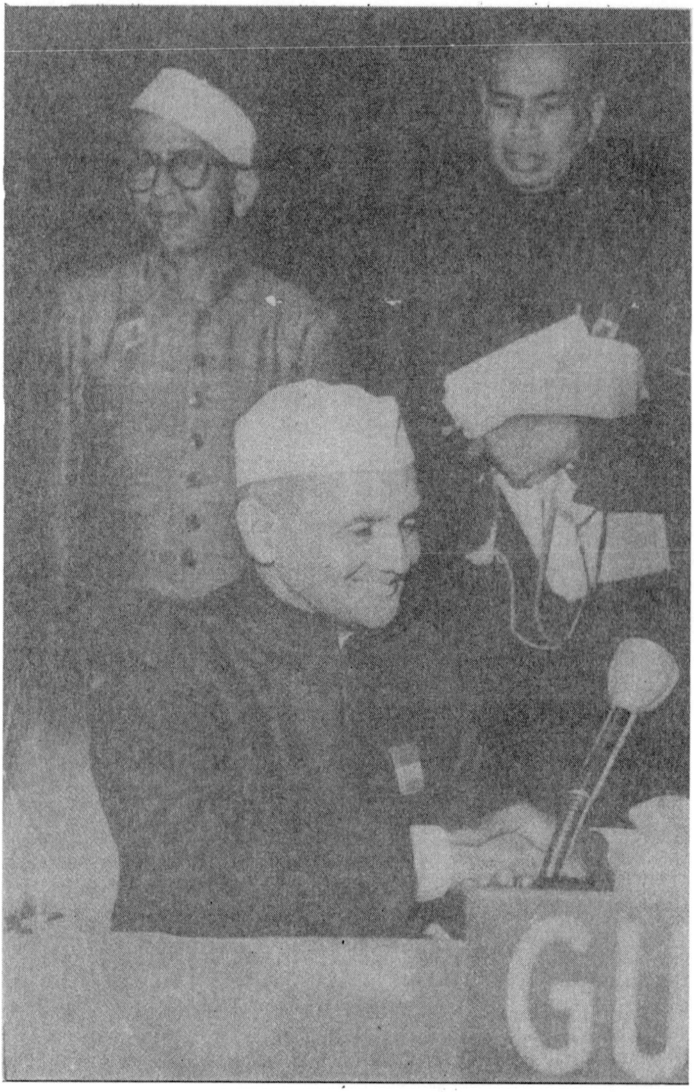

Author with Lal Bahadur Shastri, Prime Minister of India, at Non-Aligned Conference held at Cairo in 1964.

Author on extreme right with Soviet leaders on the eve of Tashkent talks.

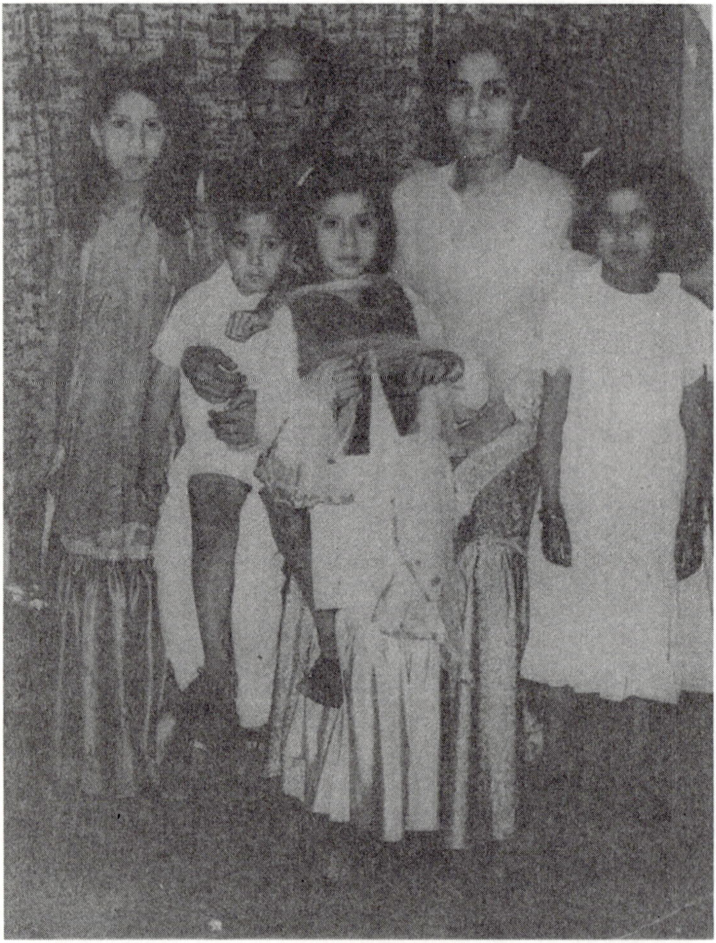

Author with his family just after he was returned to Lok Sabha in 1957.

I wrote a small note.

Sometime later, during one of the Parliamentary debates, attacked him for protecting the corruption of his own son. This touched him and he retorted that I recommended in writing the case of Serajjuddin. This evoked a chorus of shame, shame from the Socialists.

Unfortunately, I had no copy of that letter, but I shouted that my letter should be placed on the table of the House. Morarji promised to do so.

Next day, he did not place the letter on the table of the House and I again demanded it. Nehru asked him to do so. He sent his Deputy Minister to me who tried to threaten me that disclosure of the letter would not be in my political interest. Since my conscience was clear, I insisted and Morarji had to place the letter on the table of the House.

It was a very innocent note just asking him to look into the matter. I assured him while speaking in Parliament that I would continue to write similar letters to him in future also. It created an impression that how vindictive Morarji Desai was.

As I have already mentioned that in our Parliamentary activities, Feroze and myself often exchanged notes. In this connection, I would like to describe M.O. Mathai episode. He was Special Assistant of Prime Minister and there was general impression that he had great pull with Nehru. I had seen senior Ministers with the exception of Azad and Pant not taking chair in his office courting him and often being snubbed. I had seen even philosopher statesman, Sir Radha Krishnan flattering him. Feroze was annoyed with his undue and unhealthy influence on his father-in-law. He might have also certain personal reasons to be against him.

Mathai had cultivated Birla Brothers. He had floated a trust in the name of his mother who obviously was a lady of no consequence. He had purchased a valuable property from Birla Weaving and Spinning Mill for a nominal price.

On Feroze's request, I collected all the material from Municipal and other sources. Feroze passed on this information to a fire brand Member of Parliament, Bhupesh Gupta. He blasted Mathai left and right and Nehru had to dispense with his services.

In this connection, I would like to quote from memoirs of M. Chalapathi Rao, Editor of the *National Herald* owned by Nehru family. This will give background of M.O. Mathai.

> "Mathai had made for himself a home at Teen Murti House. One of the mistakes of Nehru's life was to have allowed Mathai to stay with him in the same household. Mathai had been a smart stenographer working with the Americans during the war, as Nehru found out in contrast to Upadhyay, who was not too smart as Nehru told me in 1946, but he was too smart and clever and found Nehru too good gullible. This enabled him to establish himself in a corner of the house with his dossiers, books and bar, entertaining friends of both sexes. If I had been Prime Minister and known of it, I would not have allowed it. I do not know if Nehru knew of the drama that was enacted with crude finesse under his nose. By staying in the House, Mathai came close to Indira Gandhi, and while outside, tongues wagged unjustifiably, Mathai's tongue wagged the most. Friends like Shankar warned him not to talk of Indira Gandhi, and Shankar was punished for a long time by not being allowed to attend Nehru's functions, till I advised him to contact Nehru directly. He did so with gratifying results. At one stage, Shankar invited Mathai to his house and poured enough whisky into him to make him talk. Narayanan and I were the others present. Mathai lectured Narayanan on economics for which he got a rude rebuff and then he started waxing eloquent about Indira Gandhi, what a wonderful woman, he said, 'how I adore her!' and then, more inebirated he was about to say how much she adore him; when he realised his legs were being pulled and he stopped suddenly."

Mathai's favourite method with Nehru was to pester him with background notes, damning someone or promoting someone's interest.

Feroze was very close to V.K. Krishna Menon who was Defence Minister as well as Chief Adviser of Nehru on foreign affairs. His performance at U.N.O. had made him a world figure. I was introduced to him by Feroze in strange circumstances which I have described in next chapter.

I was very much impressed by his sharp mind and still sharper tongue. While he was very much appreciated by the leftist members of the Congress Party the rightists were his bitterest critics. His efforts to build up indigenous arm industry had hit the Indian capitalists who had ganged against him. The socialists considered him pro-communists and were eager to hit him.

In the meantime, the graph of Nehru's popularity was sliding down. It reached its lowest after so-called Chinese debacle, which I have dealt in next chapter. He was a broken man. The question all over the world was being who after Nehru.

Nehru himself told me that a Prime Minister should not suggest his successor, and pointed out that Churchill's selection of Anthony Eden as Prime Minister had been a disaster.

But, the fact is that he was grooming his daughter to succeed him from her childhood. The publication of letters from Father to Daughter was the first step.

But unlike her daughter, which will be seen later he was too decent and democratic to be vulgar enough to spell his choice of his daughter. Her introduction in Congress High Command, appointment as Congress President, was a pointer.

In his last days, he was disgusted with tne tales of corruption of many of his colleagues. He wanted to clip the wing of many aspirants, particularly, Morarji Desai, the Finance Minister.

After months of sober thinking, Nehru finally acted. In the process he immortalized another honest but comparatively obscure colleague, Kamraj Nadar, the popular Chief Minister in Madras. His rough and robust demeanour, his homely dress, his conventional way of eating rice, somehow did not fit in with New Delhi environment. But, nonetheless anyone meeting him could feel that he was forthright, honest and had the tenacity and the purity of an uncut diamond. He struck me as a man of few words, but possessed of a lot of action. He had rustic peasant sense. When Nehru disclosed to Kamaraj, his dilemma and his feeling that something drastic, something spectacular and something spontaneous required to be done, Kamaraj suggested a major surgical operation while Nehru later generously attributed to Kamraj the authorship of the final plan, it was the subtlety of Nehru himself which gave to the proposed operation the noble appearance of a grand 'renunciation'. The operation affected many top Congressmen who had lingered in positions of power too long. Some of them were being openly accused of corruption others had a fine record of service.

In November 1963 the Congress Working Committee and the A.I.C.C met to implement the so-called 'Kamraj Plan'. Nehru told his colleagues that since many of the best men had been occupied too long with ministerial duties, party work had suffered, and the hold of the Congress on the people had weakened, the time, he said, had, therefore, come for some of them to volunteer to renounce office and take up party work "to clean up the Congress and prepare it for achieving its great national objectives." Nehru offered to be the first to relinquish office, since he had "borne the burden of office" for too long. This, as planned was unanimously rejected. In order that people may not be able to distinguish between the 'black sheep and the white sheep', he made even Lal Bahadur to resign, who rejoined the Government as Minister without portfolio within few months to assist Nehru.

I met Morarji Desai. He was furious. C.B. Gupta, Chief Minister of U.P. desribed it as 'Kamraj conspiracy'.

The greatest achievement of this plan was that Morarji Desai who considered himself as obvious successor to Nehru was brought to size.

Nehru's health was failing. V.K. Krishna Menon, his closest confidant was out after the Chinese debacle. He kept on trusting more and more on soft spoken Lal Bahadur who always kept a low profile and his daughter Indira Gandhi, who later on was to emerge his successor without his scruples and finer points.

Chapter 22

SCAPEGOAT

I had heard about Feroze Gandhi, but I had not known him. He was a student activist in Great Britain with Rajni Patel, Mohan Kumaramangalam and Renu Chakravarty. Later, on Nehru's suggestion, he was appointed as an assistant to Krishna Menon who was special correspondent of the *National Herald* at London on a salary of Rs. 150.

When he came back to India, most of us knew that he had become very much attached to Indira Gandhi. He came to Lucknow and became one of the Coffee House crowd.

He had managed to smuggle some Moscow posters which were till then banned in India, and we were thrilled when he organised an exhibition of them. I was one of those who became one of his close friends.

After the Congress Ministers in U.P. had resigned following the declaration of war by Viceroy of India, without consulting Indian legislatures, Kidwai had shifted to the Councillors' residence. During one of my frequent visits to his room, I found Feroze and Indira there. Kidwai asked both of them as to when they were getting married. Feroze remained silent but Indira lamented that Papa, meaning Nehru was not giving his clear consent. Kidwai pointedly asked if he had refused the permission? In reply Indira pointed out that he neither said yes nor no.

Kidwai said since he had not said no, why the engagement should not be announced. He asked me and the correspondent of United Press to announce their engagement on his authority.

Kidwai was the most important director of *National Herald,* and reluctantly the *National Herald* published the news. The very next day Nehru arrived in Lucknow from Calcutta, where he had gone to meet Chiang Kai Sheik and his charming wife. He came straight from railway station to attend a conference. I was sitting on the dais and was restless.

When Mrs Pandit's eldest daughter Chandralekha informed

him that their engagement had been published in *Herald*, much to my relief, Nehru shrugged his shoulder and remarked that what was wrong about that.

Later, he issued a public statement that Feroze and Indira would go to Wardha for Bapu's blessings and the marriage would be performed according to Vedic rites.

Feroze was elected to Constituent Assembly and to first as well as second Lok Sabha. He was a mediocre and had no brilliance about him. But he had a complex that he should make mark for himself and should not bask under the sunshine of his famous father-in-law. He was a hardworking and painstaking parliamentarian, and soon, made a mark as a constructive critic of the Government of his own party, the Congress. When I joined him in second Lok Sabha, we became very close collaborators and often jointly studied various subjects and exchanged notes.

Towards the end of fifties his relations unfortunately with his wife became very strained. It is very difficult for me to say that who was at fault.

When Mrs Gandhi assumed office as Congress President, they were hardly on talking terms. He often used to write letters to her addressing as "Comrade Congress President" and ending it as "Yours fraternally".

When Mrs Gandhi as Congress President planned to engineer the fall of the Communist Government in Kerala with the help of Nair asteists, Catholic fanatics and Muslim League communalists, both of us were very much agitated.

When I cam to Lok Sabha I had certain prejudices and reservations against V.K. Krishna Menon. My heroes in politics had been Subhas Bose and Maulana Azad and both of them disliked him.

Azad in his book *India Wins Freedom* has criticised Menon. Bose wrote that whenever Jawahar visits Europe, he is surrounded by him and who never allows him to meet anyone of consequence. and introduces him only to crooks and cranks.

Feroze asked me to meet Menon to tell him that for the first time a Communist Government had been formed through ballot and not bullet and he should exert his influence with Nehru to save the situation.

I frankly told him that I hardly knew him. We had just nodding acquaintance in the lobby of the Parliament. However, he telephoned to Romesh Bhandari his private secretary and fixed my appointment with Menon in Defence Ministry. I reached there and got a friendly greeting from him. When I mentioned the reason for my visit, he burst out by saying, "this wretched woman is undoing all good things that myself and Prime Minister have been doing for this country. I am completely helpless".

That was our first meeting and when Nehru and Menon were faced with Sino-Indian crisis, I became very close to him.

It will be necessary to describe the background of Sino-Indian crisis. Much before India achieved Independence Nehru had convened an Asiatic Relations Conference at a medieval old fort of Delhi. He had the dream of becoming the leader of Asia and it was necessary for him to obtain the support of the most populous country of Asia — China. He had already visited China and had cultivated close friendship with Generalissimo Chiang Kai-Sheik and his charming wife.

Chiang Kai-Sheik went out of his way to extend a hand of friendship to nationalist leaders like Nehru, before Independence. At the same time, it was he who double-crossed and authorised publication of maps which showed Tibet, Nepal, Bhutan, Sikkim and large areas in Assam and NEFA along the Brahmaputra river as Chinese territory. Despite later Indian protests, Mao Tse-Tung never repudiated these maps or these claims. In 1950, seeing India embroiled in some of its own troubles, Chinese armies invaded Tibet, thus forcibly establishing claim to Tibet. In a speech at the time Nehru emphasised, "Please note that I have used the word 'suzerainty' and not "sovereignty". Later K.M. Panicker, the Indian Ambassador to Peking informed China that the Prime Minister had used the word 'sovereignty' and not 'suzerainty' This created a lot of bewilderment in India.

When a clarification was later sought in Parliament, Nehru forgot what he said earlier and naively tried to equate the two expressions, as if the two terms had all the time seemed to him synonymous. "Some criticism has been made", he said referring to the Sino-Indian Treaty of 1954, "that this is a recognition of Chinese sovereignty over Tibet. I am not aware of any time during the last few hundred years when Chinese sovereignty or, if you like, suzerainty was challenged by any outside country"

Nehru had been a great personal friend of Marshal Chiang Kai-Sheik and an ardent admirer of Madame Chiang. When the communist revolution took place, Nehru was not entirely happy, but he soon reconciled himself to the inevitable. The Indian Ambassador to China during the change-over was a personal friend of Nehru. was as much due to his ability as to his extraordinary adaptability, that the new Communist rulers of China, Mao Tse-Tung, Chen Yi and Chou En-Lai found Panicker as acceptable as did the pro-American dictator Marshal Chiang Kai-Sheik. With them he shifted from Chung Kunming to Peking the new capital. Panicker arranged an invitation for Nehru. Nehru spent ten days in China. Millions of flag waving Chinese lined the routes along which he passed. had gone suspicious of the international objectives of the new Chinese rulers, especially after the forcible entry of Chinese troops into Tibet in 1950. Whether it was the very flattering reception accorded to him that influenced his judgment or because he was in a mood to develop a better understanding in the East, to counteract the puppet-seeking policies of Dulles, Nehru returned full of admiration for the new rulers of China.

Convinced in the belief that China like Russia had no expansionist designs, and believing that something positive and spectacular should be done to mobilise the uncommitted people of Asia and Africa to assert their collective strength on the side of peace, Nehru and a few others took the initiative to call a conference of Afro-Asian countries at Bandung. Ever since his first visit to Indonesia, Nehru had developed a great liking for the Indonesian people, and great personal regard for Soekarno. Indonesia was predominantly Muslim. Muslims of Indonesia who were more secular minded than Pakistan and seemed inclined if not determined to keep religion out of national and international politics. For this reason, and because of a common colonial background, Indonesia was chosen as the site of the Conference. More than twentynine Afro-Asian countries attended the meet, Soekarno's government spent lavishly to lend splendour to the Conference partly because it put Indonesia on the world map and more so because it threw the spectacular personality of Dr Soekarno in the international limelight. Menon did all the negotiating, drafting and the spadework. Nehru emerged as the architect of the grand plan. From this it was hoped would emerge a collective effort towards lessening of world tensions, if not also a movement designed to counteract colonialism and imperialism.

After almost a week of negotiations and deliberations the Conference produced a declaration which was in reality no more than a paraphrase of the Charter of the United Nations.

In India, Bandung was trumpeted as a great achievement, a sort of landmark in the history of Afro-Asian relations, and the initiator of some kind of an international movement to promote peace. In reality, apart from offering Nehru, Chou En-Lai, Nazir and Ahmed Soekarno an international forum to preach their ideas and to project their distinctly different personalities, the 'Five Pillars' of he Bandung declaration were as much sand-built as the Manila and Baghdad pacts were a house of cards.

Communist China's presence for the first time at such an international meet was heralded as a great achievement. Everybody including Nehru and Menon boosted Chou En-Lai as "Promoter of Peace and non-alignment."

At Bandung, Nehru had taken Chinese Prime Minister under his wing. He was much impressed by his courteous and almost docile behaviour. He felt like his elder brother, and was very much impressed by him.

Till then the Communist China was not admitted in the United Nations Organisation. It was on Nehru's initiative that repeated efforts were made to admit it in the world body.

In spite of Nehru's repeated gestures to sponsor the Communist China to United Nations, apparently, it was not happy that India had given asylum to Dalai Lama, after they drove away the Tibetan God King. India's assurance that Dalai Lama would not be allowed to set up a provisional Government on Indian soil did not satisfy them.

The Chinese had never accepted as stated earlier the Sino-Indian boundaries marked by the British, when their Emperors were weak and had to submit to European powers.

The Chinese Prime Minister made four visits to India in the fifties to discuss the Sino-Indian relations. During his fourth visit in 1960, Chou En-Lai, Chinese Prime Minister who came along with foreign minister, he found his reception quite cool.

Even the ordinary protocol was not observed, and he had to visit Pandit Pant, the Home Minister at his residence instead of the latter calling on him.

Nehru had not made any serious assessment of the frightening potential of China. In fact, he never imagined that India would have to confront the Chinese. He always declared that never in ancient or medieval history India had any confrontation with China.

It is true that India had inherited a strong and well disciplined army from the British. But, unlike Chinese army, our soldiers had no commitment. Their loyalty was to their regiments and not to their country. They displayed their gallantry in two Great Wars not for their country of for the British King but to uphold their regimental honour.

Red China's regular army in 1955 was estimated at 170 divisions of 12,000 men each. This was backed by indoctrinated militia estimated at ten million. It had acquired from the Soviet Union a large number of tanks, jet fighters and bombers. China was then in the process of manufacturing large quantities of its own small arms. Chinese nuclear scientists who had received training in the United States were known to be engaged in manufacturing nuclear arms, and their experiments in the preparation of an atom bomb had reached an advanced stage. While at one time Indian generals claimed that one Indian soldier was equal to ten Chinese, the Korean conflict had shown the average Chinese to be a hardy, adaptable and resourceful soldier. The Chinese generals besides, and now excelled in the new tactics of massive troop deployment and quick manoeuvrings. Unlike the Indian soldiers who had inherited British traditions, the Chinese had learnt to fight light, even to supplement daily needs locally and to dispense with elaborate supplies.

Since Sino-Indian border was not recognised, a number of border clashes took place. The Indian protests, were arrogantly brushed aside. A prolonged diplomatic correspondence took place jeopardising Sino-Indian relations.

Nehru, considered Chinese attitude as an affront to him, and to India. In sheer disgust, on 12th October, 1962, Nehru announced that he had instructed the Indian army to "throw the Chinese" out of the disputed areas. This announcement was described by the *New York Tribune* (15 October) as "tantamount to a formal declaration of war" while the British newspaper, the *Guardian,* called it an 'Ultimatum', that the Indian fired the first shot was suggested by a subsequent report in *New York Times* of 19 April, 1963, which mentioned that "General Maxwell D. Taylor, Chairman of the Joint Chiefs of Staff, indicated in secret Congressional testimony made public here today that India might have started the border fight with Communist China". On 20th October, 1962, fighting flared up between China and India at a number of points along their disputed border in Ladakh (Kashmir) and in the North-East Frontier Agency (NEFA) areas lying east of the State of Bhutan.

What happened subsequently is, however, fairly generally known. During two brief bouts of fighting, the first in October and the second in November, the Indian Army met with serious reverses. By 20th November the Indians had surrendered another 2,000 square miles of disputed territory of Ladakh, thus putting the Chinese in control of almost the entire 15,000 square miles of territory which they claimed in that part of

Kashmir. In the east even Assam seemed exposed to the rapidly advancing Chinese troops. Then suddenly, on 21st November, the Chinese declared a cease-fire and offered unilaterally to withdraw to points behind the McMahon line from the entire territory they had overrun. This undertaking they subsequently fully carried out, offering at the same time to negotiate their border differences with India peacefully.

Nehru was the darling of the nation, but he never exercised the full grip on the machinery of the Congress Party which he led in the Parliament. The followers of Patel, though had switched over their loyalty to him after latter's death, but their support to him was very dubious. He had earned displeasure of the big business by sponsoring public undertakings.

The Indian businessmen under the leadership of C. Rajagopalachary and supported by some Indian princes, had already organised a party of their own to be known as Swatantra Party, though Nehru's charisma did not allow them many seats in Lok Sabha, they had a number of Trojan horses in the Congress itself. The votaries of free enterprises were allowed by him to be entrenched in Congress itself.

The setback in conflict with China eroded his prestige. Many members of his own party were after his blood. But they preferred to make their attack on V.K. Krishna Menon, his closest friend and confidant.

Some of us who were convinced that with all his failings, that Nehru was the best bet for India stood by him. We burnt midnight oil to defend Menon, for we were convinced that attack on Menon was an attack on Nehru.

I was a member of the Executive Committee of the Congress Party. At one of its meeting when Nehru pointed out that Chinese had captured the areas where not even a blade of grass grew, Tyagi, a former Minister of Defence production, who was bald, pointed to his head and asked him, since no hair grows on his head, would he offer it to Chinese?

Ravindra Verma, a former student leader and a protege of the business house of Bajaj, told Nehru that he did not have his hand on the pulse of the people. On this remark Nehru lost his patience and thumped the table and shouted the day Jawaharlal does not have his hand on the pulse of the people, he would quit his chair.

Indian Constitution has adopted the Westminster system of Cabinet responsibility. The Prime Minister is one of them though he presides over Cabinet meetings and has every right to guide his ministers. But, after the death of Patel, of Azad and Pant, Nehru became all supreme and his cabinet was a mere rubber stamp. It is true that Menon was his close adviser and confidant, but he carried on the policies of Nehru to the letter.

As already pointed by me, all attacks on Menon were really an attack on Nehru. It was he who had given the order to army to throw out the Chinese and sounded the bu gle of war.

We tried our best to defend him. In fact we organised with the help of local trade unionists a meeting in front of Jama Masjid in the heart of walled city which was addressed by Menon explaining the whole situation. But only next day, Nehru who definitely had his hand on the pulse of his party through Satya Narayan Sinha, his Chief Whip and a pronounced supporter of the House of Birla, and after paying glowing tributes to Menon announced that reluctantly he had accepted his resignation.

Later, Satya Narayanan Sinha who was a close friend of mine told me that he had convinced Nehru's daughter, Indira Gandhi, that unless he made Menon an scapegoat his own position was threatened.

Chapter 23

END OF AN ERA

WITH the death of Nehru, the era of great national leaders was over. Patel, Rajendra Prasad and Azad, constituted the generation of those, who claimed to be known, respected and feared all over India. Sometimes earlier S.K. Patil, a close lieutenant of Patel, had compared Nehru with a banyan tree under which grass does not grow.

Within few minutes of announcement of Nehru's death in Lok Sabha, Gulzari Lal Nanda, the Home Minister was sworn in as a caretaker Prime Minister.

On hearing this announcement all of us rushed to his Teen Murti residence with tears in our eyes. We were too dazed even to think that who would succeed him. For the last few years, a question was being asked by the correspondents of national as well as international press: Who after Nehru? But, most of us had no reply.

Nehru himself told me that it would be wrong for him to suggest his own successor. He pointed out as I have referred to already that Winston Churchil groomed Anthony Eden to succeed him but the latter proved a complete failure. But even before sandalwood flames to which Nehru's body had been cast died out, the question of his succession became a subject for intrigue, and sordid diplomacy.

On the next day of his cremation, I visited Jagjivan Ram, one of the seniormost colleagues of Nehru. He asked me to canvass for him and described Lal Bahadur in rather uncomplimentary way. Nanda though eager to succeed him knew his limitations, that he was not very much acceptable to Congress Party.

Morarji, who always considered himself number two in Nehru Cabinet was busy canvassing support for himself. Though he was an ardent supporter of Patel, most of those who originally owed their loyalty to him had switched over to Nehru. They did not approve his fads, holier than holy attitude. Some even suggested Indira Gandhi's name, and Keshava Deva Malviya approached Dr Radhakrishnan, the President to permit Nanda to continue for a few months more, when Congress party could elect her. But President refused to oblige him.

It was left to Kamraj, the Congress President to choose Nehru's successor by consulting individual members of the Congress Party and find out the most acceptable condidate. By now Morarji though too ambitious to become Prime Minister was made to realise that he had no chance, against a candidate supported by Kamaraj, approved by S.K. Patil, Atulya Ghosh, Sanjiva Reddy and most of the Congress Chief Ministers.

Kamraj declared that by and large Congress party wanted soft spoken unassuming Lal Bahadur, and he was unanimously elected as the Leader of the Congress party and was invited by President of India to be sworn in as the Prime Minister.

Short statured Lal Bahadur was a complete contrast to Nehru. He came from a very poor family and has risen to some status, from being an ordinary Congress volunteer. He had great affection for me and I had known him from those days, when he used to take his bath from a public hydrant.

Unlike, Nehru, he was a commoner and had great respect for those who had participated in freedom movement.

As time passed, the press and the people in general, realised that Lal Bahadur was by far the best man to fill the post of Prime Minister at that critical juncture. He had no 'isms' about him. He had no favourites. He had no fads. His mind neither soared to the skies, nor was it obssessed by pre-conceived notions or prejudices. He was pliable enough to accept advice from any and every quarter, but when a decision had been made, he had the courage to see it through with firmness, disregardful of consequences.

Lal Bahadur, as the Home Minister and now as Prime Minister was firm in putting down corruption in high places. The Kamraj Plan had been a camouflaged purge. But no one knew who among those who retired from public office were the 'white sheep' and 'black sheep'. "Corruption and good government cannot go well together" he said, "and if one could make an example of some of the tall poppies, the lesser type of corruption could be weeded out by itself." His own unimpeachable honesty had also great effect on reducing corruption in high places. Integrity from now onwards was not taken for granted. "It had to be proven", he said Lal Bahadur did not hesitate to call for proofs. T.T. Krishnamachari whom

Nehru had invited to a second term as Finance Minister found himself suddenly involved in what came to be known as the "Barium" scandal. Serious charges were levelled inside and outside the House. Lal Bahadur felt that sufficient prima facie material was available to justify an inquiry. He informed T.T. Krishnamachari accordingly. Krishnamachari tendered his resignation.

Lal Bahadur did not get much time to tap talent from outside the party. He mostly carried on with the colleagues he had inherited except that he asked Indira Gandhi to take up 'Information and Broadcasting'; according to him, out of a sense of 'loyalty' to his erstwhile 'chief' He hoped in due course, when he had the time to go in more for quality and integrity rather than creating another party jamboree from all the nit-wits who could pull the wires and exert party pressures without strengthening the administration. As an alternative, he did something which placed at his disposal a host of expert knowledge to help him to make intelligent decision, direct the affairs even of other Ministers, and to solve some of the most difficult problem to an extent that it would not have been otherwise possible. Nehru was mostly surrounded by courtiers who took order, but dared not give advice; who smoothened queered pitches but did not oppose or question decisions. They felt no responsibility for wrong decisions, nor received credit for offering the right advice.

Lal Bahadur, on the other hand, surrounded himself with few of the best brains in the administrative field. He not only freely consulted these men but encouraged them to offer expert advice on their own. Even in the Cabinet, he believed in consultation and full and free discussion before decisions were taken. In fact, he welcomed and encouraged advice from all quarters. When it came to a decision, he had the final say.

Though I knew Nehru from my earliest days, and was very close to his wife Kamala, but he never trusted me due to my close association with Subhas Bose and later my frank and frontal attacks on Congress leadership as a member of A.I.C.C. He complained to some of my senior colleagues, that I shouted too much and often acted irresponsibly. Whenever my name was mentioned for being inducted in Parliament, he supported me in spite of the opposition of Pant. But, he never considered me for a responsible assignment.

During his tenure, a number of Parliamentary delegation were sent abroad. But, I was never allowed to cross the sea.

When Mathai, his powerful Special Assistant about whom

have mentioned earlier, suggested the name of a Muslim woman M.P. who had never even opened her lip on the floor at the House, my name was suggested instead of her; he merely shrugged his shoulder.

I met Lal Bahadur for the first time when he was chairman of the Estimates Committee of U.P. Assembly and immediately we developed a liking for each another. I felt at home with him for he was a man of grassroots and had achieved his position through really hard work and dedication. I continued my close relationship with him when he shifted from U.P. to national politics.

After the General Elections of Lok Sabha in 1962, when the Congress party was to meet to elect Nehru as leader which was a mere formality, Nehru fell ill. I came to know that Morarji Desai, who always considered himself to be number two had decided to occupy the Chair, I telephoned to Sanjiva Reddy, who was the then Congress President to claim the chair by his right.

On hearing this, Lal Bahadur advised me not to create scene, and allow me to satisfy his ego. I could not refuse his suggestion and kept quiet, but in the party meeting, I addressed Morarji Desai, as Returning Officer which evoked laughter.

On the eve of the formation of Cabinet in 1962, Nehru had asked Lal Bahadur and his daughter Indira Gandhi to draw up a list of junior ministers. Lal Bahadur included my name and asked me for my preference as to with which Minister I would like to be attached. I chose Krishna Menon, to whom by that time, I had come very close.

Nehru is reported to have told Lal Bahadur that in view of India's relations with Pakistan, a Muslim in Defence Ministry might create some suspicion in powerful Jan Sangh lobby, and even among some Congressmen. I thanked Lal Bahadur and asked him to convey my thanks, to Nehru and inform him that I would prefer to continue as a private Member.

Nehru was never swayed by communal considerations. In fact, he was the greatest friend of Muslims in Congress Party. It is true that for him and the assassination of Gandhi, the Muslims in India would have been reduced to the status of second class citizens. But, he was too discreet to annoy the communal elements in his own party. As long as he continued as Prime Minister, he could not resist the pressure not to induct any Muslim in the sensitive Ministries like Home and Defence.

The classic case was of General Haibullah, who, by his

seniority and record of service, could have been promoted as Chief of the Staff of Indian Army. However, Nehru managed to persuade Tunku Abdul Rehman, the Prime Minister of the newly independent Government of Malaysia to have him as their Commander-in-Chief.

In his own Ministry of External Affairs he did not allow communal consideration in matters of appointment. His choice of Tayabji and Azim Husain as Foreign Secretaries proved his secular credential.

When Lal Bahadur assumed office he often took me in confidence. He was to go to Cairo to attend non-aligned Conference, and decided to have two Members of Parliament as the delegates. His choice fell on me and B. Gopala Reddy, a former Chief Minister, Andhra and Minister of Information and Broadcasting.

Before his departure in his humility, he asked me to guide him for he had never rubbed shoulder with international personalities. Obviously, I felt flattered.

In Cairo, I built up close contacts with President Nasser and Ahmed Soekarno of Indonesia. Lal Bahadur deputed me to the most important political committee, where I asserted myself in spite of the resistance of top brass of Indian Foreign Office. They complained against my interference but Lal Bahadur stood by me.

On the eve of the conflict with Pakistan, which I will describe later, he sent me with a Parliamentary delegation to explain Indian case to the leaders of the Soviet Union.

In Soviet Union, we were cordially received by the leaders of the Government and the Communist Party. We specially visited the Asiatic Republics which have predominantly Muslim population to explain our case.

In fact, our visit paved the way, for his performance at crucial negotiations that he had at Tashkent. My reports on Cairo Conference as well as our visit to Soviet Union was very much appreciated by him.

The senior leaders of the Congress party were jealous of him. They felt that he had made his way in Nehru's court by his unassuming and submissive behaviour. Nehru's sister Vijaya Lakshmi Pandit went so far as to declare on the floor of the Lok Sabha that he was 'a prisoner of indecision'.

The greatest crisis in his political career came when he faced the Indo-Pakistan conflict. I informed him that some of his senior colleagues were apprehensive that he was incapable of rising to the occasion. The little great man smiled and told me that the time alone would tell, who was right.

Pakistan had never reconciled to the accession of Kashmir to India. Jinnah had sent tribals followed by Pakistan army to capture Kashmir. But the tribals got busy looting and raping Kasmiri women and were ultimately driven away by Indian Army, and U.N.O. had drawn a ceasefire line, between Kashmir and occupied Kashmir.

When Lal Bahadur became Prime Minister the hopes of Pakistani militants soared high. for they felt that here was a weak Prime Minister and they could browbeat him.

They started infiltrating in Indian territory of Kashmir. They were to establish contact with local Muslims inside the valley and await 'D' day. The 'D' day for Srinagar was August 9. August 8 was the day of the Urs of Hazrat Pir Dastgir Sahib where thousands collected to celebrate the festival. It was hoped that the infiltrators could get mixed up with the crowds and reach Srinagar unnoticed.

On the 9th fell the anniversary of Sheikh Abdullah's dismissal from Prime Ministership. On this day, the infiltrators with local helpers were expected to stage a mammoth uprising. They were to cut off the Jammu-Kashmir road, capture the airport, assassinate as many ministers as possible and set up a 'Revolutionary Council'. This in turn was to 'officially' invite Pakistani forces to enter Kashmir in aid of its newly formed 'Lawful Government'.

A Muslim shepherd and a Muslim woodcutter had sabotaged the million-dollar 'Operation Gibralter'. They had given a lie to the naive assumption that Kashmiri Muslims were either for sale or were potential traitors to Kashmir and India. Getting scent of this plan, the Indian Army and the police acted with lightning speed, but, with utmost caution and secrecy. A large number of infiltrators were arrested from their jungle hideouts. Many were held crossing the boundary, and many more were handed over by local people with whom they were seeking asylum. Hundreds were lost in the ravines forging for food and shelter, till days later they made their way back to tell their dismal tale of failure.

Meanwhile, Pakistan was all set for the great 'D' day rebellion. Taking for granted that 'Operation Gibralter' had succeeded, that Radio Station in the Pakistan wing of Kashmir announced on the evening of the 9th of August that, as a result of a "major armed revolt", the "revolutionaries have captured the Secretariat, were in control of strategic routes, and the city of Srinagar is plastered with revolutionary posters".

It was on August 13 that India took 'official' notice of these infiltrations, and Pakistan realised that 'Operation Gibralter' had failed. In a broadcast to the Nation, Prime Minister Lal Bahadur Shastri revealed that a week earlier armed Pakistani infiltrators in large numbers had crossed the cease-fire line for the purpose of sabotage and destruction. They had "attacked strategic places such as bridges, police stations and petrol depots". Appropriate action, he said, "has since been taken to locate infiltrators. Several engagements have occurred and heavy casualties have been inflicted". He further said, "Pakistan is talking of some revolutionary council and a lot of other things. All this is a mere figment of Pakistan's imagination". He then delivered a stern warning: "I want to state categorically that force will be met with force, and aggression against us will never be allowed to succeed".

Dictators thrive on success. Failure is destructive to prestige. The failure of 'Operation Gibralter', if taken lying down would have meant the early overthrow of the Ayub-Bhutto-Musa Triumvirate. General Musa, one of Ayub's favourites, was now in command of the Army. 'Operation Gibralter', they explained to their people, was only a preliminary thrust which was to have been followed by full scale invasion. Once the invasion began, Ayub declared, Pakistan invulnerable tank squadrons will cut through to Delhi and Srinagar "as a knife through a cheese cake". As a preliminary to this full scale invasion of Pakistan forces began shelling Indian positions across the ceasefire line, and attacked several positions they considered vulnerable.

India's patience was being exhausted. The menace through infiltrations continued. Haji Pir Pass was a strategic rat-hole on the Pakistan side of the ceasefire line. Through this, major infiltrations were taking place. Partly to serve a warning to Pakistan, and partly to plug this rat-hole a band of hundred Indian soldiers advanced under the command of Major Dayal. Feeling their way secretly in pitch darkness in pouring monsoon rain, they made a surprise attack on three different positions held by the enemy in a much large number, and Pakistanis of a spectacular breakthrough that Major General Nassir Ahmed, the GOC of the 1st division himself led the attack from a safe specially constructed armoured vehicle. The General became a casualty in the encounter. His valuable vehicle fell into Indian hands as a trophy.

It was during these ding-dong periods of hope and despair that Ayub threw into battle his secret weapon, in early

September, transport planes, supported by fighters, dropped at 'strategic' points behind the Indian defence lines, even as far as Delhi, a large number of crack, well-armed paratroopers. They were to "blow up bridges, capture air ports if possible" and otherwise with local Muslim assistance create a fifth column in anticipation of the great 'breakthrough' to Delhi. These men and officers were armed with light machine-guns, wireless sets, explosives and packed foods. The scare of these droppings created was certainly very great. The damage these men did was unmentionably little. They led to a mad fox hunt in all the areas in which the droppings had been witnessed and practically all the paratroopers were traced and overpowered by local cilvilians. In the process a lot of innocents were hauled up under suspicion although released after their identity had been established. What started as a fox hunt for 'paratroopers' extended itself to a search for 'spies' and fifth columnists.

During these hectic days we in the Citizen's Council of which later I was to become Secretary, whether at the Centre or at lower levels all over the country, knew no rest or sleep. The manner in which people responded to appeals for help was spectacular. Thousands enlisted everywhere as homeguards or for other duties for civil defence. In the areas along the front line, the civilians showed rare courage.

The civilian morale of Indian side was very high. In their own trucks, on horse, and in bullock carts, they carried food and drinks right up to the fighting lines, distributing the same to the brave soldiers, disregardful of enemy fire. In certain danger areas, like Khem Karan, Burki and the Sialkot sector, the troops found difficulty in locating the enemy in heavily grown wheat and cotton fields. Thousands of farmers, working in the darkness at the risk of exposing themselves to Pakistani fire, cleared these fields overnight ensuring the spectacular success of some of the later Indian surprise attacks against the Pakistanis.

When the tide of war had definitely turned and Pakistan was faced with the imminent danger of a double assult on Lahore and Sialkot, London, Washington and Moscow came to Ayub Khan's timely rescue. They pleaded for an immediate ceasefire. Even though he had declared at one stage that India could not proceed from 'one ceasefire to another' in response to urgent appeals, Lal Bahadur agreed.

The ceasefire was followed by an Ayub-Lal Bahadur meeting at Tashkent at the pressing invitation of Premier Kosygin of the U.S.S.R. Lal Bahadur hoped, when he made the journey to

Tashkent, that this time at least the ceasefire would lead to a lasting peace. That the ceasefire would lead to another war also, the oppressive fear that weighed on his mind. Mostly reluctantly, struggling between hope and fear, and probably under Kosygin's pressure, he agreed to withdraw all Indian forces from such strategic points as Haji Pir Pass, Burji, Narowal near Sialkot and Khem Karan near Kasur. Those who were with Lal Bahadur at Tashkent felt that the more he talked to Ayub, hope became less and fears oppressed him more. He felt he was making the same blunder as India had committed earlier in agreeing to a ceasefire in Kashmir under the pressure of Mountbatten. But, he felt overpowered. Finally, resistance gave place to consent. Lal Bahadur even expressed satisfaction to placate critics at home. The true story of what happened behind the scene at Tashkent, however, will never be told, since Lal Bahadur was the only one to tell it. From all available facts, it is obvious that Lal Bahadur acted under pressure, and much in the agreement was to his dislike, and a lot which roused his fears.

On the seventh day of the negotiations, after signing the pact, Lal Bahadur attended a reception given by Kosygin in honour of Ayub and himself. Ayub seemed cheerful. Lal Bahadur looked depressed and unhappy. All day he took nothing. Even at the reception he partook only of orange juice. An undercurrent of frigidity could be felt behind the cordial make-believe of diplomacy between the chief actors. On reaching his residence, Lal Bahadur took a late meal and retired for the night. He told his servant to rise early to pack up for the return journey. At 1.30 a.m. he felt a choking spasm. There was no telephone. No Doctor. He rushed out of the bedroom in search of his doctor and fresh air. Soon afterwards, he collapsed.

Although a stranger in Tashkent, thousands of men, women and children lined the route of his cortege, the next day. Lal Bahadur had fought the twenty-two days war with the resolve, courage and daring of a great soldier. He had died searching for the peace he did not find. If an honest man is the greatest work of God, then Lal Bahadur was one. For that reason alone he was great!

Chapter 24

RETURN OF THE ROSE

WITHIN eighteen months, the elders of the party again met to pay funeral tributes to the dead and to make the choice of a successor from the living. All eyes were again turned to Kamraj, still, the President of the Congress party, and the redoubtable Morarji Desai, a second-time contender for the prized office. Kamraj never expected that the party would have to make a second choice within eighteen months. He still felt committed to Nehru's wish that Morarji should be kept as far away from the throne as possible. He had also not forgotten, nor perhaps forgiven, the personal challenge that Morarji had posed to his re-election for a second term as Congress President. He tried to bring about a consensus. He failed. Morarji had also made up his mind whether consensus or confrontation, Kamray's choice was Nehru's daughter, Indira Gandhi.

She had youth in her favour. And yet she was just the age at which her own father first became the President of the Indian National Congress with Gandhi's help. She had the advantage of a great name and a great tradition. She had travelled widely with and without her father. She had played hostess to almost all the great celebrities of the world. She had been a witness from her infancy of the fire, the fury and the turmoil of the national struggle, though she was not one of its participants. She had already served as Congress President, and as a Minister in the Central Cabinet. She had not pursued a course of a conventional academic studies, but had a varied education in the humanities in India and abroad. Through intimate contacts with her illustrious grandfather, with Gandhi, with her teacher and preceptor, Gurudev Tagore, and under the tender guiding care of her own father, she had not only enriched her life with rare experience from a very tender age, but had also received a more diversified training in the culture and politics of the country than any university could offer. Her being an attractive woman, capable of holding her own in conversation or debate, added to the spectacular character of the choice.

For the first time, the Congress Party was going to adopt the democratic methods of secret ballot, in choosing its leader. Though I had my own reservations like most of the members of Nehru family and their close associates, I was thrilled with the prospect of her giving a fight to Morarji Desai, with whose fads, and politics I was disgusted.

When she arrived in Parliament House to proceed to Central Hall to witness her election, I myself with the Delhi Congress leader Subhadra Joshi received her on the gate offering her roses. We sat beside her when she watched the Members of Parliament trooping to polling booth to elect their future leader.

Indira Gandhi was put up as candidate by 'Syndicate' and supported by most of the Congress Chief Ministers, the choice by them was with ulterior motive, for they knew that never in her life she had ever contested a legislative or organisational election. She was inducted by Lal Bahadur as Minister of Broadcasting by being nominated to Rajya Sabha. Even when she joined Congress Working Committee and later became Congress President, she was a nominated member of the A.I.C.C. She inflicted a convincing defeat on Morarji. The fact that she was pitted against one of the most outstanding living veterans of the national struggle and not a non-entity was important for her. This gave her the self-confidence someone in her position was in need of, to confront a mountain-heap of problems still facing the country.

In the initial stages she appeared to be reserved, and nervous. Dr. Ram Manohar Lohia, described her on the floor of the House as 'Goongi Gudia', a 'dumb-doll'. But soon she started building her image, by inducting a 'Kitchen Cabinet', of some youthful leftists in the party. As Congress President, during a critical period, Indira Gandhi more than anyone else, realised the extent of corruption that had set into the party, and the virtual sand dunes of bogus membership on which power was being sustained. Casteism, groupism and bossism now vitiated the whole atmosphere, and the snobbery and extravagance of those in office nauseated the common people. The choice the Prime Minister now faced was either to embark on a major purge within the Congress, risk the breaking up of the party or preserve the *status quo* or wait till the elections were over. If it had taken eighteen years for the party to descend to the abyss of sloth and opportunism, she argued, she did not have as many months before the elections to clean up the mess and to revitalise the organisation from the base. It was a Herculean task! She thought it best to leave things along till the elections were over. At the same time, she felt that even though these inherited weaknesses in the Party could handicap its success, the elections by themselves may do some heavy pruning, and remove in the process a lot of deadwood which would otherwise not be possible through party action. Her main consolation at this juncture lay in the realisation that if her own party had become weak, the Opposition Parties by and large had a mediocre leadership, and were also divided both at the Centre and in the States none of them was singly so strong as to completely overthrow the Congress.

During the war the department of Food and Civil Supplies were created. In 1946, when the Congress assumed offices in provinces, these departments survived, in view of the shortage of food and other commodities, within a short time of assumption of offices, they became a source of corruption.

It is interesting to note that all those ministers who dealt with Food and Civil supplies ultimately managed to become the Chief Ministers.

In this connection, I can mention the names of Pratap Singh Kairon in Punjab, C.B. Gupta in U.P., Krishna Ballabh Pant in Bihar, P.C. Sen in Bengal and Y.B. Chavan in Bombay.

They owed their promotion for they had tremendous power to oblige the M.L.As and rally round themselves their support by temptation of making money.

The white Gandhi cap, which was once the symbol of suffering and sacrifices came to be associated with corruption and blackmarketing. Though Nehru was aware of these misdeeds of many, but he put all the complaints under the carpet.

On demand of Punjab Congressmen an enquiry was made about Pratap Singh Kairon, he was found guilty of corruption by his family. Though he was made to resign, Nehru remarked that he had only constructive res-ponsibility.

Lal Bahadur though anxious to fight the corruption had not the time to deal with it. In the initial days of her Prime Ministership, Indira Gandhi was too much dependent on the support of the 'Syndicate' and the corrupt politicians enjoyed their protection.

February 1967, almost twelve months after she had assumed charge as Prime Minister, marked the climax of 'Operation Survival'. During the previous three general elections, Jawaharlal Nehru had been the Chief Campaigner on behalf of the party. The marathon tour Indira Gandhi undertook as chief campaigner of the Congress was no less strenuous, and no less exhausting. But it was not all garlands and rose petals. While thousands shouted,'Indira Gandhi Zindabad', there were booing and catcalls, black flags and hecklings, cheers and jeers and even at one place, she had to leave the meeting with a bleeding nose. Unlike her father, she was undertaking the campaign not to insure the success of 'every donkey' or 'lamp post' with a Congress ticket, but to salvage as much of the strength, the popularity and public support for the party as she could, against heavy odds.

Indira Gandhi was facing a very difficult situation. The electorate in the states were disgusted with the tales of corruption, nepotism and administration by the Congress ministers. Nehru, a giant and darling of the nation, was no more there to act as a buffer and to absorb the anger and anguish of the people. Indira Gandhi had yet to achieve a national status.

On the eve of the election, there was a massive demonstration of Hindu youth led by saffron clad Sadhus demanding the total ban on cow slaughter.

The demonstrators tried to enter the premises of Parliament, and when they were dispersed by the police, they attacked the house of Congress President, and burn a number of vehicles. Some young men were arrested and kept in custody for few days. On their release they got heroes' reception from orthodox Hindus particularly women.

I was contesting election for the third time from my constituency in Budaun. I had to face the attack from Hindu communalists, who accused me to belong to a party which condoned the slaughters of holy cow, and was denounced by Muslim fundamentalists for having pleaded to give Aligarh Muslim University a secular character. All my efforts to counteract the campaign of Jan Sangh communalists and Muslim fundamentalists, failed and I was defeated by a non-entity candidate set up by Jan Sangh.

My performance was repeated in Delhi and entire west U.P. Prominent freedom fighters like Mahavir Tyagi, Ajit Prasad Jain and INA hero Shahnawaz Khan were floored.

Having accepted my defeat I was listening to AIR bulletin which was more like Cricket scores.

By the time the day had ended, the Congress had lost in six States — Kerala, Madras, Punjab, Rajasthan, Orissa and West Bengal. It had lost every seat for the Lok Sabha in Madras. The voice on the microphone announced that the

Congress President, Kamaraj, had been defeated in his home constituency, Virudhunagar, by a 28 year old student leader, Srinivasa! The voice continued: S.K. Patil, the Congress Treasurer, Atulya Ghosh, a senior member of the 'Syndicate' Industries Minister, Sanjivayya and Food Minister, Subramanyam had been thrown out. Finance Minister, Sachin Chowdhury and Commerce Minister, Manubhai Shah had been badly mauled. The whole Madras Cabinet had been practically defeated. The Chief Minister of West Bengal, P.C. Sen, had been thrown out. At the Centre, half of the Union Cabinet had been unseated. During the period the Prime Minister stayed, she continued to smile. Was she pleased or was she perplexed? No one could ask, nor did her smile offer an answer. However, All India Radio announced "Mrs Indira Gandhi has been elected". Next day it was declared that she had beaten her rival by 91,000 votes.

After practically twenty years of dictatorship, the Congress Party had now been cut to size. The electorate had rejected some of the tall poppies, and swept away a lot of the Party's deadwood. Democracy could now make a new start, and the Congress, as a result of the shock could revitalise itself, if it chose, under new leadership.

Indira Gandhi was elected Prime Minister without opposition. As an act of prudence and as a gesture of goodwill, she invited Morarji Desai to become Deputy Prime Minister and Finance Minister. Opposition parties combined to form coalition Governments where the Congress had been defeated. They even entered into improvised pacts to challenge Congress supremacy where it had obtained tenous majorities.

Now, Indira Gandhi was free from the bondage of the syndicate. The General Election of 1967, had cut most of them to size. Since long, they had no credibility. The rank and file of the Congress was disgusted with their arrogance and bossism. Indira had her hand on the pulse of the people and her own party.

I had known her from my early days in public life. My assessment of her had to go a complete change when she assumed the office of India's Prime Minister. The otherwise meek and shy young lady was transformed into a great political strategist.

She was waiting for a chance to fight and give a final blow to syndicate. Her opportunity came, when Dr Zakir Hussain, President of India suddenly died. The Congress Party had to sponsor a presidential candidate in his place.

At the meeting of Congress High Command her suggestion to give Jagjivan Ram, the Harijan leader, a chance was brushed aside. By majority Sanjiva Reddy the Speaker of Lok Sabha was selected. Indira Gandhi took his selection as a challenge to her supremacy. The plan that Indira Gandhi devised with the advice of D.P. Misra, the wily Chief Minister of Madhya Pradesh, was to provoke Kamraj and the syndicate to open fight. The leftists within the Congress Party were advised to denounce, the syndicate, and its members as a gang of right reactionaries. Indira Gandhi was made to believe that Sanjiva Reddy as a President would be a threat to her supremacy. She had a sense of insecurity from her childhood, and this threat made her to act as a wounded tigress.

Already at the meeting at which Reddy was chosen as the party candidate for Presidentship, Indira, was a party to this decision. But, she felt cheated. Indira now tried personal provocation. She used her prerogative as Prime Minister to strip Desai of his Finance portfolio on the plea that his known conservatism and personal association with big business disqualified him being entrusted with the implementation of the radical policies she wished to pursue.

Her dramatic action had some part of the effect she intended. It focussed nationwide attention on the conflict and gave it, at least in the public mind, an ideological basis. Instead of seeming another factional fight for personal power, all too familiar in Indian politics, Indira's challenge began to look like a strong minded and brave attempt to dislodge obscurantists. It also brought Desai's resignation from the government, for, as was expected, he refused to accept the slur on his integrity and continue to serve as Minister without portfolio. But, she still had failed to draw the Syndicate out of its lair.

Neither Chavan, who had sided with the Syndicate over Reddy's selection and who was supposed to be with it in ousting the Prime Minister, nor even close associates of Desai chose at that stage to precipitate a crisis by resigning from the Cabinet and creating a fullscale crisis. If anything, members of the Syndicate endeavoured to deflect Indira from the path of direct confrontation by publicly assuring her of their good faith towards her. Reddy himself issued press statement vowing to act, if elected, only as the constitutional head with no policy or programme of his own. He even wrote a personal letter to the Prime Minister seeking her goodwill and support.

In the plan of action that she had been executing with the precision of an experienced chess player, Indira made one false move. In a moment of weakness, when her resolve for a showdown had not hardened sufficiently and her strategy had apparently not taken precise shape, she had allowed herself to be persuaded to endorse Reddy's selection and to sign his formal nomination papers before the Election Commission as a proposer. Her action, probably, also taken when she still hoped that the Syndicate would be drawn into the open before the poll. Now hung round her neck like a moral albatross, how could she work for the defeat of one who was the party's choice and whom she had herself formally endorsed?

A way out of this curious dilemma was proved by a tactical blunder that Nijalingappa made a few days before the poll was scheduled to be held. He met with leaders of the Jana Sangh, a right-wing Hindu-dominated political organization, and the Swatantra Party, an avowedly conservative party, to seek their support in Reddy's election. Although the Congress Party itself had always abounded in communal or religious as well as conservative elements, it had in the past regarded the Jana Sangh and Swatantra Party with unconcealed disdain and dismissed any proposal for cooperation with either of them as ideologically abhorrent. Nijalingappa's action in holding private talks with the two parties was immediately announced by Indira's followers as an unpardonable sin. This made it impossible for the supposedly socialistic wing of the party to co-operate with the Syndicate. When Nijalingappa protested that it was merely his anxiety to ensure the success of the party nominee that prompted his initiative, the other side hurled at him the accusation that his meetings were really part of the conspiracy to topple Indira's government and make Desai the Prime Minister — with the help, if necessary, of the opposition parties. Indira, who had until then declined to issue to the party members the customary directive instructing them to vote for Reddy, argued that Nijalingappa's 'perfidious' activities left her with no option but to advise members to exercise 'the freedom of conscience' in voting for their choice among various presidential nominees.

Giri, who, as acting President, had earlier put forward his claim to being elected in his own right, was virtually adopted by Indira's supporters as their nominee. Arjun Arora and some leftists in the Congress party announced their resolve to vote for him. Indira's efforts to defeat the official nominee of her own party suffered from no sense of self-consciousness on her part or any doubts about their propriety.

Backing Giri against Reddy, particularly when the poll was due to take place in less than a fortnight, was a gamble. Indira and some of her associates in Delhi undoubtedly were convinced they had no option except to fight the Old Guard. But would legislators in the various State Assemblies who constituted the bulk of the electorate in the presidential poll share their sense of desperation? This was no ordinary election in which Indira with her charismatic family associations could appeal to the masses over the heads of the party bosses. Giri was not a particularly strong or appealing candidate. However, circumstances were such that Indira had to back him. She did so unreservedly. She contacted the Chief Ministers of all States, including those who did not belong to the Congress Party or were closely affiliated to the Syndicate. She also personally appealed to a large number of prominent legislators in the State.

Once the gamble over the President's election was won, events began to happen strictly in accordance with the pattern Indira and Mishra had envisaged their strategy. With Reddy defeated, Desai and Syndicate humbled, and the sword of Damocles that had hung over her government at least moved aside. M.Ps and State legislators began shifting their loyalty with tremendous speed. The Syndicate hastened to pick up the pieces and salvage as much of its hold over the organisation as it could but the inevitable split in the ruling party occurred, only ten weeks after the presidential poll. When the time came to choose sides a large number of those who had voted against Giri decided to stay with Indira, giving her the support of 204 of the ruling party's 279 members in the Lok Sabha.

The Old Guard leadership had lost much more than it seemed to realise at the time. Besides being deprived of the bulk of the parliamentary wing of the party and the usual source of its political strength, it had been routed in the propaganda war. The public image of the Syndicate, never very attractive, was tarnished further. Though it was undeniably a quarrel involving personal power, Indira had succeeded in presenting it to the public as a classical struggle between good and evil. By moving to nationalise banks to cancel the large privy purses still given (under the promise made at the time of Independence) annually to former princely rulers, and by forcing a reputedly right-wing leader like Desai out of the government, Indira had not only turned a personal fight into an ideological one but in the process had acquired for herself the image of a leader who felt deeply for the poor but whose effort to promote their interest were being thwarted by a power-hungry, corrupt clique of ageing leaders.

The Parliamentary elections were called a year ahead of time — they were normally due in the spring of 1972 — ostensibly because Indira found heading a minority government irksome and frustrating. The real reason for her using her prerogative as Prime Minister to advance the poll was her anxiety to translate into parliamentary strength the public approval her conflict with the Syndicate had generated. The party split had left her with the support of only a little over 200 members in a House of 525. She entered into no formal coalition with any other group in the Lok Sabha to secure the majority backing and, normally under the rules of Parliamentary Government, she should have tendered her resignation. But she was able to carry on her administration because, as proved in the voting for President, she enjoyed the tacit backing of the Communists, some socialists, and parliamentary representatives of certain regional parties like the Akali Dal of Punjab and the DMK of Tamil Nadu. But though it was the logical and obvious thing for her to do, her decision towards the end of 1970 to call the elections ahead of schedule took her opponents totally by surprise. The reports that she contemplated advancing the elections were frequently published in newspapers. Their appearance was invariably immediately followed, however, by vehement official denials. After a while, her opponents tended to believe the denials more than the press reports, she had won her gamble over the presidential election. In the elections the Congress Party wing headed by the Prime Minister hit the jackpot. It won 350 seats in a House of 525, thus ending its embarrassing dependence on illmatched allies and regaining for the party the type of majority that it had won in the earlier years when its role in the freedom struggle was fresh in memory. The rival faction of the Congress, which at the time of the 1969 split carried over 70 members in the Lok Sabha, contested 238 seats and won only 16 of them this despite the grand alliance that the Syndicate leaders had formed with certain opposition parties in an endeavour to avoid splintering of votes against Indira's party. Perhaps, owing to their association with the Syndicate now Indira Gandhi, like her father, was supremo of the Congress Party. She could have a rubber stamp Cabinet, for the ministers could be hired and fired at her will.

It was soon seen that unlike her father, Jawaharlal Nehru, she had no use for even a semblance of collective leadership.

Chapter 25

CULT OF PERSONALITY

INDIANS have always believed in cult of personality. They worship Ram and Krishna, the mythical heroes as God. When a Lincoln's Inn trained lawyer gave up western attire for poor man's loin cloth and started living in an Ashram with the diet of goat's milk, he was transformed into a Mahatma, and Indian masses treated him as a demi-God.

There were number of stories of sacrifices and suffering popularised by we Congressmen about Nehru family. People were made to believe that Nehru discarded velvet and brocade for coarse khadi. The stories that his linen was washed in Paris, and he was a classmate of British heir, were contradicted by him only in English version of his autobiography published in 1936. They were allowed to go unchallenged for almost two decades.

After the nationalisation of Banks, and abolition of privy purse of former Indian princes, Indira Gandhi became a symbol of a crusader against poverty. Her success in ousting Syndicate, made her a valiant fighter against all that was corrupt in Indian body politic.

She decided to go to people for their mandate in 1971 much before the election was due.

In Delhi, after Independence, a new class of politicians-cum-contractor emerged. They would hire the required number of unemployed youth, slum dwellers, rickshaw pullers and daily wage earners by paying them a petty sum, and sometime a small packet of ground nut or gram to march for any sort of demonstration.

Often their services were utilised by the protocol Department of the External Affairs Ministry. They were handed over flags to wave at the airport to receive the visiting dignitaries without knowing their identity.

They are often used by various Friendship Associations, to demonstrate before respective embassies in their support or in protest against the issue which they hardly knew.

After the abolition of privy purse and Bank nationalisation, some of the 'leftists' supporters found the services of these contractors very handy. The innocent demonstrators were brought on buses and trucks at the round about, in front of Indira Gandhi's residence, 1, Safdarjung Road, shouting slogans in her support. Indira Gandhi would emerge out from her residence, climb a rostrum and address them seeking their full support in her crusade to fight the right reaction and seek their support for her effort of 'Gharibi Hato', banishment of poverty.

The innocent demonstrators would disperse shouting 'desh ki neta Indira Gandhi', national leader Indira Gandhi.

Indira Gandhi would go back to her residence intoxicated with power and glory, and pride.

Indira Gandhi after nationalisation of banks and aboition of privy purses to Indian princes was floating on the highest crest. But the biggest opportunity was provided to her by Bangladesh War which brought her to the highest pinnacle of her political career.

As I have already pointed out that the emergence of Pakistan had made a geographical non-sense. Never in the ancient, medieval or modern history, a country was carved with two wings divided by hundreds of miles of no common boundary. The Congress leadership had accepted the partition of India in sheer frustration, and Jinnah had agreed to it to spite on his political rival Gandhi.

Jinnah pleaded to have a corridor between two wings. But the demand was so fantastic that neither Congress nor the British who acted as arbitrator of the destiny of sub-continent took it seriously.

The only thing common between two wings of Pakistan was Islamic faith. But the countries are not created on basis of religion. The entire Europe professed Christianity and Arab World was Muslim, but they were divided into many countries.

On August 14, 1947, in Karachi, Lord Louis Mountbatten laid the foundation of Pakistan. The two wings were to be known as West Pakistan, and East Pakistan. M.A. Jinnah, a Bombay based lawyer assumed the office of Governor-General and an emigrant from U.P., was appointed as Prime Minister. Under the agreement those belonging to Central Services and armed forces were given the option to serve either of the wing of sub-continent of their choice.

The overwhelming majority of the Muslim personnel opted for Pakistan. Since the armed personnel, mostly, came from

West Pakistan, they had no difficulty in adjusting themselves to new surroundings. But most of the civilians belonging to Indian sub-continent were treated as conquerors and intruders, by the vast masses of both the wings of Pakistan.

The East Pakistan had its own ethnic culture and language. They could not reconcile themselves by occupation of non-Bengali civilians, and army. They had their ethnic pride.

When Jinnah visited Dacca, the capital of East Bengal, he was received by hostile youths. They demanded that Bangla is a very rich language and it should be their official language.

In early fifties a number of linguistic riots took place, but they were ruthlessly suppressed by the Punjabi Army.

Though the Independence of India Act, 1947 provided a Constituent Assembly to India as well as Pakistan, unlike India, it could not frame any Constitution for free Pakistan.

The first Prime Minister of Pakistan, Nawabzada Liaquat Ali Khan was assassinated in mysterious circumstances. He was followed by almost half a dozen Prime Ministers, who had to resign or were sacked by the Presidents who were from services.

Ultimately, Martial Law was imposed and Pakistan had two successive army dictators. In 1971, the military under the pressure of American public opinion who were heavily financing Pakistan, held general election for National Assembly.

The East Pakistan which was the most popular wing of Pakistan gave overwhelming majority to the party headed by Sheikh Mujibur Rehman. He won 166 out of 167 seats. I had known him from his student's days in Calcutta. He was a man with progressive and leftist views.

In usual democratic process, he ought to have been invited to form a Ministry. But, he was not acceptable to army dictators and, apparently, to their masters in United States of America.

The military dictator, General Yahaya Khan, supported by the leader of West Pakistan was determined not to allow Mujib to form the Government. In East Pakistan Mujib started an agitation for provincial autonomy. It was mercilessly suppressed by the armed forces. Mujib was arrested and tried before a martial law tribunal, was charged with high treason and sentenced to death.

Most of the associates of Mujib managed to go underground, they were guided by Phani Majumdar a former revolutionary, and once a Secretary of Subhas Bose.

Ultimately, they were to reach Calcutta, to form a provisional government of free Bangladesh, and operate from Lower

Circular Road which was described as Mujib Nagar.

The Government at Islamabad placed East Bengal under military rule and appointed General Tikka Khan as military governor at Dacca, who later on came to be known as butcher of Bangladesh. The army composed entirely of Punjabis, Baluchis and Pathans indulged in atrocities which in heinousness could surpass the action of Nazi Germany in occupied Europe.

They butchered Bengali intellectuals, gang raped the innocent and young girls in their hostels of Dacca University. Their main targets were Hindus of East Pakistan whom they considered fifth columnist of Bharat.

Millions of refugees left their home and hearth to take shelter in India. Their arrival completely dislocated the economy of West Bengal.

Unlike her father, Indira Gandhi had no inhibitions about international norms. She secretly sent her military experts to train Bengali guerillas who came to be known as Bangla Bhaini. These Indian trained Bengali soldiers dislocated the means of communications, barricaded the roads and destroyed many bridges.

On October 4, Mrs Gandhi flew out of India. She visited Russia and the Western capitals, and she acted as spokesman for Bangladesh. What was happening there, she said, could not be allowed to continue. A whole nation was being systematically exterminated. It was genocide and it must be stopped. The implication was that though India wanted peace, it was prepared for war. In view of all the events that followed her trip, it was perfectly timed. She had explained the stance of her country and the tragedy of Bangladesh to the leaders of the world. She had furnished them with a background against which to interpret her subsequent actions.

The Bengalis have always been looked upon by most other Indians and by foreigners, such as Kipling, as talkers rather than doers. There is some justification in this, for they do talk, interminably, but they also have deep political involvement and the will to dedicate themselves to a cause. The Naxalite movement, one that demanded physical action rather than a dialogue, started up, after all, in Bengal. The Moghuls and the British had been mindful of the fact that the Bengalis were hard to handle; the Pakistanis were not. They had based their tactics in the east upon the illusion that the Bengalis would crumble under pressure, but they had been proved wrong. At the time of the initial attack there were about 70,000 armed Bengali personnel in East Pakistan, not only soldiers but some guards and members of other paramilitary organisations. The bulk of these, especially, those who were home guards, remained loyal to Pakistan but a number of them broke away. The police force, which numbered about 45,000 some armed, also decided to fight for independence. These forces coalesced with students and formed the guerilla army, the Mukti Fauj. Since most senior Bengali army and police officers had been arrested by the Pakistanis, the leaders of this army were usually very young men, some of whom, like 'Tiger' Siddiqui, whose forces were active in the Tgnigali area, in Mymensingh and around Dacca, became legendary figures. Politically the guerillas were a mixed bunch, but their motivation was patriotic rather than political, certainly at first.

The guerillas had the people behind them and they were equipped and trained by the Indian border forces. This meant that they were in no danger of betrayal and that they were not unskilled at their work. They harried the Pakistanis every day, but theirs was basically a nuisance value; unaided, they could not hope to push the invaders back into the sea. After April 1971 the activities of the Mukti Fauj slowed down somewhat and a new guerilla force, the Mukti Bahini emerged. This was not purely a land force; they had gun boats and sloops provided by India and operated in the rivers and waterway as well as on the open sea. Their gun boats intercepted foreign merchant vessels. The guerillas had an efficient information service. They shattered railway lines and helped to the activity of their land forces.

The Pakistanis, whenever the Guerillas struck at their forces, took their grievances out on the helpless peasantry with such ferocity that it seemed possible that the entire civilian populace would soon disappear. This inspired the peasants to an increased hatred of their masters, but slaughter and rape did not help the battle for freedom. Women of all ages, children and widows pregnant after rape, were to be found all over the country as well as in the Indian refugee camps.

The activities of the Mukti Bahini were thus, in a way, counterproductive, especially since they were embroiled, unassisted, against hopeless odds; every guerilla success was followed by a Pakistani reprisal. Resistance would soon falter without outside help; the real value of the Mukti Bahini was that they formed a pararamilitary wing throughout the country, which would be of immense help in terms of guidance and intelligence operations to any army that might come from outside. By November, 1971 it was clear whose army that would be.

The military commander in what the West Pakstanis still called 'East Pakistan' was General Amir Abdullah Khan Niazi, he sent forces out to pursue the Mukti Bahini whenever they took shelter beyond the Indian frontier. In the third week of October 1971, he declared to a crowd at a place called Said-put that "the war would be fought on Indian territory". Throughout November villages on the Indian side of the border were shelled by the West Pakistan artillery. Reconnaissance flights were made over Indian territory, in the East and the West by Pakistani Air Force planes. On November 25, Yahya Khan stated that "in ten days... I may not be here in Rawalpindi (then the capital of Pakistan), but off fighting a war..." Mrs. Gandhi told the officers of the eastern frontier that their troops were empowered to chase Pakistani forces back across the border, indeed into Bangladesh, "but only in self-defence".

The Chinese, Bhutto's friends, were at this time too involved in fighting the Russians on the Ussuri River over a frontier dispute to 'intervene'. They had, moreover, recently become members of the United Nations and did not want to fight a war that was not theirs. Bhutto led a delegation to Peking in November; what discussion the delegation had was not publicised, but they were obviously unsatisfactory to Pakistan. The State Department started to wag the flag at Mrs Gandhi. She did what she had to which was simply that she remained entirely unruffled.

A Prime Minister committed to war is special. He or she has to have a belief in what happens when soldiers, not necessarily, intelligent people, are released by one country upon another. The Prime Minister of India wanted an excuse to fight; basically, her people were fighting already. She had her excuse when the Pakistani Air Force decided to make an air strike upon India, to show the Indians that they could do so, and they also had the idea that they would make this air strike in the manner of the Israelis fighting the Egyptians in 1967. They dive-bombed nine Indian airbases on the western frontier in early December: they did so when there were no Indian Air Force planes on the runways. The Indians, therefore, went into attack.

They attacked on the western front, blasted what remained of the Pakistani Air Force out of the sky, and drove the armies back in the northern and eastern sectors. Then they turned their attention to Bangladesh; the general idea was to get there quickly. On December 4, 1971 the Indians following the Pakistani air strikes, declared war upon Pakistan. On December 6, they recognised Bangladesh as a country. By this time the Indians penetrated deep into Bangladesh. They had been preparing for this for a long while. The Eastern Command sector had been mainly for mountain warfare, but Mrs Gandhi had been reorganising it for river warfare, essential in the swamps of East Bengal. There was no doubt whatever that India had been readying itself for war, slowly but steadily, since the initial invasion, under quiet orders from a quiet woman.

Meanwhile, Nixon, on December 6, as India recognised Bangladesh, asked the Seventh Fleet to enter the Indian Ocean. The ostensible idea was that in case of a outright war, the Seventh Fleet would scoop American citizens up from Bangladesh and, keeping them happy with coke, bring them safely home. The Seventh Fleet not being a travel agency, but a fighting fleet, there was some doubt in India as to the real motive of this mission. But, the Indian troops were racing into Bangladesh as the Seventh Fleet floating over the long sea. The Mukti Bahini welcome them: so did the peasants; the big, turbaned Sikhs and the squat Gurkhas were garlanded in every village. The Indian Air Force bombed ahead: the Indian Navy were shepherds of the sea. It was typical of the pattern of warfare in the sub-continent that the first of the Indian commanders to reach Dacca had been with the Military Commander, General Niazi, at Shandhurst. The old boy network was still functional. The Indian commander sent his ADC under a white flag, into Dacca; the A.D.C. took a note to Niazi: it said: 'My dear Abdullah, I am here. The game is up. I suggest you give yourself up to me and I shall look after you' Eventually Niazi agreed.

The remainder of the Indian troops entered Dacca. At what had once been the race course, the instrument of Pakistani surrender was signed. It now remained to bring Mujib back to his own country and reinstall him as the leader of his people. Mujib under close arrest for months in West Pakistan was utterly bewildered by what had happened. He had expected death, not this astonishing release. Blinking through thick spectacles, wrapped in a very long and dirty overcoat, he was flown from West Pakistan to London, from London to New Delhi. At Palam Airport, Mrs Gandhi stood, smart and spry, to welcome him: a guard of honour awaited his salute. He flapped a hand in acknowledgement, and crowds thundered beyond the security perimete .. For him, returned from the dead, it was a tremendous moment: but for Mrs Gandhi, it must have been a climatic moment. She had performed the impossible. She had brought the leader of Bangladesh back as though from the dead. By this act she stood or she fell: it was ironic that, with the act so acclaimed, she fell, in a way, because of it, and more than ironic that the great leader, brought safely home, should have been killed by his own people three years later; and that Bangladesh should now be far more friendly with Pakistan than it is with India.

Mrs Gandhi had done it. She had achieved the status of a myth. She was Joan of Ark without the inconvenience of prison, fire and cross.

Her performance in 1971, had been brilliant, her decisions perfectly timed, as they had been when she came to power in 1966, as they had been when she engineered the split of the Congress Party in 1969. She could now do anything she wanted to without asking for advice from anyone. The Indian economy was shattered due to Bangladesh war and the people began to complain. Why, they wanted to know, had she spent so much money on foreigners? Why had she so minimal a sum to spend on the poor of India. The rampant corruption and her reliance on her favourite son Sanjay was breaking the patience of the people.

While I was attending a meeting of U.P. State Congress Committee, and was seated besides Indira Gandhi, I was handed over a note to be passed on to her. With twinkle in her eyes, she triumphantly announced that Dacca had surrendered. This was the greatest moment for her political career and she received standing ovation.

I was called upon to propose a resolution congratulating her in her victory. Obviously, I was jubilant and moved that the two nation theory propounded by Jinnah, and reluctantly for all practical purposes accepted by the Old Congress leaders was exploded by a young, dynamic and ambitious lady. She had redeemed the pledge of those who suffered and sacrificed to keep the unity of the country.

I reminded the audience that General Shah Nawaz was present there, who, under the leadership of Subhas Bose, had united all communities of India to march to Delhi.

Chapter 26

DARKNESS AT NOON

AFTER the victory in Bangladesh, Indira Gandhi was completely a changed person. It was not long after that those who called her incarnation of Durga and Saraswati started to name her a Hitler and Mussolini. She reduced her Cabinet colleagues to the status of glorified clerks. Even veterans Jagjivan Ram and Chavan became mere courtiers.

The faction of the Congress, both the Jana Sangh and Swatantra Parties, long regarded as potential rivals to the ruling party, declined noticeably in the 1971 election. The Swatantra following, for example, was reduced from forty-four in 1967 to a mere eight. Almost all political parties, on the Left as well as the Right, lost votes to the ruling party.

For Indira personally, it was a time of unprecedented political satisfaction. She now headed party with more than enough strength to form a stable government. Her detractors had been completely routed. The country's constitutional head was beholden to her for his election. Within her party not even Chavan nor Jagjivan Ram—had the temerity any longer to think of himself as possible rival. And outside the Government and Parliament the Indian masses looked to her with the kind of hope and faith that they had previously reposed only in Nehru and the Mahatma. They had turned out as voters that they never before turned out in a free and open election.

In choosing her Cabinet and allocating the various portfolios among its Members, she exercised unrestricted freedom. None of the Ministers had any doubt that he or she was in office at Indira's pleasure. Even the Young Turks in her party, noted for their brashness and arrogance, seemed overawed by her and, after the election, had little role to play. A leading Indian columnist writing about her rise to top leadership described her self-confidence and power as 'formidable' almost 'frightening', the Information and Broadcasting Minister of Lal Bahadur who had felt lost and vulnerable after her father's death, who was sometimes driven close to tears by the rough cuts from the opposition, who complained bitterly of being neglected by Shastri had come a long way.

She reacts with irritation to suggestions in India's newspapers and the legislatures that her commitment to preservation of democratic institution lacks her father's earnestness and that her action will conceal dictatorial tendencies on her part. In what way, she angrily asks, has her exercise of authority been different from that of her father?

The day she was due to arrive in Canada on a state visit a despatch in the *Toronto Star* referred to her (with awe or irony) as the 'Empress of India', an expression earlier also used by the *Economist* to describe Indira. Morarji Desai, by now, one of her most outspoken political opponents, remarked in the same period to visiting journalist that "she is not a communist; she is a fascist".

She started depending on the advice of her younger son Sanjay, a school drop-out. Even a seasoned bureaucrat P.N. Haksar, who, for long time, was her confidant had to quit in disgust.

'Indira Gandhi' after coming to power in 1971, had created a Kitchen Cabinet,' but apparently she had no use for it now. A former Secretary of Marwari Chamber of Commerce without any political background, Uma Shankar Dikshit for a short time became one of her confidants. Though only a few years earlier he had retired as an obscure officer in Ministry of Rehabilitation, he adorned the seat of Home Ministry formerly occupied by Sardar Patel, and Govind Ballabh Pant.

It was her husband Feroze Gandhi who had floated the idea of producing the small car to break the monopoly of automobile giants. But, Nehru who was against any sort of consumerism did not approve it. In fact, in his lifetime, he did not allow, even T.V., to come to India, though a much smaller neighbouring country, Pakistan, had it.

The proposal to produce small car kept on moving between various Ministries and Planning Commission without being implemented either in private or public sector.

Sanjay, the younger son of Indira Gandhi, who was described as a crown prince, had ambition to produce a small car. He had never attended any college or technical institute. He had learnt some elementary mechanics of automobile from the wayside car repairers. One of them Arjun Das became his life long friend and, at one stage, became a terror for Delhi citizens.

An obliging Chief Minister, of Haryana alloted Sanjay a huge plot of land in the vicinity of an Air Force complex, a few miles away from Delhi, and Sanjay floated Maruti Company. He applied to the Government of India for the licence to produce small car.

This was to be built without foreign aid of any kind and made readily available to the masses. In 1970 Sanjay became the only one of the applicants to be granted the licence. He declared that he would produce 50,000 cars a year and the Maruti Car factory was started. But the granting of the licence to Sanjay, whose qualification seemed mainly to rest in his heredity, was immediately bitterly criticised, in Parliament as well in the Press. Mrs Gandhi was charged with nepotism.

Moreover, shortly before the Maruti licence was issued, she was accused of attempting to suppress the freedom of the press. The Ministry of Information and Broadcasting drafted a scheme to diffuse the ownership of newspaper with a large circulation. Ninety-five per cent of the shares in each such newspaper, it was proposed should be allocated to the staff. Five per cent would remain with existing shareholders, no shareholder would have more than half a vote per share in management and policy decisions. The other half of the votes, fifty per cent of the total, would be invested in a person appointed by the Government. This scheme very naturally created a considerable amount of criticism if it was carried through, it would mean that the government was to all intents and purposes in control of the chief newspapers. Did Mrs: Gandhi, asked some leading editors wanted to become a dictator?

1971 brought up a further storm cloud. On May 24, the chief cashier of the State Bank of India in Delhi, V.P. Malhotra, was telephoned by a person who identified herself as the Prime Minister. This disembodied voice ordered him to take Rs. 6 million out of the Bank, carry it to stated spot in the city, and hand it over to a man he would meet there. This man would identify himself by saying that he was the 'Bangladeshi clerk'. Malhotra did all this, and then returned to the residence of the Prime Minister to report the completion of his mission. Haksar, the Principal Secretary, utterly horrified said, that Mrs Gandhi had never made such a call, and advised Malhotra to pay a rapid visit to the police. 'The Bangladeshi clerk' was traced the same day, for he made no attempt to cover his trail, and the money was recovered. 'The Bangladeshi clerk' turned out to be Rustum Sohrab Nagarwala, a Parsi officer from the Research and Analysis Wing (RAW), an intelligence organisation founded by Mrs. Gandhi was described by the Communist leader, Jyotirmoy Bosu as fascist in its methods. Nagarwala, the police said, had told them after his arrest that he had imitated Mrs Gandhi's voice on the telephone and that he wanted the money to support the freedom movement in Bangladesh. The tape on which this confession was allegedly recorded was never produced in court, in spite of which Nagarwala was sentenced to four years imprisonment. He made an abortive attempt to tell his story to editor of a Bombay paper of dubious reputation, and also asked for a re-trial, for as he said, his case had been dealt with by three different magistrates in three days, and had been conducted at a speed hitherto unheard of in the courts of India. Nagarwala died in mysterious circumstances in prison in 1972. Mrs Gandhi's opponents accused her by implication for having arranged for his death to stop him from involving her in the matter. The whole business was described in Sherlock Holmes style by one such person as 'a murky plot'.

Malhotra later was appointed as financial adviser in Maruti & Company owned by Sanjay Gandhi.

All kinds of rumours were in air about the influence of Sanjay on his mother, and a mysterious hold he was supposed to have over her to bend her to his will. These had been intensified by Mrs. Gandhi's reticence during the uproar over the Maruti licence. Not only had she not said enough, but she had seemed uninterested by the uproar; she had pursed her lips and turned her partisan head away. This apparent contempt for her critics had naturally maddened them still further. It was taken as a Gospel truth — in many circles that Mrs Gandhi had deliberately intervened to procure the licence for her son. Once Sanjay had applied for his licence, he was virtually certain of obtaining it. Opposition pressed for an enquiry, and mentioned Sanjay's youth, inexperience, and lack of qualifications. Mr Gandhi shrugged her shoulders. Her main argument was that it was unfair to demand that a young man, because he was the son of a Prime Minister should be forbidden from taking up work in which he was interested. She interposed herself between her son and his hunters, in doing so, she exposed herself. The attacks upon her in the press increased in intensity. Mrs Gandhi had a fixed distrust of Indian media (when it is not under her control) which manifested itself.

Sanjay Gandhi became the most powerful extraconstitutional authority in New Delhi. The Secretaries of Government of India would attend to him, and implement the orders conveyed to them.

The Chief Minister in Congress governed states with the exception of H.N. Bahuguna of U.P. counted him as crown prince and were often seen acting as dancing to his tune.

The entire political atmosphere was vitiated by sycophancy, corruption and nepotism. Jaya Prakash Narayan known as J.P. the veteran socialist leader emerged out from his hide out and practical retirement from politics to lead the agitation in Bihar. The state of Gujarat was already in flames, the Congress legislators were jeered and booed in the streets.

Indira Gandhi got greatest shock of her life on 12 June, 1975, when Justice Sinha of Allahabad High Court set aside her election on charges of corrupt practices.

In any event, said Justice Sinha, and warned the public present in the court not to create noisy scenes after he had delivered his verdict, he had no alternative but to find the Prime Minister guilty of the charges, and to debar her, as the existing law prescribed, from election to any House of Parliament or any State Legislature for the next six years. Her election from Rae Bareilly in 1971 was declared null and void. A stay order of twenty days was granted so that the Congress Parliamentary Party could find a new Prime Minister and the country would not be left entirely leaderless.

There was pandemonium in the court after this, and a rush of reporters towards telephones. The official order was signed by Justice Sinha. A seal was affixed by a court official, sentence had been passed, and supposedly the case was closed.

Mrs Gandhi heard the news in Delhi, and remained, at least outwardly, unmoved. Her entire cabinet was at her house, pledging their undivided loyalty. In the case of some people, such as Chavan and Jagjivan Ram, this loyalty might have been caused by terror; they did not know what the lady would do, but knowing her, thought she would do something to fight back, turn her enemies, and they wanted to keep their options open.

As a matter of fact, Mrs Gandhi appears, for once, to have been willing at first to bow before the blast. But the advice of her favourite son Sanjay prevailed.

After the High Court order, Mrs Gandhi appealed to the Supreme Court. There were huge rallies protesting against the Allahabad verdict, and pressing her to stay in power; these were organised by her party on the old Indian political precept of a rupee a cheer. Since she showed no sign of movement the Opposition started further agitation. J.P. declared march on Delhi to be made by people from all over the country, the purpose of which was to force her from her throne.

On the night of June 25, 1975, as a dusty air swept uncollected rubbish off the pavements and streets the daily newspapers were being put to bed when the lights failed and the presses stopped. The service systems in Delhi, indeed in India, telephones, power, water supply are notoriously unreliable. 'It all come on against in a few minutes' many thought it a routine affair.'

That night, most of the opposition leaders including J.P. and Morarji Desai, were picked up by the police and taken away to prisons. A few newspaper men were also arrested as also activists and workers of the opposition parties. The next day, June 26, newspapers were not available but the All India Radio said that a state of internal emergency in the country had been declared by the President. There was already a state of external emergency, since the declaration made at the start of the war with Pakistan in 1971, had never been rescinded, despite the protests of J.P. and the opposition.

The initial operations of the 1975 emergency resembled the initial operations of any political coup, though this was a coup made the wrong way round, by a government against its opposition rather than by opposition against its government. Had Mrs Gandhi made her move earlier, knowing the country was in a obvious state of disruption due to the tactics of J.P. and the opposition she would probably have been much less criticised than she was when she eventually made it under the shadow of her own deposition from power.

India which enjoyed a parliamentary democracy under Nehru and Lal Bahadur was transformed into a police state. She managed to get the approval of her captive cabinet and a rubber stamp President of India. From now on her son Sanjay became the real ruler of India.

Obviously, I was not a silent spectator to this tragic drama. My reaction had been ably and adequately described by my old friend and colleague in his book *That Woman,* by Khwaja Ahmed Abbas. An extract of this does full justice to my feelings.

20th March 1977

ANSAR HARVANI: LETTER OF RESIGNATION

10 A.M.

He was the same age as the Prime Minister, to be exact, six months older!

He sat down on his verandah, 204, Rose Avenue, with a writing pad and pen to write the most momentous letter in his life. He felt depressed and wary, had innumerable cups of tea before he scribbled "Dear Indiraji".

Then he stopped and remembered the nearly forty years of loyal association with the Congress that he was now going to cut asunder. The umbilical cord that joined him to the organisation, which had nourished him and supplied him with his political life-blood, had to be cut and cut today, for the day was symbolic and historic.

He remembered the day he had joined the organisation the lone member of the Congress in the Aligarh Muslim University. He had worn khaddar trousers, khaddar black shervani, and even khadi-improvised fez cap which was compulsory part of the uniform. But the fez cap was foreign and made in Italy or by Christy's in London. He was then an Intermediate student of the University, but he was a born orator, and has speeches in the Jama Masjid after Friday prayers were fiery and yet well informed. He denounced the communalists and sworn allegiance to Mahatma Gandhi, Jawaharlal Nehru and Maulana Azad.

After his graduation from Aligarh, he joined the staff of *National Herald,* because Jawaharlal Nehru was its Chairman of the Board of Directors. And the young man had an affinity for Jawaharlal and his whole family especially the frail and sick Kamala Nehru. He loved her like a mother. How brave she was. He could shed tears when the Reuter would bring more news of her death in far away Lausanne in Switzerland. But he was consoled by the thought that Indira was with her mother and would be a source of strength for her father.

He still remembered the day he had first set eyes on 'Indu' (as Indira was affectionately called by her family). She was a slim and frail child who looked much younger than her age. She looked half-famished but it was not physical food that she lacked, but emotional food the love of her father and mother, both of whom were in jail. As a correspondent of *National Herald* he had gone to write a story, 'Anand Bhawan without Nehru'. Besides servants, 'Indu' was the sole occupant of the house. But she carried herself with a dignity and modest self-assurance that went straight to the heart of the young reporter. "Can I do anything for you, Indu-ji?" "Send me a copy of the Herald first thing in the morning. I have to wait hours for it".

After Harvani was filled with a new resolve that day. "I would protect her — till her father is released from jail". The *National Herald* was published from Lucknow, the capital of U.P., and Indira was living in Anand Bhawan, Allahabad. It took at least four hours for the copies to reach that city. But, Ansar arranged for a second dak edition to be sent to Anand Bhawan by post especially the first copy which was marked in red pencil where his article about. 'Anand Bhawan Without Nehru' was printed.

"Dear Indira Ji", he wrote again, "it is with a heavy heart that this morning I have decided to quit the Congress, to which, during the last forty years, I gave my time, toil, talent and tears for all that they were worth".

Again he remembered when and how he had signed the form of membership and beloved figures came crowding in his mind:

"I joined the Congress in 1928, as a volunteer pageboy of Dr. M. A. Ansari when he presided over the National Convention to adopt the Nehru Committee Report prepared by your grandfather. I helped your father in arranging the chairs for eminent leaders like Mrs. Annie Besant, Pandit Madan Mohan Malviya, Lala Lajpat Rai, Srinivasa Shastri, Maulana Azad, J.N. Sen Gupta, Subhas Bose, young M.C. Chagla and others who are no mere".

He was exhausted by the rush of memories of his youth and overcome by the affection that he had received from all the leaders, especially one who is hardly remembered today, imbibing a fresh cup of tea to refresh himself, he wrote:

"Will you believe, Indiraji, I was personally more attached to the greatest specimen of Indian womanhood, that was your mother Kamlaji than to your father, whom I admired, and for some time even worshipped, politically?"

"Netaji and your father inspired me to build up a students and youth movement. I organised the first students' conference at Lucknow inaugurated by your father and presided over by M.A. Jinnah."

He further pointed out, that "I feel ashamed to be associated with an organisation, which has reached its lowest depth under your leadership. It is a pathetic sight for me to see the Congress Chief Minister hanging round

> Sanjay Gandhi, an ordinary automobile mechanic whose only claim to power is that he is your son by accident of birth".

More than seventy thousand men and women, including the leaders of all of the opposition parties were put behind bars. The gang of four Sanjay, Om Mehta, Bansi Lal and Vidya Charan Shukla were law by themselves and they reduced India to a concentration camp.

It was really darkness at noon. Those who admired Nehrus, only dreaded them now.

It was unfortunate that Janta Experiment failed at the altar of the ego of its leaders, Jai Prakash Narayan, who had never displayed any quality of leadership was too ill to be effective, Morarji with all his fads and a corrupt son round his neck was a liability, Charan Singh whom I had known from 1937 was a small time politician, who visited Madras for the first time when, he became Home Minister, was too small a person to assume national leadership.

Chapter 27

UNEASY INTERVAL

INDIRA GANDHI, like her father Jawaharlal Nehru, was very conscious of her international image. Nehru, in early days of Prime Ministership, had agreed to hand over the so-called Kashmir dispute to United Nations, just to keep up his international image, though later events showed that the country had regretted this decision.

The stories of atrocities during her emergency regime were heavily censored in her own country, but the press and people in free world were alarmed by it. Though she had enlisted the services of some non-resident Indians, who were beneficiaries of her regime, prominent among them was Swaraj Paul, a small time Punjabi businessman who had become overnight a business tycoon in London with her help and some say with her finances they were no match to human right activists.

I have already mentioned that she was being described as 'Empress of India', and her favourite son Sanjay as 'Crown Prince'. She was anxious to have legitimacy for her autocratic regime. She was a gambler and in the past her gamble had always paid her.

With time Emergency rule had become arbitrary, capricious and often cruel. The trappings of dictatorship were visible, India was reduced to a police state. The apparatus for such an undertaking required a political and financial investment which Indira Gandhi was clearly not prepared to make. Perhaps she recalled her father's words of warning "All of us", he had told her, "are various mixtures of the good and the great and the little and the quest for overmuch power is a dangerous one. Sooner or later downfall and ruin comes to individuals or nations who seek it".

On 18 January, 1977, Indira Gandhi surrendered to her finer instincts and called general election. Her opponents were released from prison and the press unshackled. Cocooned from healthy contact with representative sections of her fellow citizens by courtiers and an over-protective staff, she had little idea of the blow that awaited her. But the writing was becoming clearer on the wall. The greatest jolt came to her when within hours of the announcement of decision to go to poll, she was deserted by her seniormost colleagues, Jagjivan Ram, the undisputed leader of Harijans who constituted almost one-sixth of the population of the country. In her own home State, Uttar Pradesh, H.N. Bahuguna who has been the most successful and dynamic Chief Minister after Independence, also parted company with her.

Indira Gandhi had calculated that her opponents recently freed from jails had neither resources nor the necessary image to fight her. Jai Prakash Narain, about whom I have already written was considered by her a spent force. It is true that J.P., who was one of the founder of Congress Socialist Party and in frustration had joined Vinob' a's Bhoodan movement and often championed the causes like the support to Naga insurgents, praising basic democracy of Pakistani dictator Ayub, supporting some elements in Kashmir with dubious loyalty to India but he became a rallying point for those who had suffered under emergency regime. He was depicted as incarnation of a Gandhi. The poll held on the 22nd of that month brought news of a disaster, Congress had been trounced in the north where the majority of the parliamentary seats lay. She herself was defeated at her Rae Bareilly constituency by Raj Narain, while Sanjay lost at Amethi to an obscure opponent. The South remained loyal to Indira, since the Emergency's excesses were less evident there. Janata had triumphed against most predictions. The people of India, while initially accepting the need for the Emergency as a short-term shock, had refused to accept it as a way of life.

The election having been sprung on the country with scant warning, Janata decided to await the results before selecting its leader. The Front was in reality a loose grouping of parties, from the past 1969 Congress rump headed by Morarji Desai, the Socialists, Charan Singh's followers, the right wing Hindu Jana Sangh to Jagjivan Ram's hastily formed Congress For Democracy, it took a month and more after their collective victory, before these disparate groups came together formally under common Janata banner. With Jaya Prakash Narayan's benediction, Morarji Desai was elected party leader and Prime Minister. It was a windfall for Janata Party, and three claimants emerged out for the prized position of Prime Ministership. Jagjivan Ram a seasoned politician, great administrator, had all the qualities of statesmanship, but belonged to Scheduled Caste. Morarji Desai, the perpetual claimant for throne, was a fadist, and Charan Singh a small time politician, who claimed his following on his caste basis.

Instead of permitting the party to elect its own leader, J.P., who had now assumed the title of 'Lok Nayak' imposed Morarji Desai as his choice with disastrous results.

The next two and a half years were a period of low comedy. The Ministers fought among themselves and struggled to undo any progress the country had achieved. Raj Narain, the Health Minister, stopped all family planning and suggested that pregnant women ate herbs. He refused to answer questions in Parliament unless they were framed in Hindi. Like his Prime Minister, he, too, was a urine therapist and a fanatical prohibitionist. Charan Singh, opposed industrial development. The rich farmer was, according to his gospel, the salt of the earth. As Finance Minister, he was later to construct a budget so unique that everything from food-stuffs to soap disappeared from the market.

Presiding over this ministerial circus was Morarji Desai, a Calvinstic figure, with minimal respect for most of humankind. He had little time for anything he did not understand, hence science and technology received diminishing government support and at the end of his tenure morale within the country's scientific community had sunk so low that many leading scientists seriously contemplated moving abroad where their skills would be better appreciated. The particular areas of the economy suffered most from all this: plans for the peaceful uses of nuclear energy and population control.

But the Janata Government's major concern was Mrs. Gandhi. Atal Bihari Vajpayee, the Foreign Minister, relegated her to the 'rubbish bin of history'. His colleagues apparently felt she was a danger to them, even there. Like the Romans, who continued to be petrified by Hannibal despite his defeat at Zama, the Janata leaders were haunted by Mrs. Gandhi, their famous unity cemented only by fear and hatred of her.

The former Prime Minister 'shocked at her changed circumstances was clearly visible in the early weeks after her fall. There was talk of her retiring from politics and fading into private life, a sign of her low spirits. The Congress debacle had brought its usual stock of defections, led by former ministers, Yashwant Rao Chavan, Karan Singh, Swaran Singh and K.C. Pant. Chavan suddenly discovered failings in her about which he had apparently been oblivious as a member of her Government. The party split yet again in January 1978 with Congress (R) now challenging the legitimacy of Indira Gandhi's Congress (I).

However, Janata's fear and petty vindictiveness brought Indira Gandhi well and truly back on to the national stage. On October 3, 1977, she was arrested on the orders of Charan Singh, then Home Minister, on charges of corrupt practice, but as no evidence was furnished, to back these up, Delhi's Chief Metropolitan Magistrate released her the next day. The whole drama was played out, thanks to Mrs Gandhi's thespian instincts, before television cameras and droves of newspaper reporters.

In contrast to this one act play, the sittings of the Shah Commission, set up under a former Chief Justice of the Supreme Court J.C. Shah to inquire into the Emergency excesses, became the nation's longest running serial. The judge had clearly seen better days at the bar. An irascible old man moved by a deep dislike of his principal witness, he was driven to distraction of Mrs Gandhi's refusal to answer questions which she felt breached the confidentiality of her office. He sentenced Sanjay to a month's imprisonment for tampering with witnesses. The Commission did finally produce a damning indictment of the former Prime Minister's misdeeds but by this time it resembled both a star chamber and comic opera and people had simply ceased to believe in its credentials. When Indira Gandhi returned back to power, all of the copies of report were destroyed and future historians will have to search it.

Meanwhile, Mrs Gandhi, her back to the wall, was fighting back. She trudged up and down the country, addressing public meetings, visiting scenes of man-made and natural disasters which seem habitually to strike India. She moved among the crowds with an astonishing lack of concern for her own security; she shared their woes, comforted them in their troubles, while her opponents in Government sat hermetically sealed in the capital, paralysed by their mutual bickerings and quarrels.

By now, the odour of sanctity could no longer hide the corruption in Janata's ranks. Morarji Desai's son, Kantilal, it was said, had taken advantage of his father's position and helped himself to a sizeable fortune. He should, therefore, face an investigation, affirmed certain ministers, notably Charan Singh and Raj Narain. The sexual proclivities of Jagjivan Ram's son together with a compromising photograph had become front page news in the national and Delhi press, causing his father acute embarrassment. Mr Ram Senior for his part had also to explain how he had evaded paying income tax for the last ten years. However, the pressure on Desai had little to do with any concern for probity in public life; it was simply a signal that certain of his colleagues coveted his crown and was part of the internecine conflicts which had racked the Janata Ministry from birth.

In July 1978, the authorities filed six cases in courts relating to Emergency excesses and abuses of power against Mrs. Gandhi, Sanjay and other Congress leaders. Undeterred, she contested and won a by-election at Chikmagalur in Karnataka in November. But Desai moved a motion to have her arrested and expelled from the Lok Sabha because of her breach of privilege and contempt for the house when officials investigating the affairs of Maruti in 1975 had been allegedly harassed. The Parliamentary Privileges Committee found her guilty and a warrant for her arrest was issued on 19 December. Once again, with a fine eye to publicity, Mrs Gandhi insisted that she be taken by the police from the floor of Parliament. The press, radio and television recorded the event for the benefit of the country. She was released from prison on 26 December.

Early in the new year 1979 the rabble rousing George Fernandes accused Indira Gandhi of having accepted bribes from the multinationals and called for her expulsion from Parliament. The Chief Election Commissioner thereupon ruled that the expulsion meant that she was automatically required to vacate her seat. There was more drama, however, Devraj Urs, the Congress Chief Minister of Karnataka, left Mrs Gandhi as he could not tolerate Sanjay's arrogance.

In June 1979, Congress (I) ordered Urs to resign from the party presidency, which led to the final break between them.

But the tribulations of Congress were more than offset by the death agonies of the Janata regime. Charan Singh and Desai were on a collision course. They had split, then came together, again, with the former officially designated Deputy Prime Minister. He now moved openly to the offensive. Raj Narain left the party on 9th July and six days later on 15 July Desai, an embittered man, resigned. On 28 July, Charan fulfilled his life ambition by becoming Prime Minister at the head of another leaky coalition which collapsed on 29th August, after a mere 24 days in power. Whereupon, the Prime Minister unable to face the prospects of losing a parliamentary vote of confidence, advised the President to call mid-term elections. These were to be held on 6 January 1980. The Janata experiment had dissolved into incoherence.

Chapter 28

MY FORAYS INTO JOURNALISM

I was interested in journalism since my childhood days. My father subscribed to an Urdu Children's Weeklies, "GHUNJA", "BUD", as soon as I started reading Urdu. It was one of the few children's magazines in those days.

For the first time, my name apeared in print, when I copied a joke from some Urdu book, and sent it for publication under my name. I was thrilled by it and showed it to all my relations, friends and acquaintances.

While still at school, being underage, I filed a declaration for publication of a students' monthly in Urdu "TALIB ILEM", but was advised that being a minor my declaration could not be accepted. However, I found someone to be its publisher, and brought it out as Chief Editor. Certain newspapers had described me as the 'youngest editor' of India.

Since I knew nothing about the business side, it ceased its publication within seven or eight months. When I went to Aligarh, I found Abbas equally ambitious to be a journalist. He was editing college magazine, and encouraged me to write for it. Later on, I became the editor of Urdu section of the magazine.

Abbas and myself were not satisfied with working for the college magazine, which was to be published under the guidance of a University teacher. We decided to bring about a weekly newspaper probably the first students' journal in India. We named it *Aligarh Opinion,* We collected money from fellow students, cycled down to the press and on Sundays hawked it ourselves in University campus.

The British Pro-Vice Chancellor, Mr Rambasbottar was very unhappy with it. He called us and asked us that with whose permission we were bringing out this newssheet and threatened us with the expulsion from the University.

While still at Aligarh, I worked as a correspondent for the *Hindustan Times* and *Bombay Chronicle,* but, I never disclosed my identity to anyone except to close friends. Often inconvenient news about the University appeared, but no action against me could be taken by the University authorities.

Abbas left the University to join the *National Call,* since *Hindustan Times,* was acquired by Birlas and they appointed Pandit Madan Mohan Malaviya, a Hindu Maha Sabha Leader as its Chairman. Dr. Ansar felt it necessary to have a committed nationalist daily from Delhi. He persuaded J.N. Sahani to resign from *Hindustan Times* and to take up the editorship of *National Call.*

In my summer vacation, I came to Delni, and joined the National Call as an unpaid apprentice. Then Delhi was a very small city having less than half dozen police stations, one hospital and a small district court.

As an apprentice reporter, I used to cycle down to police stations, hospital and court for news. In the night shift there used to be only one or at the most two sub-editors. I used to assist them also.

Later, Abbas decided to go to Bombay to join the *Bombay Chronicle,* edited by Abdulla Brelvi. Here again I started working as an unpaid apprentice covering city courts. Brelvi gave me a special assignment to interview enlightened ladies on women's problems. In this connection, I interviewed Mrs. Sarojini Naidu, Mrs. Kamala Devi Chattopadhyaya and Sofia Somjee and many others. Here I built up a contact with the great lady Mrs. Naidu who kept on treating me as her own son till she died, as the first Governor of U.P. after Independence.

I met a remarkable Muslim lady, Aitaya Faizi, who lived in a palatial Moghul style house on Ridge Road, Malabar Hill. She was probably the first Muslim liberated Indian woman who had discarded purdah and freely moved in society. She was running a 'Three Arts Club'. at her residence, which used to organise music and dancing and other entertainments every Sunday afternoon, and invite the celebrities, visiting Bombay as Chief Guests. It was here that for the first time I had heard Dr. Radhakrishnan speaking and saw George Bernard Shaw in flesh and bones. While the *Bombay Chronicle* was being edited by Syed Abdullah Brelvi, the *Bombay Sentinel* had B.G. Hornimn, a great friend of India as its guiding force.

In those days, Bombay was the journalistic and political metropolis, and it had become a Mecca for aspiring journalists. I was happy in atmosphere of both of these established and pupular newspapers.

During one of his frequent visits to Bombay, I met Jawaharlal

Nehru, at the residence of his sister, Krishna Hutheesing. He asked me what I was doing in Bombay. On learning that I was working with his old friend Syed Abdullah Brelvi, in the *Bombay Chronicle,* he suggested to me to proceed to Lucknow and meet Mohanlal Saxena, who was trying to bring out a daily English newspaper, the *National Herald,* and within a few days, I left for Lucknow.

In those days, there were two powerful English dailies published in U.P. The *Pioneer* was being edited by Desmond Young, the *Leader* by Sri C.Y. Chintamani both these papers were anti-Congress. It was felt that the recently formed Congress Government under the Government of India Act, 1935, granting limited provincial autonomy should have an organ of its own.

A company was floated in the name of the Associated Journals Limited, with Nehru as Chairman and Mohanlal Saxena as Managing Director. Among its directors were Rafi Ahmed Kidwai, Mohanlal Saxena, Purushottam Das Tandon, Acharya Narendra Dev and Sri Prakasa.

It was difficult to find funds to bring out a national daily. reported to Mohanlal Saxena who was worried about raising finance. I was the first person to sign as an employee of the Associated Journals Limited.

Mohanlal Saxena was the President of the U.P. Provincial Congress Committee also. We decided to issue coupons worth Rs. one to Rs. ten and all the District Congress Committee were instructed to sell them. Rafi Ahmed Kidwai was Revenue Minister. He sold some shares to sympathetic taluqdars and zamindars.

After Nehru's death, these shares were inherited by his legal heirs, and thus they control Associated Journals Limited and its huge buildings in New Delhi and Lucknow, has passed on to his family.

An old press in Calcutta was lying idle. It was purchased and installed in a building of an Anglican Church School which has folded its tents in view of the changed political atmosphere. Kidwai had persuaded the trustees to sell it at a nominal price.

The newspaper that Nehru was going to start — an English daily — created enthusiasm in journalistic circles. Hundreds of applications poured in offering their service to the forthcoming nationalist daily. Most of the patriotc journalists considered it to be an honour to be associated with the newspaper started by Nehru.

Rafi Ahmed Kidwai was keen to seek the services of Pothan

Joseph who was editing the *Hindustan Times*. But under Karachi Congress Resolution even the Ministers were drawing Rs. 500 as monthly salary and a Congress paper could not pay more. It was obvious that Joseph would not work on this salary.

Now the choice was between K. Rama Rao, News Editor of the *Hindustan Times* and K. Srinivasan, of the *Free Press Journal*, on my advice the management sought the opinion of Syed Abdullah Brelvi who felt that K. Rama Rao would be better for a newly started newspaper because he was an all rounder.

The Directors, assisted by K. Rama Rao, went through the bio-data of various candidates. Acharya Narender Dev and Sri Prakasa took special interest about the background and credentials of applicants. Apart from their journalistic experience their dedication to the Freedom Movement was also examined.

Among the assistant editors selected were M. Chalapathi Rao, T.N. Singh who later on became a central minister and the Governor of West Bengal. Among the sub-editors were R. D. Kwatra, Y.P. Verma, Sibtey Hasan and W. A. Kidwai.

I selected Subhan to assist me as a reporter. Though fresh from the university and poor in writing, he was a good contact man. In those days, Lucknow had a very small corps of press correspondents. Lala Durga Das, who later on became the Editor of the *Hindustan Times*, represented the *Statesman* and Dr S.N. Ghosh was the special correspondent of the *Pioneer*.

I had to cover the U.P. Secretariat and Legislative Assembly and Council. Most of the speeches were delivered in English. The Treasury Benches were headed by Pandit Govind Ballabh Pant, Lal Bahadur Shastri the Chairman of the Estimates Committee, was most helpful to me.

In the evenings, the entire Cabinet treated the National Herald office as a club. They used to come for a cup of tea and freely mixed with the staff and exchanged views with them. There was perfect comraderie between the Herald staff and the Ministers of the Pant Government.

When the *Herald* hit the stands, it gave a new direction to journalism in northern India. While in Bombay and Calcutta, the nationalist or pro-Congress press had a tradition, English journalism in northern India was mostly controlled by the British.

However, the call of 'Quit India' and 'Do or Die' broke the patience of the British. They confiscated the *National Herald* office and its premises and those of its employees who had managed to avoid jail were given marching orders.

It was towards the end of 1945 that the ban was lifted, the keys of the building were handed over to the management and Nehru followed by Rama Rao and other members of the staff triumphantly entered the building. The rusty press was made workable and Rama Rao, brought out the *National Herald* with the headline "GOOD MORNING HALLET", Hallet was Governor of U.P., under whose order, Herald's press was locked.

On my release from jail, I did not join the *National Herald* as, I felt that it will not provide me freedom to criticise the Congress which apparently was heading to grab absolute power.

During war days, afraid of Japanese bombs, most of the rich citizens of Calcutta had migrated to the 'Safety', of upcountry leaving millions to face the famous Bengal famine. Tushar Kanti Ghose had come down to Allahabad and started the Allahabad edition of *Amrit Bazar Patrika.*

In the absence of *National Herald,* and with professional management, it had picked up wide readership. He needed a man in the provincial capital, and he approached me, I readily agreed to work with him with full assurance that I would not have any editorial interference.

Though Congress always criticised the hills exodus of the Government in summer to the hill stations, Pant Government carried on the British legacy of transferring the capital from Lucknow to Nainital. In 1946 summer, it was decided to hold the U.P. Assembly session there. The Nainital club, an exclusive white men's domain was taken over by the U.P. Government, besides Air Force convalescent barracks, but there was not sufficient accommodation to house the M.L.As and the Secretariat staff which has very much grown during the war days.

It was a fact that on such a short notice so much arrangement would not be made. The members of the Assembly had reached Nainital and they were running from pillar to post for accommodation. Ultimately, it was decided to abandon the whole project.

In spite of Patrika being a pro-Congress paper, I filed a dispatch highly critical of U. P. Government decision to have summer capital on the pattern of British colonists with headline "TREK BACK FROM TUQLAKBAD". It very much annoyed Pandit Pant, and from that day, our relations became strained.

Next year, in 1947, the hills exodus was again restored, the

U.P. Assembly met and discussed Mountbatten Plan. It was supported by Leaguers as well as Congress benches, but the only dissenting voice was raised by Maulana Hazar Mohani, who declared that Gandhi should be ashamed that he had accepted a divided India and Jinnah should hang his head in shame for he was given a motheaten Pakistan.

An interesting incident in my journalistic career happened at Nainital. Jinnah had sent Khaliquz-Zaman, a former Congressman and Khilafat leader who was the leader of Muslim League party in U.P. to tour West Asian countries to obtain the support of Arab leaders for his proposal of Pakistan. On his return, I found him giving an exclusive interview to Prem Bhatia of *Statesman* which was more sympathetic to Muslim League than to Congress. Later, I enquired from Prem that what was he doing with Khaliquz-Zaman. In a very boisterous way he declared that he was doing some international coverage.

I at once rushed to telegraph office and dispatched a wire to Allahabad and Calcutta, pointing out that Jinnah Emissary was jilted by the leadership of Arab World. This was a front page story appeared earlier than *Statesman* interview could be published much to the discomfiture Prem Bhatia.

I admit that in the beginning I had full freedom to write. I was a vehement critic of League and British administration which earned a wide readership for Patrika in U.P.

But after the transfer of power by the British to Congress things had changed. My zest for writing had disappeared with the exit of the British and the Muslim League. However, I watched with dismay the growing corruption, nepotism and inefficiency of the Congress administration in U.P. headed by Pandit Pant.

I earned displeasure of Pandit Pant and his government. One day I was called by Tushar Babu, Proprietor and Editor, he told me that Pandit Pant was unhappy with my presence in Lucknow. For the first time, I heard the word 'Foreigner', being used by an Indian in his own country. He frankly told me that since he was a foreigner, he could not stand by me in opposition to Pandit Pant, and suggested to me that I should go to Allahabad on the desk. Since my centre of political activities was in Lucknow, I declined his offer and said goodbye to *Amrit Bazar Patrika*. How Pandit Pant was annoyed with me has been described by D.P. Misra former Chief Minister of M.P. and a member of Working Committee of Congress, in his memoirs.

> "Govind Ballabh Pant bitterly complained that Kidwai was indulging in calumny against him and that he had published in the Allahabad edition of the *Amrit Bazar Patrika* (now Northern India Patrika) that during the thread ceremony of his son, he had received ornaments worth hundred of thousands of rupees as presents. Nehru, who had till then sat silent, now angrily remarked that he himself had enquired from the Patrika's editor according to whom Kidwai was not informant. To the dismay of everyone, present, this made Pant burst into tears. Amidst sobs, he said, "The informant was Kidwai himself and he had told the Patrika's correspondent and not the editor", still sobbing he added "I have carried out all your politics in my state. I have not allowed the communal poison of Punjab and Bengal to enter U.P. I have seen to it that Muslim life and property were not endangered and yet you are defending one who has left nothing undone to blacken my face". Even Pant's tears left Nehru unmoved and he went on mumbling that in respect of what the Patrika had published, Kidwai was not to be blamed. It was a bewildering scene—Nehru's eyes flaming with anger and tears running down Pant's cheeks."

I did not remain unemployed for long. On the recommendation of my old friend, K.A. Abbas I was hired by Rusy Karanjia as U.P. representative of *Blitz*. I got full opportunity to expose the corruption, maladministration of the Congress Government headed by legendary administrator Pandit Govind Ballabh Pant. My dispatches were published with credit to my name and often with screaming headlines. I was told by the U.P. Chief Secretary a member of Indian Civil Service that they were asked by Pant to find out the legal opinion if any case in court of law could stand against me or *Blitz*. But he was advised that no case would stand in court of law.

After Purshottam Das Tandon had resigned from speakership of U.P. Assembly following his election as Congress President, Pandit Pant who had acquired a love for erstwhile Muslim Leaguers and former British stooges, like other Congress leaders, got Nafis Ahmed a Muslim League MLA elected as the Speaker.

Most of the Muslim leaders had migrated to Pakistan as conquerors to acquire valuable properties left by Hindu refugees, some of them who preferred to live in India to protect their own properties, donned Gandhi cap, and became blue-eyes of Congress leadership. Nafis Ahamed was one of them.

In one of my despatches, I had made some indiscreet remark on his conduct. This gave an opportunity to Pant to ask him to issue warrant of arrest against the acting editor of *Blitz.* He was arrested, on a warrant issued by the U.P. Speaker, in Bombay, and flown to Lucknow. Chari a supreme Court lawyer challenged the authority of U.P. Speaker to get his warrant of arrest executed outside U.P. The Chief Justice of India, Meharchand Mahajan, upheld Chari's stand. When pointed out that the warrant of arrest could be executed in U.P. alone and may be arrested again Mr Justice Mahajan, Chief Justice of India declared the hands of Supreme Court are long enough to reach Uttar Pradesh

The acting editor was released in Lucknow, with the intention of being arrested next morning. With my experience as an underground worker, I whisked him away from Lucknow. The government sealed airport, Jhansi, Moghul Serai, and Ghaziabad Railway Station the only exit points from U.P. I brought him to Delhi via Agra bypassing Ghaziabad.

Next day Pandit Pant was vehemently grilled by Opposition for his inefficiency to check our escape. We held a press conference at Delhi describing our escape comparable to escape from a Nazi concentration camp much to the embarassment of Congress Government.

However, Pandit Pant persuaded the accredition committee to withdraw my accredition. But it made no difference to my activities.

In this connection, I may make mention of an interesting incident. Kamalapati Tripathy was a mere MLA and his son Lokpati who is a Minister in U.P. was involved in a number of shady business deals. Their exposure embarrassed Kamalapati and he issued a legal notice for civil as well as criminal action against Blitz. I provided a documentary evidence of the deal challenging Kamalapati to declare that Lokpati is not his son Or Lokpati to declare Kamlapati that he is not his father and offered to apologise and withdraw my allegations. Obviously there was no response to this challenge.

Everybody knows that Karanjia is not very straight forward journalist. He is one of those who can easily be influenced by his personal interest. However, some powerful friends of Pant in business circles persuaded him at dispensing with my services.

I had faced unemployment in past but this time it was different. Now I was a married man and had acquired family responsibility. Under the influence of Pant doors of the most newspapers owned by big businessmen were closed to me, I was almost on street and during these days I knew that what unemployment and even starvation means. For some time I maintained myself by pawning and selling jewellery of my wife. But soon I was a pauper.

In this connection, I mention an incident. I received an invitation from the Governor of U.P. to attend a reception at the Raj Bhawan on the occasion of Independence Day on August 15. I asked my wife to dress up to accompany me for attending the function. While we were just to leave, our Ayah came and informed us that the milk tin to feed my three month old daughter was exhausted. I immediately rushed to local store to buy it. But I was bluntly told by the salesman that the limit of my credit was exhausted and he cannot make any supply without cash. I had to rush back to my house and proceed to a money lender for some cash postponing to attending the independence day celebration for which I had sacrificed my time and tears.

After my dismissal from *Blitz,* I was in terrible financial conditions. In those days, I came to know what unemployment and almost starvation mean. I ran from pillar to post, but no newspaper will touch me with a pair of tongue for the fear of antagonising Pant. However, Lala Durga Das who was the joint editor of the Hindustan Times and knew my talents as newspaper man when he represented *Statesman* at Lucknow, sympathised with me, and gave me a job in his paper. But the managment was run by Devdas Gandhi, the youngest son of Gandhi, who was very closed fisted man. He called me and told me that the salary which he was offering me was ridiculously low, and remarked that I had made enough sacrifice for the country and should sacrifice something for his paper. I told him that I had done enough sacrifice for your father and I did not intend to do any more for him, and walked out from his office.

This was the end of my journalistic career. In sheer desperation, I sought an interview with Nehru and requested him to give me some paid assignment. He pointed out to me that all assignments were controlled by Union Public Service Commission and he had nothing to do with the Commission. I told him that neither he nor me had anything to do with Union Public Service Commission, and pointed out to him, if he had anything to do with he would have retired by now as joint secretary. This remarked pleased him, and he rang Sir V. T. Krishnamachari a former Diwan of many princely States, whom Nehru had picked up as Deputy Chairman of Planning Commission. Through his munificence I got a very junior assignment in their publication division till I contested the election for Lok Sabha in 1957.

In my journalistic career I came across with some of the most important journalists, prominent among them were B.G. Horniman, Pothan Joseph, Abdullah Brelvi, and Syud Husain who edited *Independent* in early twenties but was exiled to U.S. for he and Nehru's sister Sarup later to be known as Vijaya Lakshmi Pandit had fallen in love and were about to get married.

I was also one of the founder of working journalistic movement and organised its first meeting at Lucknow presided over by Dr. Syud Husain, later this organisation forced the government to enforce working journalistic act, which gave a sense of security to journalists, otherwise like me most of them were hired and fired on the whims of proprietors.

Chapter 29

MEMORIES OF NEPAL

HAVING spent most of the World War II years in far off Alipore Central Jail, Calcutta, I was then transferred to my home province of U.P. and lodged in Lucknow jail. It was here that I met some young Nepalese students from Patna and Banaras Universities who were imprisoned by the British Government on the request of the Ranas of Nepal for they were suspected to threaten their oligarchy.

Prominent among them were S.P. Upadhyaya, later to become Minister for Food and Civil Supplies, Dr. D.R. Regmi, Foreign Minister and M.B. Shah, Nepalese Ambassador in New Delhi. They told me stories of the autocratic regime of the Ranas, who controlled the entire forest wealth of Nepal and pocketed most of the pension of valiant soldiers who had served in the British Army in India, Malaya, Singapore and Shanghai.

I had known the Ranas, who often visited Lucknow for medical treatment, acquired palatial houses, and demonstrated their power of wealth by throwing lavish parties to Oudh taluqdars and British officials. They often gave their daughters to Rajput aristocracy, with the temptation of costly jewellery, huge dowry and beautiful brides. I had known some Oudh taluqdars and members of the landed aristocracy, who entered these matrimonial alliances to wipe out their debts to money-lenders and save their properties.

I had already worked in my humble way for the freedom of my country and was tempted to offer my meagre assistance and to share my experience with these freedom fighters to serve their country.

After Nehru had joined as the Vice-President of the Viceroy's Executive Council, and formed his interim government, all of us were released from jail. During the days of imprisonment, the Nepalese freedom fighters had cultivated Rafi Ahmed Kidwai, while B.P. Koirala had built up close relations with leaders of the Congress Socialist Party, particularly of Bihar led by Jai Prakash Narain.

On my release, I visited the border areas of Nepal and visited Dhangari in Lakhimpur Kheri district and Nepal Ganj adjacent to Bharaich district of U.P., Raxaul and Jogbani in Bihar. We felt that if a small armed force entered these areas they would be welcomed by local political elements. The Ranas had only a small ceremonial army in Kathmandu which would take days to climb down to these areas.

It may be interesting to describe the set-up in Nepal. The Tarai area, meaning sub-Himalayan region, was inhabited and still is inhabited by people who have not only ethnic, religious and linguistic affinities with the people of eastern U.P. and northern Bihar, but also blood ties. Some of them own properties on both sides of the international border. Marriages between them are very common.

The Gorkhas inhabit Upper Nepal and Kathmandu Valley. It was a princely family from Rajasthan, who had overpowered the local ruler in the seventeenth century and established his dynasty. Later, a mentally retarded king abdicated in favour of his Prime Minister who established an oligarchy. While the king was known as Maharaj Adhiraj, the Prime Minister and his family members assumed the title of Rana. In the usual course, the eldest of them used to succeed, But in later days the Rana family often elected him. The king had abdicated all his powers in favour of the family of his Prime Minister, but he continued to be treated by his people as the God King. On Dussehra, he gave 'darshan' when his people worshipped him. Later, he was imprisoned in his palace, cut off from the outside world, without specific permission of his Prime Minister.

The entire wealth of Nepal was owned by the Ranas, who gave some petty maintenance expenses to the king. The Ranas lived a life of luxury while the king's family led a caged life.

The main wealth of Nepal was its forest resources. They were lavishly distributed by the Ranas to their sons born from wedded as well as unwedded wives. These forests were the main source of wooden sleepers for Indian Railways in northern India. Some of the children of unwedded wives were very rich, among whom were Subrana Shamsher and Mahavir Shamsher. They lived in exile in Calcutta. When the Japanese threatened Calcutta many Britishers abandoned their properties and these people acquired Metro and the Light House cinemas, the prestigious properties at Chowranghee, and the famous departmental store, Hall and Anderson.

Since they were looked down upon by the ruling Ranas, they actively supported and financed the freedom fighters who were determined to overthrow the Ranarchy, as they described their oligarchy, to usher in democracy in Nepal.

Rafi Ahmed Kidwai was inducted by Nehru as Communication Minister. He was keen to introduce night air mail. But all the four private Indian airlines refused to take the risk. However, Kidwai persuaded Mahavir Shamsher to purchase a few war surplus dakotas and to hire Polish and German aviators who were facing pangs of unemployment after the conclusion of the war, and to launch Himalayan Airways which undertook to enter into a contract with the Government of India to carry night air mail. Later this company was christened the Royal Nepal Airline.

As ill luck would have it, the Ranas permitted two sons of the King, Prince Mahendra and Prince Himalaya, to visit Calcutta to consult Dr B.C. Roy on some ailment, where they were secretly contacted by Subrana Samsher, a childhood friend. He assured them that the Government of India will provide all help to his father, His Majesty King Tribhuvan, if he managed to take shelter in the Indian Embassy. The plan was hatched in strict secrecy. It was proposed that the King should persuade his Prime Minister, General Sir Mohan Shamsher Jung Bahadur Rana, to allow him to come out of the place in a closed car to go for a picnic and duck shooting with his family, and instead of going to the jungle, he enter Sital Nivas, the residence of Indian Ambassador.

Prince Himalaya, the younger son, was given some rudimentary training in car driving. The king reluctantly accepted the advice of his sons. The Indian Ambassador, Sir C.P.N. Singh, who himself was a past master in court intrigues having served the British for a long time, was taken into confidence by Kidwai. Tempted that he would control the Rana's wealth, he agreed to act as the King's host. It is said that without the knowledge of Nehru and South Block, Prince Himalaya drove the car inside the Indian Embassy

The news of the King's escape made world news. It was stated that the Ranas intended to sack the Indian Embassy but at that time there was only one other embassy in Kathmandu, the British and their Ambassador warned the Ranas not to do so.

After a few days, the King was safely flown to Delhi and his entourage was lodged in Maidens Hotel in Kashmere Gate. For the first time he breathed fresh air, Kidwai arranged the meeting between the crowned King Tribhuvan of Nepal and uncrowned king of the Indian people, Jawaharlal Nehru. His Majesty was impressed by the dynamic personality of the Indian Prime Minister.

King Tribhuvan had already heard about the generosity of Sardar Patel towards Indian princes, who after the merger of their states were given suitable privy purses and reasonable privileges to keep their dignity and honour. He is reported to have offered to merge Nepal with India, but Nehru's hands were too full — with the suspicions created by Pakistan, with the problems created by the merger of Kashmir, police action in Hyderabad and annexation of Junagadh. He was in no mood to burn his fingers in Nepal.

In the meantime, the Nepalese freedom fighters had obtained the services of some INA soldiers formed by Subhas Bose, who were refused employment in the Indian Army and had acquired some obsolete twelve bore guns from princely states which were still to enforce the Indian Arms Act. They marched to Raxaul, Dhangarhi, Birat Nagar and Jogbani without any resistance and established their government.

I, accompanied by 20 soldiers headed by C.B. Singh, a brother-in-law of Mahavir Shamsher, crossed the border in Lakhimpur Kheri district and captured the administrative headquarters of Bhangarhi. The Nepalese Governor, who was known as Suba, was nowhere to be seen. He abandoned his treasury leaving a few hundred coins in chest.

On the advice of the British Ambassador Sir Mohan Shamsher Jung Bahadur Rana, the Prime Minister, accompanied by General Sir Baber Shamsher Jung Bahadur Rana, the Commander-in-Chief of Nepal, rushed to New Delhi to meet Nehru. On the way, they halted at Lucknow and met Pandit Pant, the Chief Minister of U.P. who promised to intervene on their behalf.

Nehru frankly told them that the days of oligarchy were over. He advised them to frame a democratic Constitution and accept the King as titular head like the King of Great Britain. Mohan Shamsher reluctantly agreed.

The government of India lent the services of Dr. U.N. Singh, the Dean of the Faculty of Law of Lucknow, a brother Rajput and a constitutional adviser, Govind Narain, who later became Home Secretary to the Government of India and Governor of Karnataka, was lent as Financial Advisor, and some other Indian officers to reorganise administration. Nepal also set up a

High Court and a Congress Socialist lawyer of Patna was appointed first Chief Justice.

On return to Kathmandu Mohan Shamsher the Prime Minister, formed a provisional government and agreed to take B.P. Koirala as Home Minister, S.P. Upadhyaya as Minister for Food and Civil Supplies and Dr D.D. Regmi as Foreign Minister. Except for him, the entire Cabinet was composed of Nepal Congressmen.

Mohan Shamsher signed the treaty of 1950 which has created the present controversy. After some time Mohan Shamsher resigned and migrated to Bangalore with his family and entourage carrying all his movable wealth handing over power to the leaders of the Nepal Congress.

Earlier Mohan Shamsher invited Nehru to visit Nepal, and I was there. Never in its history had Kathmandu witnessed a bigger crowd than when Nehru drove through its solitary street, Youdh Road, accompanied by B.P. Koirala and Mahavir Shamsher in an open jeep. The valley vibrated with shouts of 'Jai Hind' and 'Jai Nepal'.

Soon after King Tribhuvan died. He was succeeded by his eldest son Mahendra. Unlike his father, he had political ambitions. He resented the behaviour of Indian Ambassadors who acted like British Residents in the erstwhile princely states. On Nehru's suggestion, Nepal had built up diplomatic relations with other countries also. India sponsored Nepal for membership of the UN.

In due course King Mahendra assumed dictatorial powers. The Constitution was suspended, and after a series of Cabinet changes, political parties were banned, and due to mishandling by the Indian Embassy a powerful anti-Indian group has now emerged.

With the exit of Dalai Lama, China also became a neighbour. Earlier India had built a motorable road known as Tribhuvan Path, linking Kathmandu Valley with India. King Mahendra permitted the Chinese to link Tibet with Nepal. Now it has opened its doors to Chinese diplomats, teachers and technicians.

But in spite of their recent close relations with China, the ethnic, religious, and cultural relations with India are too strong to drive them into the lap of China. India needs statesmanship and flexibility to win over Nepal.

Chapter 30

DYNASTY

IN less than three years, Indira Gandhi was provided with an opportunity, to appeal to Indian electorate, to appeal against their own verdict in 1977. Though persecuted by the Janata Government, deserted by her own faithfuls like Chavan, Brahma Nanda Reddy, Karan Singh, the erstwhile Maharaja of Kashmir, K.C. Pant, the son of her father's faithfully, Govind Ballabh Pant, she stood like a rock during her brief period of out of office.

From her modest bungalow of 12 Willingdon Crescent at a stone throw from Teen Murti House, the last abode of her father, all the time, she was planning to stage a comeback. Her persecutors who consisted of unimaginative persons like Morarji Desai and the Jat leader, Choudhari Charan Singh, provided full opportunities to her to appeal to her countrymen, as a persecuted and maligned woman.

Her expulsion from Lok Sabha, and imprisonment for a few days in Tihar Jail of Delhi, where during Emergency she had sent hundreds of innocent men and women made her a martyr before the people. Her son had already organised a gang of lampoon youth, who, under the flag of Youth Congress were raiding courts and creating disturbances.

As soon as the caretaker Government of Choudhari Charan Singh announced the dates of elections, she started to implement her strategy as a seasoned general.

In 1977, she had lost two of the important sectors of vote banks, which she had inherited from her famous father, the Muslims and Scheduled Castes known as Harijans. While she was not in office, she had already gone to some obscure villages crossing rivers and swamps on elephant bank to give solace to Harijan families, whose bread-earners were butchered by the caste Hindus, demonstrating the indifference of Janata Government towards them.

Her next step was to climb seventy steps of the famous

Moghul monument, the Jama Masjid of Delhi, accompanied by Abdul Rehman Antulay who was later to be appointed as the Chief Minister of Maharashtra, and her son, Sanjay to offer unconditional apology to the Shahi Imam, for having earned his displeasure, for ejecting poor Muslim families forcibly from Turkman gate.

She was also not to take a chance with Hemvati Nandan Bahuguna, whom earlier, she had dismissed as the Chief Minister of the most populous State Uttar Pradesh. Bahuguna has been the most popular Congress leader among Muslims. Bahuguna was a protege of her father, she met her in Shanti Vana the venue of Nehru's cremation and asked her son, Sanjay to touch his feet and to address him as Mamou, (the maternal uncle). To humour Bahuguna, she went still further and created a new office of Secretary-General in Congress and appointed him on this newly created post.

After having fully fortified herself, she made extensive tours and after hectic campaign came with flying colours and was sworn in for the third time as Prime Minister of India.

Most of us felt that the defeat in 1977, almost three years out of office, might have tamed her. But, we were rudely shocked, when once again, her son Sanjay started behaving as a *de facto* Prime Minister. Indian politics since Independence has been bedevilled by the relationship of father and daughter, mother and son, father and son, father-in-law and son-in-law, and husband and wife. It was thought that Jawaharlal Nehru, who served as the first Prime Minister of the newly independent India for seventeen years, until his death, in 1964, had ambivalent feelings about whether his only child, Indira Gandhi should succeed him as Prime Minister. On the one hand, he seemed to have groomed her for the office, he permitted his official hostess (he was a widower), to become his unofficial secretary and his confidant; although she was elected to no office and held no position in the government, he helped her assume an ever more important behind-the-scene role in party politics, and finally, in 1959 and 1960, she served, in part thanks to him, as the President of the ruling Congress Party. On the other hand, Nehru seemed to have been alert to the danger of setting a precedent of family succession and so perhaps giving rise to a Nehru dynasty; he frequently warned his colleagues to be on guard against his own dictatorial tendencies, he laboured to foster India's nascent democratic tradition, her father, and that Sanjay had persuaded her to do so. In any case, Sanjay became the

Emergency's main beneficiary.

Propagandists of the Emergency began presenting Sanjay as a rising political leader; they compared him to the son, the moon, and 'the rising orbs', hailed him a Messiah Sanjay. Although he held no political office and no position in the government, Mrs. Gandhi, helped him assume an even more important behind-the-scene role in Congress Party politics, as a member of the executive committee of its youth wing. His mother was grooming him much as her father, consciously or otherwise, had groomed her, but at a greatly accelerated pace and despite the fact that Sanjay had clearly demonstrated a total lack of patience with the constitution and with democracy and was generally considered to be a spoiled, tyrannical child. In practice, he became almost as powerful as his mother. He quickly acquired his own set of chamchas, or spoons — in common Indian parlance, sycophants who would feed their children. He dictated orders in his mother's name to officials and politicians everywhere. He toured the various States as her chief emissary (in time, he got himself a pilot's license and started piloting the planes he travelled in. On the road, he had gone in for speeding; in the air, he went in for daredevil stunts). He inaugurated what he called a Four-Point Programme — of mass sterilization, slum clearance-cum-tree planting, abolition of dowry and extension of literacy. Three of the points immediately met with popular protest; mass sterilization was seen as, among other things, an attack on the sanctity of the family, slum clearance as an attack on the sanctity of the home, and abolition of dowry as an attack on the sanctity of marriage. (Extending literacy had long been a government objective).

Shortly after seven o'clock on the morning of June 23, 1980, Sanjay came out of the Prime Minister's residence, at 1, Safdarjung Road, and got behind the wheel of his car — a green Matador. He drove to the Delhi Flying Club, about half a mile away, where the young and chic well-to-do go to sport with planes. There he met a friend, Captain Subhas Saxena, who he invited to go up in his Pitts with him. Sanjay had recently acquired a Pitts S-24, a two-seater, two-hundred-horse-power, light, aerobatic American plane. It was the only one of its kind in India and the star of the club's fleet of small planes, Saxena, who was a flying instructor at the club, demurred, saying that he shouldn't fly, because he might be going in for a hernia operation any day. But Sanjay wanted someone with him at the controls, and prevailed upon Saxena to go up. As they were walking toward the hangar where the plane — red, sleek, and new-looking — was housed, they were intercepted by the club's chief instructor, a Captain Shamim, who suggested that Sanjay go up in an Indian Pushpak with a flying trainee instead of taking up the Pitts with Saxena. The Pushpak was an old club stand by, which Sanjay had flown innumerable times, while the Pitts had been in service only a few days. Sanjay himself had flown it for six of the ten hours it had been in the air, and he was very keen on it. But it was a tricky piece of equipment, and flying it required special training and experience. "I have to take up this red bird today", Sanjay said, "It's Pitts day".

The senior deputy director of the Civil Aviation Department Mr G.R. Kathpalia, had made a point personally supervising the arrangements for Sanjay's flights since Mrs Gandhi's return to power; junior officials in the department generally steered clear of Sanjay, for fear that they would be blamed if anything happened to him. Sanjay had a reputation for being a something of a daredevil. Once, he had brought down a plane in a town that had no airport, another time, he had performed a particularly dangerous stunt — swooping down, without releasing the landing gear, until he was flying just few feet off the ground, and then zooming up again. Kathpalia was now on hand as the Pitts was got ready, and he watched Sanjay and Saxena board the plane and strape themselves into the two seats. They received clearance from the control tower and took off. It was two minutes to eight.

The Pitts climbed rapidly and headed towards Willingdon Crescent, near the Prime Minister's residence. When it was about a thousand feet up, it attempted a stall turn. A stall turn — a quick, somersault like reversal — is considered advisable in a Pitts only for experienced Pitts pilots and at a height of not less than fifteen hundred feet. The Pitts banked, pitched, nosedived, spun, and crashed in a cluster of trees, just missing some barracks behind Willingdon Crescent. Both Sanjay and Saxena died instantly.

Mrs Gandhi was at the site of the accident within minutes, and she accompanied the bodies to a nearby hospital, where eight surgeons worked almost five hours to prepare Sanjay's body for public viewing. They also embalmed the body — although the practice is unknown among Hindus — because Rajiv was vacationing in Italy with his wife, Sonia, and their children, and Sanjay's cremation had to be put off for a day to allow for their return.

In the early afternoon, Mrs Gandhi went back to the site of the crash. She walked up to a rope cordoning it off, jumped over the rope, and went up to officials investigating the crash. "Sanjay was wearing a wrist watch and had a bunch of keys", she said. The officials informed her that they had found the watch and the keys and had deposited them at the local police station. Without further ado, Mrs Gandhi returned to the hospital

The capital was soon abuzz with rumours.

"She returned for the watch because on its back are engraved the numbers of Sanjay's secret Swiss bank accounts".

"The keys are to Sanjay's secret cupboards holding tens of millions of rupees."

"The watch and keys were two things that Sanjay wouldn't even allow his wife to touch."

The explanation for Mrs Gandhi's return to the site so soon after the crash may have been nothing more than that a grief-stricken, benumbed mother wanted some memontos of her son, but many people, including a number of the family's most loyal supporters and retainers, thought that she wanted the watch and the keys because they provided access to some illegal hoard of Sanjay's.

In the afternoon, Sanjay's body was moved from the hospital to the annexe to the Prime Minister's residence, where, in all but name, it lay in state — an honour ordinarily reserved for the Prime Minister or the President.

The next day on the floor of the Lok Sabha, A.P. Sharma, Minister for civil aviation announced a judicial enquiry. But, within hours, mysteriously, this decision was reversed. It was whispered in many circles that it might have disclosed many things not complimentary to Indira Gandhi and her regime.

Sanjay's death, though a great shock to her, did not discourage her from the attempt to perpetuate her dynasty. Her eldest son, Rajiv was a pilot in Indian Airlines. He married an Italian and was leading a quiet happy family life listening to the tapes of Western music and enjoying the company of his two lovely children.

Though he was staying with her mother, he completely avoided to mix with her mother's political friends. Thousands of people who were daily visitors, had never a glimpse of him. But Indira Gandhi was determined to induct him as her political heir. The services of the Youth Congress workers were utilised to urge him to enter politics. Even some of them threatened to go on fast unto death unless he relented.

He was determined to complete his training in aviation, and when he went to Hyderabad, to attend his courses, the Ministers and Congress leaders of the State were on the airport to garland him. He was shocked and rudely brushed aside their gesture.

However, for long the poor young man could not resist the pressure of his mother and her enthusiastic supporters. Reluctantly he joined the Congress Party and immediately was appointed its General-Secretary.

Now, there was no looking back for young Rajiv. Within a short time, he tasted the power, he started rebuking the Chief Ministers, pulling his weight about. Once while, visiting Hyderabad he rebuked a Chief Minister who burst into tears. He hurt Andhra pride and Mrs. Gandhi lost the State of Andhra in her own lifetime.

His novice was handling Andhra and later, Kashmir was noticed by all but no Congressman had the courage to point it out to his mother. One of the greatest challenges to her supremacy was posed by the explosive situation in the border province of Punjab, where the Sikhs headed by an obscure religious preacher Bhindranwala were almost in revolt. It may be interesting to give its background in a short passage.

After the disintegration of the Moghul Empire, they had carved out a Sikh State ruled by a valiant General and Asministrator, Maharaja Ranjit Singh. But, after his death, the British took advantage of the court intrigues and annexed it. Within few years, they became the most loyal subject of the empire.

In the First World War, they demonstrated their martial spirit in Europe as well as in Middle-East. But, after the war, they showed great discontent, and organised themselves in revolutionary parties. The Sikh emigrants in America and Canada sent their men and material, to fight the British on Indian soil.

Gandhi, after launching his Khilafat and non-cooperation movement, wanted to transform the revolutionary spirit of Sikhs to non-violent channels. A band of Akalis, the Sikh puritans, who were agitating to liberate their holy shrines, Gurudwaras from the corrupt priests, provided an opportunity to him to enlist their support.

The Congress formed a Committee headed by Hakim Ajmal Khan to raise funds for their agitation, and subsequently, they became an ally of the Congress.

On the eve of the transfer of power, Nehru as well as Patel, fully used the Sikh card for the partition of Punjab. The Sikhs were the worst sufferers of the partition of North Western India. They had to migrate from Pakistan, part of Punjab, to East Punjab not leaving even their vast landed and Urban properties, but some of their most holy shrines. However, to appease them one of their leaders, *Baldev Singh was appointed as Defence Minister.* He accompanied Nehru to London when Jinnah and his Deputy Liaquat went there to parley with British Prime Minister, thus recognising a separate identity of their community.

After things settled down, they started displaying their discontent. They demanded a Punjabi Suba which Nehru refused. However, when Indira Gandhi came to power, the Punjabi Subha was conceded. But, Indira was anxious to create split among Sikh ranks, who, by and large, supported the Akalis.

She and her son spoinsored an obscure priest, Jarnail Singh, Bhindranwala as their candidate to capture the management of Sikhs shrines, the source of finance for Akalis.

In the meantime, the semi-educated young Sikh who was appeased by Indira Gandhi and her faithful Chief Minister, of Punjab, Giani—Zail Singh to wrest the leadership of Akalis from their adversaries. He was allowed to collect the band of armed Sikh youngmen, to roam about freely not only in Punjab, but to visit Bombay and Delhi also collecting money and arms.

When Rajiv Gandhi who overnight was elevated as the Chief General Secretary of Congress Party was asked about him, he merely remarked that he is just 'a religious leader'. Later, Bhinderwala entered the holiest of the holy shrine of Sikhs, the Golden Temple of Amritsar which ultimately became an armed fortess. He was joined by a retired military General Subheg Singh who had trained in Mukti Bhahini in Bangladesh and started preaching from Akal TAkhat whoe edicts had complete religious sanction to Sikh masses to fight for a sovereign Khalistan State.

For sometime, Indira kept her cool. But, on advice of her and probably foreign intelligence, she decided to strike. A military campaign was launched, with the help of Indian tanks, armoured cars and after fierce battle, Akal Takhat was razed to ground and Bhinderwala and General Subhag Singh with hundreds of innocent pilgrims to the holv shrine were put to death.

This completely alienated the Sikh community. In sheer desperation, they took to the path of terrorism. Indira Gandhi herself was slain by her own security guards on the morning of October 31. While her dead body was lying in All India Institute, an obliging President of India administered oath of office to Rajiv Gandhi who became the Prime Minister of the second most populous country of the world. It may be noted that following the death of Nehru as well as Lal Bahadur Shastri, after thirteen days mourning, the Congres Party met to elect its leader. But, Indira Gandhi's faithful followers did not consider it necessary even to have this formality.

I have no doubt that Indira Gandhi was determined to establish the Nehru dynasty. But, I have my own assessment that Rajiv Gandhi never relished it. His brother who was described as crown prince all over the world died in June 1980, but Rajiv continued to serve the Indian Airlines till April 1981. It must have been the pressure of her mother which forced a reluctant and very much family man, who was more interested to listen pop cassettes than to political orations to join the public life.

It was left to Indira Gandhi to impose a reluctant politician to India as its Prime Minister, and to lay down the foundation of Nehru dynasty.

The assassination of a woman Prime Minister created a shock wave all over world. In Delhi, some of her devotees, in their anger, started indiscriminate killing of Sikhs and I witnessed many of them being burnt and roasted alive. The estimate of those died in thirty-six hours varies between 3,000 and 29,000.

Her only surviving son, heard the news in West Bengal. He hurried back to be sworn in as the Prime Minister. In the past, India had developed a convention, that after the death of a Prime Minister in Office, the country awaited for thirteen days of mourning, with bated breath for the decision of the ruling party to elect its leader. In the meantime, the seniormost Minister, functioned as an interim Prime Minister. This convention was laid down after the death of Jawaharlal Nehru, and was followed, when Lal Bahadur expired in far off Tashkent in Soviet Union.

But the former Airlines Pilot, reluctant to enter politics had come long away in the last thirty months. He had tasted the glamour under glory of power and was not willing to wait for a moment to succeed his mother who had died in most tragic circumstances.

The assailants of Indira Gandhi had pumped thirty six bullets in her body. It was obvious that she died on the spot. But the announcement of her death was delayed till Rajiv Gandhi reached New Delhi. While her dead body was still warm, two of her aides, R.K. Dhawan, a former stenographer, and Arun Nehru who had shifted from amulti-national to Indian Parliament approached, the President of India with the request that the late Prime Minister's son should immediately be installed as Prime Minister. In London, the court Chamberlain would have shouted the King is Dead, Long Live the King'.

Here, an obliging President of Republic could only whisper "the Prime Minister is dead" Long live the Prime Minister.

After all, India is a Sovereign Republic, though asa result of Independence Act, 1947, passed by British Parliament assented to by British monarch, it is a democracy, with all colonial, social and economic and administrative structures intact, it owes everything to Nehru dynastry as pointed out by Rajiv Gandhi in April 1988 in Indian Parliament.

"Mr. Speaker, Sir, I am also the only surviving son of an assasinated mother... As the House is aware, I had no love for politics, I treasured the privacy of my happy family life. Then my brother Sanjay was killed in the Prime of his life. There is a unique loneliness only a bereaved mother can know. There is a unique loneliness only a bereaved woman Prime Minister can know. That Prime Minister was my mother. She called out to me in her loneliness. I went to her side. At her instance I left my love of flying. At her insistence, I sacrified my family life".

More pathos followed about filial duty and duty to the nation and about learning from Indiraji to Ekla Chalo Re (walk alone) but this was pitiful rather than worrying; the worrying bits, as I said, only struck me at the second reading. And whatcaused the second reading in the first place, was a sentence which went: "The enemies of our democracy were out to destroy her (Indira) and through this, the democratic foundations of our polity". Also, "the votaries of religion in politics were out to eliminate her and ineliminating her, to eliminate the secular basis of our nationhood."

In other words, Indira was not just India, to quote the memorable words of Shri Dev Kant Barooah, but Indira was also democracy and secularism. So if democracy, secularism and India have survived Indira's tragic demise, they have done so only because her dynasty remains intact. "The nation is safe in our hands. We have guaranteed its independence, we have reinforced its unity, and have upheld its integrity."

When analysed, the message is quite simple. Listen, all you non-believes in the Nehru-Gandhi dynastry, if it was not for the dynastry, there would quite literally be no India. It is a message which is so reminoscent of 'Mummy', that the sound of the words is enough to evoke memories of that period of our political history which is popularly regarded as 'the dark days of the Emergency'. It was in those days, when in the name of putting 'democracy back on the rails', Mrs Gandhi arrested the entire Opposition and enforced Press censorship.

It is obvious that Rajiv Gandhi as a son of Indira Gandhi, and grand and great grandson of jawaharlal Nehru and Motilal Nehru considers it divine right to continue as Prime Minister. To him if Nehru dynasty lives, India lives, if Nehru dynastry dies, India dies: For thirty years of my life I worked for freedom and after forty years I witnessed this scenario.

Index

4